"The brilliance in this book cannot be overstated. Resting takes time. Lord knows, it takes great grace as well. When Israel came out of Egypt, it took a long time to learn the new rhythms of God under the lordship of Yahweh. This book invites us to a conversion of rhythm. And if you are like any of us, it may take a whole year. Highly recommended."

A. J. Swoboda, assistant professor of Bible, theology, and world Christianity at Bushnell University, author of *After Doubt*

"Under the culture's relentless pressure to hurry, we need a resource that not only reminds us to slow down but also offers a touch point with Jesus that nourishes our souls with the grace and truth of God's kingdom every day of the year. Alan Fadling's latest devotional is that resource—full of daily thoughts and questions that invite us into the life-giving presence of God. I highly recommend it!"

John Carroll, director of Dallas Willard Ministries' School of Kingdom Living

"Don't be fooled by the title of this book into thinking it's about slowing down the pace of your life so you can 'smell the flowers' or somehow break away from the world. It's about adopting a pace of life that allows you to listen to the Scripture more fully, with your mind as well as your heart. That is what Alan has done in the writing of this book. He models it for us on every page. If this is the result of a deliberately unhurried pace, then I'm in!"

Michael Card, musician and author of *Scribbling in the Sand*

"As someone who has walked and stumbled with Jesus for over fifty years, I found myself embarrassed and amazed at my inability to keep pace with him. Having given up on quick fixes to my long-term pacing problem, I was excited to embrace these daily readings—readings that became a yearlong slowing journey focusing on God, our Savior, and our community."

Tim Winters, executive pastor at Shepherd of the Hills Church

"We all know we need mentors and coaches in our lives. In *A Year of Slowing Down*, Alan opens up his life to give us a daily master class in what it means to apprentice ourselves to a deep, refreshing life in God. Alan's insights and questions will reveal new possibilities and expectations about your spiritual walk with Jesus. This book is the spread-out toolbox of a craftsman who lives this slowed-down life."

Rob Jacobs, pastor of spiritual growth at Saddleback Church

"If we are to offer hope and healing in a world of anxious, driven souls, we must incarnate—not just preach—the message of rest and grace found in Christ. In this timely devotional, Alan Fadling offers us a simple, powerful reminder each day of who we are and who we are becoming. Slow down, Alan reminds us, so that we can savor the wonder of the life of God . . . and touch those around us with the love of God."

Jerome Daley, executive codirector of the Vining Center

"If anyone could take five minutes of your time and turn it into a retreat, it's Alan Fadling. As I read the daily devotionals in *A Year of Slowing Down*, I found myself drawn into the *selah* of the psalmist, the richness of God's Word, the whisper of Holy Spirit, and the pace of Jesus. In each reading you're sitting down with a soul friend who has a simple way of chatting with you that feels easy and relaxing. Then, all of a sudden, profound insights rain down from heaven and wash your heart and soul with the smile of God. These holy moments can flood your soul with Jesus' living waters and overflow from you into the lives of the people around you."

Bill Gaultiere, psychologist and author of *Journey of the Soul*

"I can't think of anyone better than Alan Fadling to lead us on these five-minute daily retreats that he has provided. Far from being escape moments, these times will help us sink more deeply into reality."

Jan Johnson, president of Dallas Willard Ministries and author of *Abundant Simplicity*

"Having done contemplative retreats with Alan Fadling for more than fifteen years, I can almost hear his voice as I read each of these devotionals. More than anything, Alan's personal reflections are an invitation to live life at a different pace, cultivating a deeper awareness of God's Word and presence as an extraordinary invitation to 'learn the unforced rhythms of grace.' Alan's insights and reflective questions are a gentle invitation into that grace with the result of deep soul transformation and a richer life for those willing to take the journey."

Carol Taylor, former president of Evangel University

"Everyone needs a voice of wisdom in their life, and for many people, one of the most trusted voices belongs to Alan Fadling. And now we can hear his voice every day! Alan's new book, *A Year of Slowing Down*, is a daily devotional resource that helps orient our thoughts toward God and goodness. Everything about this book—the format, the organization, the choice of words—rings with Alan's pastoral presence, which ushers us gently but firmly into God's presence. I highly recommend this grace-filled book."

Richella J. Parham, author of *Mythical Me: Finding Freedom from Constant Comparison*

"In a world that privileges hustle and hurry, we need thoughtful, soulful guides for gospel living that shape us into fruitful Christians. Alan Fadling's *A Year of Slowing Down* ushers us into a life of sustainable spiritual rhythms for weary and overworked people."

Ashley Hales, author of *A Spacious Life*

A YEAR
OF SLOWING
DOWN

DAILY DEVOTIONS
FOR UNHURRIED LIVING

ALAN FADLING

An imprint of InterVarsity Press
Downers Grove, Illinois

InterVarsity Press
P.O. Box 1400 | Downers Grove, IL 60515-1426
ivpress.com | email@ivpress.com

InterVarsity Press® is the publishing division of InterVarsity Christian Fellowship/USA®. For more information, visit intervarsity.org.

All Scripture quotations, unless otherwise indicated, are taken from The Holy Bible, New International Version®, NIV®. Copyright © 1973, 1978, 1984, 2011 by Biblica, Inc.™ Used by permission of Zondervan. All rights reserved worldwide. www.zondervan.com. The "NIV" and "New International Version" are trademarks registered in the United States Patent and Trademark Office by Biblica, Inc.™

Scripture quotations labeled BCP 1979 are from the Book of Common Prayer, copyright © 1979 by the Episcopal Church in the United States. Used by permission. All rights reserved.

Scripture quotations labeled BCP 2019 are from the Book of Common Prayer (2019), copyright © 2019 by the Anglican Church in North America. Used by permission. All rights reserved.

While any stories in this book are true, some names and identifying information may have been changed to protect the privacy of individuals.

The publisher cannot verify the accuracy or functionality of website URLs used in this book beyond the date of publication.

Cover design and image composite: Cindy Kiple
Interior design: Daniel van Loon

ISBN 978-1-5140-0318-3 (print) | ISBN 978-1-5140-0319-0 (digital)

Printed in the United States of America ♾

Library of Congress Cataloging-in-Publication Data
A catalog record for this book is available from the Library of Congress.

8 7 6 5 4 3 2 1 | 29 28 27 26 25 24 23 22

TO RICHARD E. FADLING

My father, who always modeled

a love of reading good books and imparted that love to me.

I dedicate this book to him in his eighty-fourth year.

AND TO WAYNE ANDERSON

(1940–2008)

With gratitude for his mentoring influence in my life,

showing me the way to live, serve, lead, and breathe deep in

the atmosphere of God's measureless grace.

CONTENTS

INTRODUCTION

THESE DEVOTIONALS HAD THEIR beginnings in my personal journal. I began to practice the regular discipline of spiritual journaling in my twenties. Since then, I've journaled thousands of pages and millions of words. My journal is a place where I wrestle, meditate, reflect, create, and, in it all, pray. It's a place where I acknowledge the presence of God with me. I trust that the Spirit of God with me along the way will be with you as you read.

I envision these daily readings as five-minute daily retreats. They are not an escape from reality but a sinking more deeply into Reality. It is my hope that, over this year, you'll experience a renewal and refreshing of your ideas, your assumptions, your expectations, and your vision of God and the spiritual life. I hope you'll sense a holy slowing of your soul in the presence of God as you take part. Each daily reading ends with a reflection question that you can engage in at the moment and take with you into your day.

I invite you to allow these readings to be full of grace and truth, just as Jesus is. Grace without truth is simply unchallenging inspiration. Truth without grace is unbending advice that we're left to figure out on our own. Grace and truth overflowing together enable us to slow and discern the path before us and find strength to walk that path in God's presence.

These readings are arranged in three seasons. The first season is rooted in the Old Testament, especially the Psalms (Days 1-91). In these I reflect on the unhurried way of God with Israel and their spacious response to him in worship. The second season journeys mostly through the Gospels and John's letters (Days 92-273). In these readings you'll gain an appreciation for the ways of our unhurried Savior. Finally, the third season walks through the New Testament letters (Days 274-365). A primary theme in these readings is the church as an unhurried community.

This year of slowing down is not mainly about how fast you drive, or walk, or think, or talk, or work. It is about a pace of life more in keeping with the pace of Jesus. It is a pace of grace over drivenness, of peace over anxiety, of gentleness over harshness, of patience over anger. It is the pace of love because it is the pace of the kingdom of God who is love. It is the pace at which our true self longs to live.

I hope you'll come to believe that God has given us enough time for everything he's given us to do. I pray that you'll find growing freedom and courage to make time for that which matters most—to God and to you. I trust that you'll come to discover that most things shouldn't be hurried and some things simply can't be.

A core calling that my wife, Gem, and I have sensed over our lifetime has been to share our lives with others. God invites us to share not just truths, or insights, or ideas, but *life*. I pray that you'll sense that the one who is Life will refresh in you an eternal quality of life as you read.

PART ONE

THE UNHURRIED WAY OF GOD

REST IS HOLY

By the seventh day God had finished the work he had been doing;
so on the seventh day he rested from all his work. Then God
blessed the seventh day and made it holy. (Genesis 2:2-3)

THIS IS THE LAST WORD in the first creation story of Genesis. God's blessing of the seventh day as space to rest is a holy moment. Sabbath is the culmination of the creation story. We live in a culture that sometimes sees rest as a necessary evil to be minimized as much as possible. Or it sees rest as the moment we run out of gas for any more work. But rest isn't an absence of goodness. It is space to stop our working, enjoy God's goodness, and rest in his presence.

Resting is hard work. It requires strong personal leadership to say no once a week to measuring our lives by what we produce. It takes intentionality to slow down and cease our striving to achieve, acquire, and impress others and simply enjoy what God has given us. But God calls this Sabbath gift a holy thing.

I've sensed a daily invitation alongside this weekly Sabbath call. The creation story that starts our Scriptures describes the days of creation in a way that feels different. As each day of creation ends, we hear that "there was evening, and there was morning." This way of envisioning a day places rest first.

I've been experimenting with seeing my workdays as beginning with rest rather than ending in a collapse after a long day. My various practices of numbing, escaping, or avoiding don't bear good fruit. I'm finding it more fruitful when my work grows out of places of soul rest.

. . . .

How do you find yourself escaping, self-distracting, or numbing in the evening? How might God invite you to enjoy rest in his presence in the hours before you go to bed?

DAY 2

WHY DOES GOD BLESS YOU?

I will make of you a great nation, and I will bless you and make your name great, so that you will be a blessing. (Genesis 12:2 NRSV)

THE WORDS ABOVE ARE God's blessing to Abraham when he called this wealthy son of an idol worshiper to leave his father's house, abandon all that was familiar, and obediently go to . . . well, God didn't tell him where. God's command to leave came with a promise but not with an itinerary. Abraham was obedient despite the vague instructions, and God was faithful and kept this promise.

Notice the heart of that promise. Like Abraham, I am blessed not just so that I'll be blessed; I am blessed so that God's blessing will flow to others through me. My bishop, Todd Hunter, often reminds us that we are blessed for the sake of others.

Of course I want to be blessed. We all do. But I also truly want to bless others. I want others to receive the good things from me and through me that I've received from a generous Father.

Most recently, though, I've realized I need to let myself be blessed. I've been resisting God's blessing because I'm focused on whether I deserve it. That's the wrong question. God isn't assessing whether I deserve his generosity. He is simply generous. This is how God treats us. Blessing is rooted in him, not us. God would love nothing more than for you and me to open ourselves fully to all the ways he desires to be generous. Doesn't that sound inviting?

. . . .

Reflect on someone you have seen blessing others with the blessings God has given them. If you've been on the receiving end of their blessing, share with them how God is honored in their actions.

DAY 3

THE GIFT OF THE LONG PATH

When Pharaoh let the people go, God did not lead them on the road through the Philistine country, though that was shorter. For God said, "If they face war, they might change their minds and return to Egypt." (Exodus 13:17)

GOD KNOWS WHAT BARRIERS will be too much for us. In kindness, he sometimes leads us on what feels like the long way so we're not overwhelmed by obstacles that would overcome us. We may complain about the long way because we don't understand that God is sparing us something.

We think the best path from here to there is straight. Sometimes the best path is quite crooked. God's goal may not be our arrival at a destination but our formation along the way. We can be goal-focused when God is process-focused. He is forming us. And the long way is sometimes the best path for God to help us grow.

Perhaps God has invited us to join him in the work of the kingdom. We think the main thing, then, is to get to work. God gives us the gift of working with him, but he also gives us the gift of making us ready and able to do that work well. God calls us not only to collaboration but also to friendship in the work.

We can learn to discern how God is inviting us to join him in his work. We can also learn to cooperate with the process by which we are made ready to do that work. And the process sometimes involves a longer path than we anticipated.

How has your path felt more indirect than you would have wanted? How might this be a gift rather than a burden?

DAY 4

BETTER BACK THERE

Didn't we say to you in Egypt, "Leave us alone; let us serve the Egyptians"? It would have been better for us to serve the Egyptians than to die in the desert! (Exodus 14:12)

IN THIS MOMENT OF CRISIS the people of Israel believe they were better off under Egyptian oppression than they are now, being threatened with Egyptian attack. They have forgotten their complaints of mistreatment and their cries for deliverance. They have forgotten their bondage in Egypt and instead imagine the abuse that is about to land on them at the hands of their enemy. Don't we sometimes have second thoughts about whether we really want to be rescued?

Isn't it like us to begin to have second thoughts when we face obstacles on our journey toward freedom? We think, "It was a lot better back there where we came from. There were a lot of good things back there." We forget two things: how bad it really was back there and how good it really is where God is bringing us! We become myopic and lose our sense of context.

Moses speaks to the fears of the people, saying, "Do not be afraid. Stand firm and you will see the deliverance the LORD will bring you today. The Egyptians you see today you will never see again. The LORD will fight for you; you need only to be still" (Exodus 14:13-14).

Fear and insecurity are enemies of faith. We can be so overwhelmed in the looming presence of our enemy that we fail to realize God is more real than any enemy before us. The power of God's promise is stronger than the threat of our enemies.

. . . .

In what ways are you tempted to look back at some stuck place in your past and experience selective amnesia? How might God's presence with you now be far better than that situation?

LED IN UNFAILING LOVE

In your unfailing love you will lead
the people you have redeemed. (Exodus 15:13)

GOD LEADS US AS his rescued people in love that will never fail. We are on a journey of renewal and restoration. Love restores what it treasures, and God treasures us. God has sought us out in his limitless delight over us. This has always been God's intention for us. I haven't the wisdom nor the strength to rescue myself. I couldn't buy my way out of the slavery in which God has found me. Mine is a hopeless slavery except that my loving, powerful God chooses to rescue me.

It helps to remember that this is the reality in which I walk with God. God's love and strength are reliably and always present with me. God leads and guides me with persistent care and wisdom. I am always being treated by God with affection, encouragement, and empowerment.

It is remarkable that the destination of this journey is the very place where God dwells. God is leading me closer to his home (and mine). God invites me to walk on paths that draw me closer to his heart and mind. God is leading me away from the false gods of Egypt and toward himself—the only true God!

God deals with every enemy we encounter on this journey. We are not abandoned or alone. God knows what will oppose or attack me before I do. God will put fear into the heart of those enemies who seek my harm. What good news!

. . . .

When you think of hard places you've traveled, how might it help to have a greater awareness that God is lovingly present with you in these very places?

TRAINING OR TELLING?

Teach [God's people] his decrees and instructions, and show them the
way they are to live and how they are to behave. (Exodus 18:20)

JETHRO SPEAKS THESE WORDS to help Moses serve the people of God better. Exodus says that Moses sat alone morning to night hearing and deciding cases in light of God's law. His strategy was to "inform them" (Exodus 18:16) of God's laws and decrees. Jethro's counsel was to "teach them" and "show them the way." God wants to train us in righteousness rather than just inform us of righteous. I think of how I parented our sons when they were very young.

One morning my oldest son, Sean, was doing something to frustrate his brother Bryan and make him cry. Brothers do this to one another sometimes. My angry impulse was to lay down the law and tell Sean what he was doing wrong. But I had this passage in mind and wondered to myself if I could somehow teach him and show him instead of just informing him.

So I brought him over to me. Instead of my usual (and not very helpful) lecture, I told him I wanted to teach him and show him how to treat his brother kindly. I gave Sean a hug and said, "This is something kind you could do for Bryan." He wasn't too excited about my wonderful counsel.

A bit later I noticed Sean doing something that made Bryan laugh. I told him what a kind brother he was being. He lit up! Then he helped Bryan with a puzzle he was working on. Again I affirmed Sean's kindness. Sean was beaming! And without my urging, he gave Bryan a hug.

. . . .

Can you envision your heavenly Father looking for opportunities to train you in love and grace rather than informing and then reproving you? What happens to your desire to live well?

PROMPTED BY GENEROSITY

*The LORD said to Moses, "Tell the Israelites to bring me an
offering. You are to receive the offering for me from everyone
whose heart prompts them to give." (Exodus 25:1-2)*

I'M IMPRESSED BY THE LITTLE PHRASE at the end of today's line of
Scripture. God welcomes offerings from everyone whose heart prompts them
to give. Too much giving these days seems prompted by external guilt, ma-
nipulation, or peer pressure. Here the prompt is rooted not in a perceived
need but a person's heart. Yes, we can rightly give to meet a need, but sometimes the needs we perceive may not be the direction God has for us.

God is not desperate for us to give. God does not need something from us
that he lacks. An offering is perhaps something we need to give. We may need
to be freer from the possessions that possess us (rather than the other way
round). We need an opportunity to recognize that we are stewards more than
we are owners.

This passage nudges me to pray: *Father, may I be more aware and attentive
to your promptings in my heart today. May I remain open to your invitation to
be generous. What I think I own is yours. Grow in me a vision of stewardship
to replace the burden of thinking I own things. I long to grow in this freedom. I
welcome your sovereign leadership in my life in this way. Amen.*

. . . .

**Think of the most recent offering you made, whether it was in a church
service, in response to an online opportunity, or whatever. What was the
primary prompting of that offering? What might it look like to let God's
Spirit grow an increasing character of heartfelt generosity in you?**

A COSTLY SACRIFICE

Hannah did not go. She said to her husband, "After the
boy is weaned, I will take him and present him before the
Lord, and he will live there always." (1 Samuel 1:22)

THE LORD WAS GRACIOUS to Samuel as he grew up at the temple in the presence of the Lord and under the guidance of Eli the priest. The Lord was also gracious to Hannah, giving her five more children after she—true to her word—gave up her firstborn to the Lord's service.

I cannot imagine what it would be like to give up a child. What if after you had prayed so long for a child you had to give him up to be raised at a distant monastery? How would you feel if you saw your firstborn only once a year? You'd be proud of his service to God, but you'd miss him terribly.

And yet this is much like what God himself did with his Son. In love God gave us the gift of his Son. Jesus grew up in a world that didn't understand him or recognize him for who he was. He grew up away from the immediate presence of his Father for our sake. What a remarkable gift. What a wonderful invitation.

There may be a moment when God invites us to make an unexpected sacrifice for the sake of love. It may be hard, but good fruit will be borne from such loving abandonment.

. . . .

What difficult feelings have you experienced in response to sacrifices you've made on your journey? How have you experienced God's grace and generosity in moments of necessary surrender or invited obedience?

LEARNING CONTENTMENT

The LORD sends poverty and wealth;
he humbles and he exalts. (1 Samuel 2:7)

AS I REFLECT ON Hannah's humble prayer, I see that God brings me some things I like and some I don't. I want God to bring poverty only into the lives of the "bad guys," but sometimes faithful people have lived with little as well.

Paul shared with the Philippians that he had learned deep contentment right in the middle of unfulfilled needs, hungers, and wants (Philippians 4:10-12). Of course, I find contentment easier when I like my circumstances. God allows a variety of welcome and unwelcome circumstances to cross my spiritual journey. Perhaps in this way I learn that God alone is my portion and treasure.

God humbles one and lifts up another. I long to be honored and recognized in this world. But honor that lasts is found in union with God. I can be lifted up in friendship with God and largely invisible in this world.

I long to live in a community of God's people where our ongoing need of grace is the assumption rather than the exception. In such a culture the pressure to keep up appearances would diminish. We would not be embarrassed to admit our need for grace because this would be an acknowledged and shared reality for all of us. We would each recognize that honor doesn't come from appearances but from real, received grace. We can trust in the kindness and goodness of God amid whatever happens to cross our path in the moment.

. . . .

In what ways have you felt humbled lately? Are there ways you have felt lifted up? How might you talk with God about all of this?

DAY 11

GROWING UP
IN GOD'S PRESENCE

Meanwhile, the boy Samuel grew up
in the presence of the LORD. (1 Samuel 2:21)

I LOVE THAT SAMUEL "grew up in the presence of the LORD." I find myself wishing I had grown up in the presence of the Lord rather than with little awareness of God and the knowledge that he was with me. I can only imagine how different my childhood and youth might have been had I known my Good Shepherd.

That said, I am grateful that I have grown up in the presence of the Lord over the years of my adult life. I'm grateful for this journey. And I'm still growing up in the presence of God today.

As we grow up in the presence of the Lord, we may find ourselves being approved of less and less by the world and without a lot of company. The same was true in Samuel's day. Eli's sons, who are described as "scoundrels" (1 Samuel 2:12), treated the offering of the Lord "with contempt" (1 Samuel 2:17). Yet as Eli's own sons were walking away from God, young Samuel was growing up in the Lord's presence.

Whether you have been aware of God's presence from childhood or have become a friend of God later in life, you are growing up, even now, in the presence of God. What a fertile place to mature and develop.

. . . .

What has God done along your journey to help you grow into a Christlike individual? Whom did God use in your life?

TROUBLES AS AMPLIFIER

In his time of trouble King Ahaz became even more
unfaithful to the LORD. (2 Chronicles 28:22)

KING AHAZ IS NOT REMEMBERED as a hero of Israelite history. He reigned over a particularly ugly period in the life of God's people. The Chronicler describes Ahaz as one who "did not do what was right in the eyes of the Lord" (2 Chronicles 28:1). Ahaz's unfaithfulness to God grew in a time of trouble. Trouble has a way of exposing the dynamics of our inner life.

The good news is that trouble doesn't automatically cause unfaithfulness. Trouble tends to amplify what's going on in us already. What may have been quiet or hidden in times of relative ease gets louder or is uncovered in times of trouble.

If we are orienting ourselves toward God, seeking to trust him and entrust ourselves to him, trouble has a way of refining and strengthening that trust. If we are hiding a tendency to wander from God, trouble has a way of intensifying that reality. The chronic trauma that many of us have experienced during the pandemic has amplified inner dynamics that had perhaps been largely hidden before.

If we are leaning in toward God, trouble will tend to draw us closer. If we aren't, trouble can strengthen our resistance and waywardness. It's a good idea to seek God in times of trouble, but it's even better to cultivate that habit when times are easier. God is our Rescuer in times of trouble, but even more, God is always our very life.

. . . .

How has your life felt full of trouble lately? What does that trouble amplify in you? How might you offer yourself to God to strengthen your trust in him?

THUNDERING HEARTS

At this my heart pounds
and leaps from its place. . . .
God's voice thunders in marvelous ways;
he does great things beyond our understanding. (Job 37: 1, 5)

THESE ARE THE WORDS of Elihu, the young friend who has listened to all the back-and-forth between Job and his three "comforters." Elihu speaks out of frustration with Job's complaining and his friends' inability to answer those complaints. Elihu's words of praise ring true, but he uses them like a weapon against Job. Truth here is not in service of love.

There are moments when my own heart pounds and leaps from its place. There is emotional energy and resolve that rises within me at times. I have moments when I genuinely feel interaction with God like that. Something stirs in me that feels alive, vital, and even heart-pounding. Can I believe there is something of the divine voice in such conversations that is causing my heart to leap within me?

But sometimes my heart seems disengaged. There is another part of me that resists, perhaps out of fear. I find myself afraid of such passion, energy, and drive. That fearful part of me is childish, even adolescent. That part of me isn't growing whole and holy in Christ.

. . . .

The following prayer may help you in your own transforming journey in the way of Christ: *May your voice thunder in marvelous ways today, Lord. May I hear the thunder. May I not resist your voice in fear. Let me hear your voice saying what you've said to many others before me: "Do not be afraid. I am with you." I'm grateful for this good news. Amen.*

BATTLING INTERNAL ENEMIES

Many are saying to me,
"There is no help for you in God." (Psalm 3:2 NRSV)

ONE OF MY CONTINUAL BATTLES is the one that happens in my own heart and mind. I continue to discover and fight negative patterns of thought and emotion that are shaped less by Jesus and more by the world around me. The words of David's psalm ring true for me.

The enemies David mentions are human, probably military. Like his enemies, my negative thoughts and emotions insinuate that I'll be finding no help from God. Such thoughts and emotions pester me and hound me. They rise against me. They whisper that I am abandoned and alone. They oppose everything good that God intends for me.

So I'm grateful when I am awake enough to respond as David does with a hearty "But you, O LORD, are . . . " (Psalm 3:3). What is God? He is my shield. He surrounds me with protection. He is my glory. He makes my life shine so that it has impact. He is the one who lifts my head. He encourages my soul in the face of discouragement or accusation.

When I feel surrounded by trouble, like David I can cry out to the Lord. He answers my cry with holy help. He is my strong friend when the thoughts in my heart and head feel like enemies.

. . . .

In what ways do your thoughts or feelings feel like enemies? Take a moment to write about some of those internal adversaries. Name them. Now take a moment to cry out to the God who is with you. How might he desire to help you against these enemies?

WELCOMED INTO GOD'S PRESENCE

I, through the abundance of your steadfast love,
will enter your house;
I will bow down toward your holy temple
in awe of you. (Psalm 5:7 NRSV)

DRAWING NEAR TO GOD and entering his house used to be reserved for the privileged few. Only the priests were allowed, and they went through elaborate cleansing rites beforehand. I wonder if we in the twenty-first century might be helped by a little more of that kind of reverence and awe when we approach God in corporate worship and personal prayer.

This psalm gives us a starting point for recovering that reverence and awe. It might be good to consider how—on what basis—we enter the Lord's house. Do we enter because of our worthiness? Do we stay away because of our unworthiness? If we are thinking about worthiness, we may be focusing on the wrong thing. Let's shift our attention to God.

"I will enter your house through the abundance of your steadfast love." What an encouraging phrase! As if God's love for us weren't amazing enough, David adds the modifier "steadfast" and multiplies that by "abundance." May we be overwhelmed by God's love for us and grateful that he welcomes us, just as we are, into his presence. May we learn to bow before our God in awe of him and his abundant, steadfast love for us.

. . . .

Are there ever times you feel you might be too casual or too formal when you approach God? How might you enter God's presence—both in corporate worship and in personal prayer and meditation—with a heart full of both comforting grace and reverent awe?

WORDS THAT BLESS

May these words of my mouth and this meditation of my heart
be pleasing in your sight,
LORD, my Rock and my Redeemer. (Psalm 19:14)

WATCHING TELEVISION NEWS IS often painful. I'm thinking specifically about the words that are used and the way they are spoken. So much conflict, so many harsh words, so many accusations and insults in the headlines. Too many people speak to others with disrespect and contempt. A gracious and honoring word seems hard to come by.

All this has made me think that, as a culture, it would be helpful to rediscover the language of blessing. I'm not talking about saying a prayer before you eat. Not that kind of blessing. I'm not talking about greeting card wishes. Blessing is not empty, cotton-candy language.

The blessing I'm referring to here involves speaking words of substantial goodness to one another, words that bring about goodness in another's life. That's worth restating: I'm talking about speaking words that bring real goodness and blessing to another.

I've learned a lot over the years about the power of blessing—especially spoken blessing. Hearing words of blessing spoken over us gives those words greater power. You are invited to hear words of blessing from your Good Shepherd. You are invited to share those good words with those who cross your path. What a difference you could make in your world!

· ·

As you look around you, where is blessing needed? Who is one person you could meet with, call, or write to offer heartfelt words of blessing? When can you do that?

DISCERNING YOUR HEART'S DESIRE

May he give you the desire of your heart
and make all your plans succeed. (Psalm 20:4)

YEARS AGO, I SPENT eight days in silent retreat. The retreat center was about five miles south of Walden Pond where Henry David Thoreau conducted his experiment in simple living in a natural setting. I was hoping that my days in silent attention to God might bear similar fruit in my own life.

On the first morning of my retreat, the senior retreat guide suggested I spend the next twenty-four hours asking myself, "What do you want?" He gave me a few passages to reflect on but invited me to focus on this question. At first it seemed an easy one to answer. But the longer I lived with the question, the deeper my answers went.

At first, surface desires like catching up on a favorite TV series or enjoying pizza and beer came to mind. These weren't available to me at the retreat center. Eventually, I wrote down forty things I wanted (or didn't want). The longer I wrote, the more compelling my desires became. They felt focusing. They felt energizing. I realized what a gift my retreat mentor had given me.

Do you know what you want in life? I believe that the plans that succeed most fruitfully are rooted in desires that resonate with the heart of God. God wants good for us. Jesus wants us to share in his overwhelming joy. The Spirit longs for us to know the peace of God's presence. May God fulfill desires like these in our lives.

. . . .

Experiment with the question I was given on my silent retreat: "What do you want?" Start writing. Keep writing. Revisit your list. What surfaces in the beginning? How does your list develop over time?

GUIDED BY MY SHEPHERD

I will fear no evil,
for you are with me. (Psalm 23:4)

PSALM 23 IS A GOOD WORD for every stage of our lives. In it, David reminds us that "he guides me along the right paths for his name's sake" (Psalm 23:3). My Good Shepherd has it in his heart to guide me along the best paths because his good care for me reflects well on him. Just as I want my own sons to live well because it says something about how I've served them as a father, so the Lord shepherds me away from rutted, empty, wayward paths and toward nourishing, refreshing, fulfilling ones.

Even those best paths, however, will take me through dark seasons. Darkness can come with losses such as a prodigal child, a chronic illness, divorce, job loss, aging parents, or the death of someone close to us.

I'm guessing you're like me: I would rather never walk through dark valleys. But since I must at times journey through such places, I am grateful I'm not walking alone. My Good Shepherd guides me, protects me from evil, and brings me comfort when I'm tempted to give in to anxiety, fear, doubt, or insecurity.

Finally, consider the image in the next verse of this psalm: "You prepare a table before me in the presence of my enemies" (Psalm 23:5). Of course, I'd prefer sharing a sumptuous feast with my friends, but when my enemies threaten my joy, my gracious Host provides a place of hospitality for me. I enjoy the Shepherd's goodness in the presence of evil. I can then share that goodness in ways that might even overcome evil. Trust this reality today.

. . . .

Spend some time thanking your Good Shepherd for ways he's been shepherding you.

I'M BEING FOLLOWED

Surely your goodness and love will follow me
all the days of my life,
and I will dwell in the house of the LORD
forever. (Psalm 23:6)

THE LAST LINES OF PSALM 23 answer to a general sense of dread that something bad is about to happen. I have often felt I live in a world that feels unsafe and threatening. These feelings are like an echo of something old; they are not feelings rooted in adult realities. I didn't know Jesus as my Shepherd for the first seventeen years of my life. Instead I experienced a world where worry and abandonment seemed to follow me all the time.

But now I know that I live in a world where Jesus personally shepherds me. There is nothing I truly need that he does not provide. All I desire I find in him and receive from him. And if I'm being followed, it's by his goodness and love, and this will be true for eternity. I will always have a home in God's presence, and this reality is quite a contrast to beliefs formed in my childhood and experienced in emotions I still carry around as an adult.

I want to keep growing in this wholesome reality. I want to work together with my Good Shepherd as he replaces my childhood leftovers of angst, insecurity, fear, anxiety, and self-doubt. I want to trust Jesus more deeply and rely on God's goodness and love following me, surrounding me always.

What does it mean to you—despite the challenges you face now—that God's goodness and love are with you and will follow you all the days of your life?

I LIFT UP MY SOUL

To you, O LORD, I lift up my soul. (Psalm 25:1 NRSV)

WHEN I'VE READ THIS LINE previously, I've sometimes assumed that the main way I would lift up my soul was in personal prayer or corporate worship. I would measure whether I had lifted up my soul to God if I felt good feelings or experienced some sense of God with me. But what is my soul and how might I lift it up?

The imagery of being lifted up here seems to be about buoyancy. Water lifts up a floating object like a piece of wood or a boat. A boat doesn't expend immense effort to float. Floating is what happens when a boat is set in the water. It is carried without a great attempt at floating. I lift up my soul when I let God's Spirit hold me and make me buoyant. I can cooperate with this lifting up, but I cannot control it.

Sometimes my soul needs to be lifted up out of shame. In the next line David prays,

> O my God, in you I trust;
> do not let me be put to shame;
> do not let my enemies exult over me. (Psalm 25:2 NRSV)

Where shame might make me sink, I can trust God to lift me up to places of courage and hopefulness. Shame weighs us down. But God lifts us up.

When voices around me or within me would heap shame on me, God lifts me and speaks words of value and encouragement to me, and my heart is made whole.

· ·

What has weighed down your soul lately? How might you take on David's prayer as your own, lifting your soul to God and welcoming him to lift you up?

BEING FAITHFUL TO GOD

Test me, O LORD, and try me;
examine my heart and my mind.
For your love is before my eyes;
I have walked faithfully with you. (Psalm 26:2-3 BCP 1979)

UNLIKE DAVID HERE, I don't always feel the confidence to go before the Lord and state, without qualification, "I have walked faithfully with you." Why? Because I'm painfully aware of how I stumble.

I could focus instead on placing the Lord's love before my eyes. I could imagine the face of God smiling with favor. I could envision his pleasure over me as his child. I could trust that his love is always greater than my shortcomings.

I could ask God to "examine my heart and my mind" and talk with me about my faithfulness and how it might grow. What might he say to me? Perhaps this:

"You have let yourself become discouraged by your weakness when you could be encouraged by my gracious strength and faithfulness. You have let yourself be intimidated by empty fears when you might walk in the courage of my protective, mighty presence.

"Take time to refresh your vision of me day by day, even moment by moment. Receive and welcome my presence, my power, my vision, my mission for your life. Step into the promise I have given you. I will be with you as you do your work. Abide in me as you do this good work I have given you to do. Let's do it together, beginning right now."

Maybe I can just let my small faithfulness reflect God's great faithfulness to me.

. . . .

How might God's faithful presence with you be the key to your being faithful to him?

PRACTICING PRESENCE

One thing I ask from the LORD,
this only do I seek:
that I may dwell in the house of the LORD. (Psalm 27:4)

DAVID OFFERS A SINGULAR PRAYER to God. It's a prayer for presence. In my own life, I realize that presence has a few different facets.

I can be present to God. Brother Lawrence talked about practicing the presence of God. God is inviting me to cultivate growing awareness of God with me. Recently I've found the psalmist's invitation helpful: "Be still, and know that I am God" (Psalm 46:10). In the morning, I can take a few moments to be still and silent, acknowledging God's presence and leadership in my life and work. I find that my scattered thoughts are a little less overwhelming as a result.

I can be present to myself. This is a fruit of recognizing the presence of God. In another psalm the writer asks, "Why, my soul, are you downcast?" (Psalm 42:5). There is a holy awareness of impulses in me that do not echo the reality of God's grace. When I let myself become downcast, I am not paying attention to the thoughts that provoke such a movement.

I can be present to others. When I'm with someone, I'm sometimes tempted to give thought to a task or appointment that is coming up next in my plans. I allow my attention to wander away into the future instead of being present to the one in front of me. I miss the grace God would give to the other through me. May we discover the gift of being present to God, others, and ourselves.

What does the temptation to be absent look like in your life? How is Jesus inviting you to be more present to him, to yourself, to others?

WHAT I DON'T WANT FROM GOD

Do not hide your face from me,
do not turn your servant away in anger;
you have been my helper. (Psalm 27:9)

DAVID FEARS THAT GOD will hide his face and reject him in anger. But David also seems hopeful, asking that God never abandon him. As this psalm begins with David describing a terrifying situation in which he finds himself, perhaps he feels an absence of God and his help. Perhaps David wonders whether the bad things happening to him are caused by his own shortcomings, so he prays, "Do not reject me or forsake me, God my Savior" (Psalm 27:9).

I've experienced moments, even seasons, when I felt like God was more absent than present, more rejecting than embracing, more abandoning than ever-present. Sometimes troubles have tempted me to imagine that God was finally fed up with me. Rather than pretend he doesn't feel this way, David prays those thoughts and feelings aloud to God. He reminds himself that God has been his helper and savior.

Unlike David, I've sometimes been tempted to pretend I'm trusting in God when my heart is filled with doubt. I've put on a hopeful façade when my heart is full of despair. I've pretended instead of praying. Others might be impressed, but I'm not fooling God.

How much better to follow David's approach and simply pour out my heart and mind to God. What I say will not surprise God. God knows what's in me and loves me right there. I won't be shocking God with unexpected honesty. I'm safe bringing what's in me into the presence of my Father in heaven.

. . . .

When have you felt like God was more absent than present in your life? How have you spoken honestly to God as David does here, or how might you do so in the future?

LEADERSHIP: RECEIVING AND GIVING GOOD

I will exalt you, LORD,
for you lifted me out of the depths
and did not let my enemies gloat over me. (Psalm 30:1)

DAVID EXPRESSES HIS INTENTION to exalt the Lord. Why? He tells us, "For you lifted me out of the depths and did not let my enemies gloat over me." David experiences God's Spirit lifting him from the deep place in which he finds himself. Was it depression? Despair? Discouragement? Whatever the dark place was for David, the Lord lifted him out of it.

When I read those first two lines, in my heart I hear something like, "How could I help but exalt you, Lord, when you have first exalted me?" It sounds like an echo of the words of John in his first letter—"We love because he first loved us" (1 John 4:19)—but with "exalt" in place of "love." I think it works just as well.

How do I respond when I find myself in a deep, dark place? Do I hang my head and stare into the darkness? Or am I looking for God and crying out for his help? When we look up, we'll find that God continues to be a Good Shepherd. The time between cry and healing is not instantaneous, but God's faithfulness will be at work to bring healing in his time.

Whatever we offer God or give to another is always something we've first been given by God. An expression of joy is an overflow of the joyful heart of the God in whom we are at home. As we learn to not be anxious for anything, we experience the fruit of God's peaceful presence in ourselves and among one another.

. . . .

Where have you recently felt trapped in "the depths"? How might you look up and cry to God for help?

GUIDED BY UNDERSTANDING

Do not be like the horse or the mule,
which have no understanding
but must be controlled by bit and bridle. (Psalm 32:9)

THIS LINE OF SCRIPTURE is rightly used to warn against stubbornness and resisting God's guidance. But it also speaks to God's desire to help us grow into people who are guided by wisdom.

You can't give a horse or mule turn-by-turn directions to your desired destination. The animal doesn't have the capacity to understand that sort of verbal guidance. Instead, it needs to be guided with a bit and bridle. It needs to be nudged turn by turn.

But people are different. God doesn't want to give us turn-by-turn instructions for every step of our daily journey. God doesn't constrain us without our cooperation. He teaches us wisdom and understanding. He shows us what the good way looks like. His Spirit gives us a vision of the goodness of the heavens, his home, where we might also be at home. In this way we can be guided rather than controlled.

Perhaps even better, the primary outcome here is not about reaching a destination, but willingly coming to God. God does not want to force our communion with him. He seeks to draw us, attract us, woo us toward him. He doesn't tie a rope to us and pull.

God loves the heart that comes to him freely and willingly in love. We are not animals to be controlled, but beloved children to be invited. Even more than giving us guidance, God wants to give us himself as Guide.

. . . .

Are you ever tempted to think God is trying to coerce you into his good way? How instead could God be inviting and attracting you to come to him as Guide?

AN EARTH FULL OF LOVE

The LORD loves righteousness and justice;
the earth is full of his unfailing love. (Psalm 33:5)

THE EARTH IS FULL of God's unfailing love. God loves making things right. He loves restoring attitudes, thinking, and ways of relating so they are what he intended. This is the fruit of communing with the God who does everything well. When we align ourselves more closely with God, he finds pleasure in this, and we find ourselves being made more whole and holy.

Sometimes all we can see is the bad in this world. We hear news stories or witness global events and we see the injustice. Where is God in this? Despite the apparent evidence, God is working toward righteousness and justice. God is at work transforming our individual lives so that we, together, might bring change to the world around us. But that takes time. Hasn't it taken time for God to bring about the transformation your life has needed?

Later in this psalm, we're told that

The LORD foils the plans of the nations;
he thwarts the purposes of the peoples.
But the plans of the LORD stand firm forever,
the purposes of his heart through all generations. (Psalm 33:10-11)

Sometimes we struggle to see how this is true considering what we are witnessing at the present time.

A small group seeking to follow God's just guidance in their lives will lead to a just community. Small communities seeking to follow God's good counsel together with other communities lead to a more just world. Justice must have its work in me, then it can have its lasting work through me in the world around me.

. . . .

How do you sense God wants to do justice in your life? How might this work bear fruit in justice in the larger world around you? Ask God to help you discern this connection.

EMPTY ENVY

Do not fret because of those who are evil
or be envious of those who do wrong;
for like the grass they will soon wither. (Psalm 37:1-2)

DO YOU EVER FRET because someone else is doing things wrong but apparently getting ahead? What if their bottom line is better than mine because of their unscrupulous practices? Don't I have to follow suit if I am not going to be driven out of business? Let me paraphrase David's psalm prayer here:

"They are doing wrong, no question. And the results are quite enviable. This worries you. I get it. But your perspective is too small. The day will come when their wrongdoing will be exposed, and all that profit will come to nothing. They aren't building anything that will last. Their profits are like young grass in blistering weather that will wither almost as soon as it comes up.

"What others gain through dishonesty and unscrupulous shortcuts won't last. Don't follow their way. Instead, trust in the Lord and his ways. Do what you know is right. You'll find that you're building something substantial and lasting if you do. Dishonesty is often more profitable for a season. A thief has a better hourly wage than most . . . for a time. But it's a wage that is on borrowed time. At any moment he can be caught, and his lucrative activity will catch up with him in the end. It's not a way to actually live.

"And instead of delighting only in financial prosperity—which can be a great God-given source of joy and gratitude—delight in the God who is abundance personified. You'll find that everything you really want is in God anyway."

· ·

What did someone else have that you didn't? Why did you think their success was doing you harm? Talk with God about that.

CAN'T HURRY, SHOULDN'T HURRY

Be still before the Lord
and wait patiently for him. (Psalm 37:7)

It helps me to remember that one of the very practical reasons I shouldn't hurry is that there are some things in this world that simply *can't* be hurried.

We cannot rush certain natural processes. Tectonic plates may move only a dozen feet in a human lifetime. A tree may take decades to transition from seed to full growth. The sun will rise when it rises. Time cannot be rushed. There are always sixty seconds in a minute, sixty minutes in an hour, and twenty-four hours in a day. There is no accelerator pedal for time.

And so we learn that creation has its pace. Would I like to enjoy a fine bottle of wine? I'll need to give it plenty of time to mature and ripen. Simple table wines may be ready much more quickly. We sometimes try to hurry the process by which food is ready. We genetically modify plants and animals to accelerate their development, but naturally grown food is better for us in the end.

A conversation that is given time for unhurried interaction will be more satisfying than a quick chat while we're on our way to something else. Getting the amount and quality of sleep our bodies need will serve us better than stealing time for work away from our rest. Using resources sustainably (more slowly) will be better for us over time.

Life operates best at the unhurried pace of God's creation. We do well when we let ourselves slow to that pace.

. . . .

What are you tempted to hurry along that simply can't be rushed? What are you trying to rush that should be left to proceed at its own pace?

GOD MEETS ME WHERE I AM

I waited patiently upon the LORD;
he stooped to me and heard my cry. (Psalm 40:1 BCP 1979)

I LOVE THE IMAGERY of the Lord stooping to me. I remember when our three sons were little. Sometimes they would come to me crying about something that had scared or frustrated them. When they came, I would stoop or even kneel down to get on eye level with them to love and comfort them. I love that David uses an image like this to describe God's response to him when he cries out.

I am down here. God is "up there." I am a little child and God is a good Father. He meets me where I am. The way of God is fatherly and gracious. Sometimes I imagine that I need to reach up to him and get his attention, as if I must somehow jump to reach him. But God reaches down to me. He leans down to meet me where I am. He hears my cries.

Unlike the image of a little boy and a father, David says that he has learned to wait patiently for the Lord to come down to him. Little ones aren't usually good at patient waiting. So David has gained maturity in this area. This is an invitation to me. I can learn that when something in my life stresses me, I can cry out and patiently wait for God to come to me.

God comes down to my level. I simply must be patient in my watching and waiting for him. He *will* come. He will.

. . . .

When have you been in a hard season of crying out to God? How have you experienced God stooping down to meet you there? How would you like him to meet you in it?

DAY 33

GLAD RIVERS

We will not fear, though the earth should change,
though the mountains shake in the heart of the sea. . . .
There is a river whose streams make glad the city of God,
the holy habitation of the Most High. (Psalm 46:2, 4 NRSV)

CHANGE, ESPECIALLY UNPLEASANT CHANGE, can provoke fear in us by challenging our feelings of certainty and security. Storms instead of calm, tumult instead of peace—and for who knows how long—may cause us to tremble emotionally and even spiritually. It is into such a context that this peaceful river of Psalm 46 comes into view, its streams making God's city (and my heart) glad.

There is a river. Have you noticed the presence of these glad rivers in your life? I think of the many days I spent as a child playing alongside the American River in Sacramento, California. There was a park right on the riverbank just a short bike ride away from my house. I spent hours there throwing rocks in the water, watching rafters float by, looking for lizards. It was a glad river full of glad memories.

I also have glad memories about the spiritual rivers in my life. God has not let me be swept away by the rapids of change. He has enabled me to test the waters with my foot, watch and learn from others who have handled the whitewater, and catch signs of his presence with me. In the places where I'm tempted to fear, I am invited to live my life next to holy streams that will refresh and delight me.

. . . .

Describe a storm of change you have endured. In what ways did you experience your Good Shepherd's presence, even his gladness, despite your fears?

WHAT ARE YOU THINKING ABOUT?

We ponder your steadfast love, O God,
in the midst of your temple. (Psalm 48:9 NRSV)

WHAT WORDS COME TO mind when you think about God's love?

Maybe some of these: reliable, trustworthy, eternal, redemptive, transformative, undeserved, unearned, gracious. The list doesn't end there. God's love is something for us to think about long and deep. The more we do, the more we marvel.

God loves you and me in ways we can't begin to fathom. We need only look at the cross: "God demonstrates His own love toward us, in that while we were still sinners, Christ died for us" (Romans 5:8 NKJV). Psalm 139:14 tells us that we are "fearfully and wonderfully made," and Jesus even numbers the hairs on our heads (Matthew 10:30).

But do I really trust that God is love? My behavior has sometimes suggested—or perhaps even shouted—that I don't. Can that change? Can I grow to trust that God really is love? Of course, I can if I want to! Though I may never fully comprehend the measureless height, depth, length, and breadth of God's affection, his delight in me, or his availability to me, I can explore these realities more deeply than I have so far. So can you.

We can make pondering our Good Shepherd's steadfast love part of a regular engagement with God day by day.

. . . .

What, if anything, tempts you to not deeply trust that God is love?

OFFERING THANKS

Sacrifice thank offerings to God,
fulfill your vows to the Most High. (Psalm 50:14)

IN THIS PSALM OF ASAPH, God has been speaking to the people of Israel about their mistaken perception of their relationship with him. They seem to think God needs their sacrifices and offerings (Psalm 50:13). They imagine that God is somehow hungry and that their offerings provide him with something he doesn't yet have.

Instead, God reminds his people that if he were ever hungry, he wouldn't look to them for help (Psalm 50:12). Everything in the world is already God's. Our offerings or sacrifices do not provide something God cannot do without.

We may make a similar mistake in our own interactions with God. We can come to believe that God needs us to give money or go to religious meetings. God enjoys our presence but does not need our presents.

If that's true, then our best offering to God is just what Asaph suggests: offerings of gratitude. Our sacrifices are a response to God's generosity. We do not initiate grace—God does. God's economy is not dependent on something we offer or promise. God's own will and God's good intention are far more than enough for him and for us. We are responders to the sacrifice of God on our behalf. Our simple yes to God's invitation is what he wants.

It's freeing to live life recognizing the grace of God with our gifts of gratitude. Offering words and actions that express our thanks is good for us, and it is a pleasure to our Father in heaven.

. . . .

Are there ways you imagine that God needs something from you rather than inviting something from you? Ask God's Spirit to give you insight about your assumptions or expectations.

WAITING IN SILENCE

My soul, wait in silence for God alone,
For my hope is from Him. (Psalm 62:5 NASB)

MANY OF US FIND IT challenging to practice silence in the presence of God. We may find it hard to concentrate. We may find ourselves overwhelmed with distracting thoughts. We may take this to be evidence that we are just not cut out for such practice. But this experience might simply be evidence of our great need.

My own practice of silent prayer has felt this way. My difficulty in concentrating is not evidence that I'm not cut out for silent prayer but shows that I profoundly need it. Silent prayer is the remedy for my distracted mind and attention. The discomfort I feel in the presence of many distracting thoughts is part of the training. Being able to settle into peace amid anxious thoughts is the pathway to grow in my ability to notice distracting thoughts without being hooked by them.

When I intend to practice silent prayer, I can find many other activities to turn to instead. I may look for a solution to anxious thoughts by busying myself with some task. I may distract myself searching for something on the internet. But if I really believe that good work grows out of good rest, then the practice of silent prayer might just be an important element of my soul training. In silence, I remember who I am. I remember who God is. And in the silence, I might hear the voice of the one who calls me beloved.

Try sitting comfortably for five minutes in silence. Notice what happens in your heart and mind. Seek to offer God the gift of your attention as best you can.

OVERWHELMING GRACE

When we were overwhelmed by sins,
you forgave our transgressions. (Psalm 65:3)

DAVID WRITES A SONG PRAYER remembering a time when he was overwhelmed by his shortcomings or transgressions. David knew he'd come up short. He knew he'd crossed the line many times. Being overwhelmed by sins feels like guilt and sometimes even shame. I know how that feels. I don't like it.

But instead of being overwhelmed by what's wrong in us, God overwhelms our sin with his mercy and grace. Overwhelming sin is met with overflowing grace. What a gift! Letting guilt and shame overtake my soul doesn't not do me much good. And God doesn't find pleasure in how it creates even more distance between us.

I'm especially grateful that David talks about being forgiven of his *transgressions*, not just mistakes, failures, stumblings, or other such unintended slips. Transgressions usually involve some knowing disobedience, crossing over the relational boundary God has established to protect our relationship, our well-being, our health.

When I recognize I've chosen poorly, I often feel heavy. What good news it is to know that God wants to lift that burden by forgiving me. I acknowledge what I've done, and God puts it behind us. God isn't nearly as interested in rehearsing our failures as we can be. God is grace and mercy.

When have you recently felt overwhelmed by shortcomings or offenses in your life? How might you let God care for you by putting that behind and overwhelming you instead with his kind mercy and grace?

DAILY SUPPORT

Praise be to the Lord, to God our Savior,
who daily bears our burdens. (Psalm 68:19)

GOD IS NEAR US as our *Savior*. Our God is a God who saves. God does not sit on a distant throne giving occasional attention to this world. God does not wind up the clock of this planet and leave for an extended vacation. In as many ways as we need saving, God is present to save. God is our *Savior*.

God is *our* Savior, not just *my* Savior. We are being saved together in community. We are being saved with God working through each of us for the benefit of others. I need the help God can give through nearby brothers and sisters. God is *our* Savior.

As Savior, God *bears* our burdens. He sees what weighs us down and is near to carry what overwhelms us. God does not burden me but bears what would crush me. God *bears* our burdens. I don't always know all my burdens, but God is bearing them all, nonetheless.

Maybe the most precious word in this entire passage, though, is *daily*. God our Savior is with us, day by day, bearing our burdens. I wish it weren't true that I often experience burdens daily, but I do. God can't bear daily something that doesn't happen daily. There are many ways the world around us makes things heavy. When I feel that my load is just too great to carry, I must remember that I'm not even carrying the whole weight of it. God is bearing that burden with me so it doesn't end me.

What has been making your life heavy lately? Ask God to help you see how he has been present to carry some of that weight.

REVIVED AGAIN

Will you not revive us again,
that your people may rejoice in you? (Psalm 85:6)

I WISH THAT BEING revived was something I needed only once, but that hasn't been my experience. I think of the rhythm of the book of Judges where God's people begin to stray from the path of life. God sends a warning that the people fail to take to heart. Hardship in some form or another comes as God's loving discipline to awaken them. They finally turn back to God and God provides a deliverer to rescue them from the mess in which they find themselves. They experience revival.

Unfortunately, this cycle happens perhaps a dozen times in Judges. The people need to be revived again and again. Our psalm prayer asks for another chance—revive us again. I have needed to be revived often over the years. My life grows thin and drains away. I need to be refreshed and brought to vitality again.

God is always willing to receive us back into rootedness in his abundant kingdom. When we grow weary of what we thought would bring us life, our Father in heaven welcomes and embraces us. The True Vine stands ready to receive us into abiding communion once again. The Good Shepherd welcomes us back into the fold. Our Savior rescues us yet again.

I'm always grateful for the work of the Spirit to awaken me to my need for revival. God wants to restore peace and joy to my heart. God wants to awaken me to his grace and mercy. God is longing to revive us again.

In what ways have you felt more drained than refreshed, more deadened than alive? Why not ask God to draw you to the place of fresh revival yet again?

ETERNAL RULE, UNCHANGING LAWS

Your statutes, Lord, stand firm;
holiness adorns your house
for endless days. (Psalm 93:5)

THE PSALMIST ACKNOWLEDGES THAT God himself has ruled everything "from all eternity" (Psalm 93:2). He has ruled everything from before there was anything except the triune God himself. As sovereign and eternal God, he needed no one to establish his reign for him. The Almighty required no help or additional authority. Nor was he elected or appointed or named successor to someone else. God exists from all eternity past, and he will exist throughout all eternity future. What a remarkable truth!

Then, as verse 5 teaches, not only does God's throne—his rule—exist from eternity past throughout eternity future, but so does his holiness. We also see that the Lord's statutes stand firm.

Yet I still emotionally resist the word "statute" because it reminds me of legalistic teachings and modeling from my early Christian experience. But a beautiful, simple statute that leads to fuller joy, peace, and energy for the kingdom is not something to resist. I choose to receive God's statutes as good news and a great opportunity to really live. He guides me into the place of secure and abundant life.

Finally, there are no commands in Psalm 93. The psalmist simply acknowledges God—his eternal existence, his authority over all, his holiness, and his steadfast reign.

Like the psalmist, you and I have a God who reigns and who has chosen us and adopted us as his children. We can behold God's beauty. We can approach God's eternal throne freely and confidently.

· ·

When have you appreciated the value of God's statutes and laws? When, for instance, did his guidelines provide you much-needed guidance, protection, wisdom, or grace?

THE BEAUTY OF BELONGING

Know that the LORD is God.
It is he who made us, and we are his;
we are his people, the sheep of his pasture. (Psalm 100:3)

I GET INTO TROUBLE when I pretend that I'm god instead of remembering that the Lord is God. When I try to run life on my own, I find that I don't quite have the wisdom or strength to do it as well as I thought I would.

God made me, and I belong to God. We sometimes talk about a person being "self-made." We think that such people, by virtue of their own efforts, wisdom, creativity, or drive, have made a name for themselves. But an identity that needs to be earned needs to keep being earned.

Instead, our true identity is given. We are God's people, and God is our Shepherd. We belong to God. Belonging to God is more about having a reliable home than it is God running our lives in ways that limit or constrain us.

It is good news for our souls to remember that the Lord is God, is our Creator, is the Father to whom we belong, is our very good Shepherd.

. . . .

Which of these words to describe the Lord intersect with where you are in this moment? Take a moment to be still and remember this reality of God in your life.

PRAISE AND THANKSGIVING

Enter his gates with thanksgiving
and his courts with praise;
give thanks to him and praise his name. (Psalm 100:4)

THIS PSALM INVITES US to enter the presence of God with gratitude and praise. We offer these to "his name."

I've come to understand praise as the way in which I remember the words God has spoken of himself and then affirm them with words that acknowledge who God is in words that echo his own. I agree with who God says he is.

This has a way of combating false assumptions about God that linger in my young emotions. Sometimes I seem to be praying to a God who is short-tempered instead of the God who reveals himself as slow to anger. Or I'm coming into the presence of a God who holds a grudge against me instead of the God who delights in mercy and longs to be gracious to me.

Then, thanksgiving is also the way in which I give words to the gratitude that rises within me in recognition of God's generous grace. God is good to me in more ways that I even notice. Gratitude expands my awareness of just how graced my life is.

I acknowledge the grace of God by speaking words of thanksgiving to God. I give God the gift of my thanks. It's good for my soul to come into the presence of God with words of affirming appreciation and generous gratitude.

. . . .

Take a moment to do what the psalm invites you to do: offer some words of appreciation for who God is (praise) or what God has done in your life (thanksgiving).

THE POWER OF RECALLING GRACE

Praise the LORD, O my soul,
and forget not all his benefits. (Psalm 103:2 BCP 2019)

DAVID'S HEART IS FULL of praise as he remembers the good things he experiences in the presence of God. My heart is also full of praise when I am fully awake to the multifaceted grace of God in my life. My heart becomes full of complaint when I forget and let disappointing circumstances fill my awareness and my meditations.

Remembering I am forgiven inspires worship; thinking I am accused or condemned doesn't. Remembering I am shepherded in my weakness and illness provokes praise; feeling abandoned to what hinders or hampers me doesn't. Remembering I have a Savior brightens my perspective; thinking I am stuck in a dark pit doesn't.

Remembering that God honors me with mercy and everlasting love fills my heart with joy; imagining that God is impatient and disappointed with me doesn't. Remembering that the Lord is my portion and provides an abundance of goodness for my deepest needs encourages a bright perspective; believing myself to be mostly stuck in scarcity doesn't.

I need to often remember all God's benefits to me. I get into trouble when I am forgetful. Forgetting is like coasting downhill—it requires no intention or effort. Remembering requires remaining awake in my soul toward God and God's goodness. I can choose to remember, and it's good when I do. I can tell my soul to bless the Lord and remember how gracious, forgiving, healing, protecting, and generous he is in my life.

· ·

How are you reminded of the goodness of God in your life right now? How might you be rehearsing certain hardships, losses, or weaknesses? Which would you prefer to do now?

THE HOLY ENERGY OF SEEK FIRST

All creatures look to you
to give them their food at the proper time. (Psalm 104:27)

ALL CREATURES. When I read these words, I tend to think of critters like the finches nesting in the eaves above our front door, the hummingbirds that buzz around our backyard, or our little dog, Lex, who brings us so much joy.

But I am one of God's creatures. I am one of the living beings made by God. God nourishes me and provides for me just when I need him to ("at the proper time"). Who decides on that timing? God does. God opens his hand to me, and I receive good things that satisfy my hunger and thirst. I am grateful!

Whatever satisfaction I experience in my life, it is the fruit of receiving what God gives. It is the fruit of divine generosity and God's gracious initiative and activity. The invitation of Psalm 104 is profoundly simple: *Look to God.* I direct my attention to the God who is always with me. I focus my gaze on the face of God, the hand of God, the presence of God-with-us. I keep looking until grace meets me "at the proper time."

Whatever I need for today will be something given, not taken. I'm invited to lift my open hands into the presence of God throughout this day and to be ready and receptive. I'm invited to wait patiently, wait attentively, wait readily, like a sprinter in the blocks. When grace comes, I will know the presence of God's generous peace.

. . . .

How might you direct your current hunger toward the one who has made you? What would it look like to wait patiently for grace to meet you here?

RESPONDING TO GOD

When you send your Spirit,
they are created,
and you renew the face of the ground. (Psalm 104:30)

WHAT WE NEED IS a gift from God. We live in a world where God provides generously. We learn to turn our eyes toward God whenever we feel hunger, thirst, or longing. There is a rhythm in this psalm that rings in my heart as I read: "When you . . . they" (see Psalm 104:27-30). God initiates and we respond. God acts and we receive. God creates and we benefit.

On a retreat once I noticed this rhythm and wrote some couplets of my own: "When you provide good food for me, I enjoy it with gratitude. When you provide me with a beautiful bride and gifted sons, I welcome them as your gift. When you provide me with times to be still and remember that you really are God, I enter into them and learn how to listen better. When you provide me with good books to read, I sink into them, seeking to read like a learner and not an expert.

"When you create beauty in the world around me, I learn to live with my eyes and heart awake to visible goodness. When your Spirit inspires and guides me, I write words I trust will give grace and encouragement to those who read. When you promise to provide us with everything we need, I watch for and receive good things you provide with the intention to be generous with others. When you give me a heart full of true feelings, I learn to notice them, discern them, and express them in loving relationship."

. . . .

Write your own "When you . . . I" journal entry. Where are you noticing the grace of God at work in your life?

ENVISIONING GLORY

Glory in his holy name;
let the hearts of those who seek the LORD *rejoice.*
Look to the LORD *and his strength;*
seek his face always. (Psalm 105:3-4)

GLORY IN HIS HOLY NAME. I can revel in the beauty and weightiness of who God is. I can exult in the vast extent of God's greatness. When I recognize how glorious God is, my heart is overwhelmed with praise. When I lose sight of God, my life becomes dimmer and thinner—less glorious.

Let the hearts of those who seek the LORD *rejoice.* I orient my attention toward God. The psalm here invites me to a focus on God that inspires overflowing joy in me. Does my vision of God inspire joy? Do I see God as he is—profoundly generous and magnificently good?

Look to the LORD *and his strength.* I remember how God has been powerful in my life before, and then I recognize how God will strengthen me today. When I feel weak, I am not alone. I am companioned by a powerful God who is also my Father. When I am tired, I can remember I'm in the presence of God who is my rest.

Seek his face always. Looking into someone's face is an act of intimacy. I don't gaze into someone's face unless I am welcomed by them. Staring into a stranger's face at the grocery store would make us both uncomfortable! I can grow in my continual awareness of the smiling, caring face of God in Christ before me.

. . . .

Which of these four prayer phrases seems most timely for you today? Why not let it guide you into conversation with God now?

THE GRACE OF A
STEADFAST HEART

My heart, O God, is steadfast;
I will sing and make music with all my soul. (Psalm 108:1)

I LOVE THE IMAGE of David's steadfast heart. When my heart is distracted or unsteady or timid, I can find, as David did, a heart that is confident, stable, even steadfast. How does that happen? What would that look like? I find that a good place to start is opening my heart and pouring out what is in it before God. I talk with God honestly about the thoughts and feelings present in my mind and heart.

But then, like David, I often find myself rehearsing the reality of God. I acknowledge the grandeur of God above all my puny thoughts and feelings. I ask for what I need: salvation and help. David's way of praying in this psalm inspires a prayer in me:

O God, your love for me—for us—is so vast that it reaches higher than the sun, the moon, and the stars. Yours is no small love. And your faithfulness—your reliable, powerful availability to me—is greater than the atmosphere above me and the clouds in the sky today. Be exalted, O God, in my life and work today. May who you are and what you do be the largest reality for me. May the beauty and weightiness of who you are fill me and overflow as I write or work or speak or whatever I may do. Amen.

. . . .

What words do you want to say to God about whatever need for rescue or help you may have in this season?

GOD CALLS US HIS OWN

Gilead is mine, Manasseh is mine;
Ephraim is my helmet,
Judah is my scepter. (Psalm 108:8)

GILEAD WAS A REGION of the Promised Land east of the Jordan River that belonged to the tribe of Manasseh. Ephraim, Manasseh, and Judah are all tribes of Israel—the people of God.

What would it feel like to hear God say, "You are mine" about the people who are dear to me? When it comes to my family, can I hear God saying, "Gem is mine, Sean is mine, Bryan is mine, and Chris is mine"? Can I imagine God saying "my helmet" and "my scepter" about those who are close to me? Through them God fights his battles and conducts his reign. They are intimately involved in the work of God. Amazing!

And then there are Moab, Edom, and Philistia, all enemies of Israel (Psalm 108:9). God uses his enemies as a place to wash his hands, toss his sandals, and proclaim his victory. My enemies may feel overwhelming to me, but God sees them as insignificant.

Just as I can have deep confidence that I belong to God, everything in my life also belongs to him. God is more concerned about what concerns me than I am. Those enemies who come against me are small and inconsequential in the presence of an almighty God who happens to be my Father in heaven. When I let my concerns loom large on the horizon of my emotions, imagination, or thoughts, I am forgetting this simple, potent reality.

· ·

Think about the people or situations in your life. What would it feel like to hear God say to you, "This one is mine. That one is mine. These belong to me"? Take a moment to envision this.

EMPTY PRAYERS,
POWERFUL PRAYERS

Not to us, LORD, not to us
but to your name be the glory,
because of your love and faithfulness. (Psalm 115:1)

TWICE THE PSALMIST SAYS, "Not to us." We live in a culture that is glory-seeking. The singer here wants to remember that all true glory—all beauty and significance—finds its end in God. We don't have glory coming to us like the Lord does. The Lord is loving and faithful in ways we can't begin to be.

Not to me today, but to you today, Lord. You are the weighty one. You are the shining one. You love me. I can count on you. And your love and faithfulness are descriptions of how you treat those you have made, including me.

The singer goes on to unpack this glory perspective:

Why do the nations say,
"Where is their God?"
Our God is in heaven;
he does whatever pleases him.
But their idols are silver and gold,
made by human hands. (Psalm 115:2-4)

The culture around us takes God lightly but pours glory onto empty idols. There is much empty glory in today's world. But idols cannot contain the glory we pour into them. They are a bottomless pit and a drain leading to nowhere. The "glory" of more money and possessions is no different from building an idol out of silver and gold. "Money, save me!" is a foolish prayer. "Fame, deliver me!" is empty. "Power, protect me!" will not bring me an ounce of help when cancer or natural disaster or economic ruin strikes.

. . . .

In what ways do you wish to notice God's glory and acknowledge it? Ask God's Spirit to give you eyes to see his beauty and his power in ways that provoke praise within you.

THE LORD REMEMBERS US

The LORD remembers us and will bless us:
He will bless his people Israel,
he will bless the house of Aaron. (Psalm 115:12)

OUR GOD IS A GOD who remembers us. He has us in mind. His heart is to bless those who are seen as great and those who are seen as nobodies. Such human distinctions mean little to God. God is at work to make each one of us flourish. We can learn how to welcome and embrace this work so that flourishing becomes our home.

God blesses us and causes us to flourish so we can be a blessing in the lives of those around us and serve them in ways that enable them to also flourish. The best way we can do that is to point them to the Flourisher in Chief. God, the master artist, makes a beautiful and creative world of abundance. God is not one to skimp when it comes to creative work. And we are his creative work.

Today may we see God's hand of blessing in our lives, our relationships, and our work. May we find our way to trusting in divine abundance as the atmosphere of God's kingdom. May we and our children know this grace and peace. And may all this goodness so fill our lives that they overflow with goodness that blesses others.

· ·

In what ways have you been tempted to feel that God has forgotten you? What evidence do you see that God is remembering you to bless you?

GRACE AND RIGHTEOUSNESS

The LORD is gracious and righteous;
our God is full of compassion. (Psalm 116:5)

WHAT HAPPENS IN MY HEART when I read these lines? I realize there are young emotions within me that cannot conceive of a God who is both gracious and righteous. Inside is still a young child terrified of the angry God that was preached in the fundamentalist church I attended in my childhood.

The words "gracious" and "righteous" may sound as if they are in opposition to each other. We may think "gracious" means unconcerned about what's right and what's wrong. We may misunderstand "righteous" as meaning right and wrong are the only categories through which to view the world. But God is graciously righteous and righteously gracious.

God's grace is full of light, goodness, wellness, and, in this sense, righteousness. Grace is medicine that makes good living possible. And God's righteousness is not pinched, external, or starchy. God is simply right about what is good, true, and beautiful. God's righteousness is full of compassion and kindness.

When my soul is restless, I can remind myself of how gracious God has been in my life. When my soul is restless, I can remind myself of how good and wise God is to lead me in the way that is just right for me. My soul's restlessness seems rooted in a vision of God as demanding something of me without empowering me to do it. What rest my soul finds when it trusts in the grace and goodness of God!

. . . .

When you think about God as gracious and righteous, how do these sound to your ear? Do you sense resonance or dissonance within? Talk with God a bit about this.

CALLING ON THE LORD

Out of my distress I called on the LORD;
the LORD answered me and set me in a broad place. (Psalm 118:5 NRSV)

HOW DO YOU RESPOND to times of distress? Do you complain to those close to you? Do you find yourself calling out to the Lord? In my experience—not surprisingly—the second response has been far more fruitful than the first. After all, the promise is there: "The LORD answered me."

Our calling out won't be in vain. God's answer is sure. And his answer is an action: he puts us "in a broad place." The Book of Common Prayer 1979 renders the second line of Psalm 118:5 as "The LORD answered by setting me free." Setting that alongside the "broad place," we can see that freedom and spaciousness go together.

Yet some of us might be surprised to realize we're afraid of true freedom. Spaciousness can make us feel exposed rather than safe. We sometimes prefer our closed-in, constricted spaces because they provide a false sense of security. But safety and security are not so much a matter of being separated from danger as being protected *in* danger.

The next verse of Psalm 118 addresses exactly that: "With the LORD on my side I do not fear. What can mortals do to me?" (Psalm 118:6 NRSV). By God's grace, a broad and spacious place is at the same time a place where we are protected by him and are led by our Good Shepherd.

. . . .

What experience or current situation comes to mind when you read, "Out of my distress"? What has God done to bring you out of that distress—or what are you praying he will do for you now?

WHERE TO FIND HELP

It is better to take refuge in the LORD
than to trust in princes. (Psalm 118:9)

BETTER. IT'S A WORD of comparison. It says one thing is more helpful, more useful, more beneficial than another thing.

It's nice to have human reasons to be confident about our ability to do life. I am, for instance, grateful for education, natural abilities, experience, and physical resources God has graciously and generously given me. But none of these is a refuge from what attacks my soul. I can't buy my way out of the enemy's assaults with any amount of money. My King, the Lord, is a far better refuge than anything mere human resources (i.e., "the flesh") can offer.

As for putting confidence in princes, I've often been tempted to think, *if only our nonprofit had more major donors, then our troubles would be over.* But my refuge and the source of my provision are the Lord, the Prince of Peace, who has decided to have me on his side. I haven't any lack of resources in him.

Frankly, I'm not always so clear about how to access resources God is making available. I know how to use a debit card to access funds in our bank account. I know how to pull cash out of my wallet to purchase something. But I'm still learning how to access divine resources. We can ask God to mentor us in living and working from a place of divine provision. What a great way to pray!

· ·

What is your personal version of putting your trust in human resources ("the flesh")? What is your version of putting confidence in princes? Why do you seek confidence and trust in these lesser things? What can you do to loosen their grip on your imagination?

GOD'S GOOD JUDGMENT

I do not shrink from your judgments,
because you yourself have taught me. (Psalm 119:102 BCP 1979)

WHEN I READ THE WORD "judgments," I'm tempted to assume the psalmist is talking about condemning judgment. I imagine God sitting on a throne of accusation. Who wouldn't shrink from condemnation by an all-knowing God? Instead, the psalmist is speaking of judgment in terms of God's declarations about reality. The psalmist is inviting us to embrace how God tells us exactly the way things are. When God speaks, his words describe how things really are.

We can let go of the belief that God's main purpose is to condemn us. God did not send Jesus into the world to condemn the world but to save it (John 3:17). In Christ there is absolutely no condemnation for us, because God's Spirit has set us free from the reign of sin and death in us (Romans 8:1-2).

When God speaks reality to me, even if it seems unpleasant in the moment, it is always good. God has better judgment than anyone. I see my fantasies and bent perspectives in the light of what actually is. I learn to trust his assessment of my life. He intends my good. In that way, the judgments of God are always good news. Rather than shrinking from the declarations of God, I'm learning to lean into this sort of divine counsel.

. . . .

Can you think of something in your life that you may be tempted to hide from God's sight, perhaps for fear that you would be condemned? Imagine a vision of the God who comes to forgive, heal, and restore that very place in your life. How does this change your approach to God?

DAY 59

UNLESS GOD

Unless the LORD builds the house,
the builders labor in vain.
Unless the LORD watches over the city,
the guards stand watch in vain. (Psalm 127:1)

GOD IS BUILDING, so we can build with him fruitfully. *God* watches over us, so we can watch with him in confidence. *God* grants rest and sleep to his loved ones, so we can work enough but not too much (Psalm 127:2). God's work and God's activity come first. Grace always precedes our activities.

What am I trying to build these days that will prove empty if God isn't building there? What am I trying to protect or guard against that will be useless if God isn't in it? In what ways am I working long hours without regard for God's work that enables me to relax a bit?

When I'm building or guarding or working, it's easy to focus on what I'm doing. In my building, God invites me to notice where he is already building. In trying to protect something, God invites me to consider what he wants to guard. My work is not fruitful because of how many hours I put in. It is fruitful because I'm learning to join God in the work already being done.

Apart from God's grace, my efforts are in vain. *Vain* simply means "empty," without meaning, reality, or substance. My efforts and toil don't have much meaning or substance apart from how they are aligned with God's work.

· ·

Which of these human activities—building, guarding, working—are you wrestling with these days? Ask God to help you see how *he* is building, guarding, or working in those places.

DAY 60

QUIETING MY SOUL

But I have calmed and quieted myself,
I am like a weaned child with its mother;
like a weaned child I am content. (Psalm 131:2)

OFTEN I SET ASIDE part of a day to be alone in God's presence. Here is a memory from one of those days:

As I hike up this hillside, I want to be still and remember that God is God (Psalm 46:10). I hike and rest, but my mind is still busy with my many thoughts. Sometimes the physical activity helps me quiet my mind and heart.

As I reach the top of the hill, I see a lake to the southwest. Vista views like this help me sense the spaciousness of my soul in the presence of God. Alone with God, I often feel moved to a higher place where I can see where I'm at, where I've been, and where I'm going all at once.

As I sit, I feel the coming and going of the breeze. I notice a fir tree swaying with the wind. The needles are in constant motion. The smaller branches move when the breeze blows a bit stronger. The larger branches and top of the trunk rarely move—only with the strongest gusts. The trunk doesn't budge at all in the wind.

If the wind represents the winds of change, the influence of my surrounding culture, then I want to be the trunk—immovable and deeply rooted in God. If the wind is the moving of God's Spirit, then I want to be the smallest, humblest branch, moving wherever the Spirit moves me.

. . . .

When might you find an hour or two to enjoy the presence of God in creation? How can you allow God's Spirit to speak to you through what he's made?

HOW GOOD AND PLEASANT!

How good and pleasant it is
when God's people live together in unity! . . .
It is as if the dew of Hermon
were falling on Mount Zion. (Psalm 133:1, 3)

IT IS INDEED GOOD and pleasant when people—especially God's people—dwell in unity. When people are of one mind for a specific goal—when God's people are of one heart overflowing with love for him and one another—good things can happen.

In the same way, it isn't very good or pleasant when our human brokenness divides us or distances us from one another. Instead of feeling like the "dew of Hermon," it feels more like the deserts of Sinai.

In this psalm David acknowledges the unexpected beauty of unity when he refers to Mount Hermon and Mount Zion. The temperate climate of Hermon meant green lushness, and David imagined Hermon's fresh dew falling in the desert-like climate of Mount Zion. The life-giving and perhaps somewhat surprising relief of that morning dew would indeed be good and pleasant for residents of Mount Zion.

Zion is God's dwelling place. It's the place where God offers his blessing of life forevermore (Psalm 133:3). God invites us to be part of the work of bringing his people together. As we each draw near to him individually, we'll find we are drawing close to one another as well. How good and pleasant it is.

. . . .

When has God given you unexpected refreshment in a desert season of your life? How can that touchstone encourage you if life is desert-like right now?

GOD'S APPARENT ABSENCE

If I say, "Surely the darkness will hide me
and the light become night around me,"
even the darkness will not be dark to you. (Psalm 139:11-12)

ARE THERE PLACES IN your life where it feels like you've made a left, but God seems to have taken a right? You feel like you're wandering, but you don't feel like you chose to wander away. I was in a place of God's apparent absence when I prayed Psalm 139 a while back:

Father, you have searched me and you know all that is in me. You have seen each time I sat at my desk and each time I rose. You know just what I'm thinking, even when I'm not sure. You are aware of when I arose this morning to go to a meeting, and you'll be the one who knows the moment when I lie down. Before I said a word today, Father, you knew what it would be. There are no surprises for you when it comes to me.

If I rocketed to the heights of the heavens, you'd be there to greet me. If I went down to the deepest depths (which I have felt lately), you have not lost touch with me. If I could travel at light speed from sunrise to the other side of the Pacific Ocean, you would be there to meet me. If I think there is darkness where you cease to feel present, I am mistaken. Darkness cannot overwhelm the light of your presence. You lovingly see everything.

Enable me to see the unseen. Open the eyes of my heart to discern your presence with me in these dark places in which I find myself. Enlighten me in ways I cannot achieve by my own efforts.

. . . .

When has God seemed more absent than present to you recently?

ALREADY WONDERFUL

I praise you because I am fearfully and wonderfully made;
your works are wonderful,
I know that full well. (Psalm 139:14)

I WAS TOUCHED WATCHING *Won't You Be My Neighbor?*, a documentary about the life of Mr. Rogers of children's television fame. He meant a lot to me as a child in the 1960s. As an adult, I learned we shared the same birthday.

At some point in the documentary, someone blames Mr. Rogers's affirming message that children are special just the way they are for the lack of initiative or work ethic among today's young adults. Was Mr. Rogers's quiet voice of affirming love really that destructive? Might not the noisy, demanding, threatening voices of most of the rest of television and other media impact the courage, creativity, and initiative of our children?

I'm sure the one making this complaint didn't intend it this way, but his accusation sounds to my ear like this: "We need more insecurity among our youth. We need them to feel bad about themselves so they'll feel the pressure to work hard and prove themselves." Perhaps that kind of self-doubt is a great way to raise consumers, but it might not be the way we want to raise loving human beings.

My own experience is that coming to believe in my value *before* I produce something bears better fruit than my insecurity ever did. I've taken more risks. I've been more creative and energized. My work is an expression of something already wonderful about me from the beginning.

. . . .

In what ways do you trust in your value as a gift to be received rather than a paycheck to be earned? What do you sense God wanting you to know and trust about this today?

HOW WE BLESS

May our barns be filled,
with produce of every kind. (Psalm 144:13 NRSV)

I LOVE THESE LINES, these words of blessing. Did you notice that they are not just "me" prayers but "us" prayers? These blessings are wishes for robust life, great abundance, and protection from real harm. It takes faith in the ready generosity of God to speak words of blessing to others.

These psalm blessings got me thinking about blessings I want to pray for the good of my family, friends, community, nation. Here are some that came to mind:

- May you bless every desire in our hearts to do good in honor of your kingdom.
- May our families seek you first, O God, in everything we do.
- May our next season be one of recovering whatever the locusts have eaten in the last ones.
- May we know deep peace, abounding joy, boundless love, and holy power in our lives.
- May we see you and your ways even more clearly than we have so far.
- May we be strengthened within to grow in our confident experience of your ever-present love.
- May we be as carefree in heart and mind as the birds in our backyards. May we, like them, simply trust that you, our Good Shepherd, will care for us day by day.

Take time to formulate words of blessing for you and your family, for you and your church, or for you and your community.

WHAT DELIGHTS GOD?

He has no pleasure in the strength of a horse;
neither does he delight in any [one's] strength.
But the LORD's delight is in those who fear him
and put their trust in his mercy. (Psalm 147:10-11 BCP 2019)

THIS PSALM ISN'T SAYING that God despises horses or human strength. Rather, the psalm is speaking of war horses and infantry might. God is not impressed by military resources we use to attack and defeat others. What pleases the Lord is not what we accomplish in our own strength but our trusting, reverent orientation toward him.

Awaiting God's gracious favor is different from attacking in our own strength to get what we want. In today's world, people too often do the latter. But it's a delightful thing to the heart of God when we humble ourselves and follow him as closely as we can.

Reading the rest of Psalm 147, we hear a recitation of all God's initiatives on behalf of his people: strengthening their protection, blessing their children, giving them peace with other nations, providing the best food, commanding the good of the earth, providing snow and rain, and so forth.

I wonder if a prayer like this one might arise in your heart as you reflect on these things: *Today, Lord, grant me a greater awareness of your work, rather than being so impressed, obsessed, or even overwhelmed by my own work. Help me to remember that my work is microscopic compared to yours. Cure me of empty pride and relieve me of the illusion that my yoke is heavier than it really is.*

. . . .

In what ways are you tempted to focus on your own resources, capabilities, or strengths instead of cultivating a humble posture focused on God?

WHERE WISDOM MEETS US

At the highest point along the way,
where the paths meet, [wisdom] takes her stand;
beside the gate leading into the city. (Proverbs 8:2-3)

THERE ARE THREE PLACES where God's wisdom meets us:

Perspective places (at the highest point). A while back I used one of our upstairs bedrooms as my home office. Because our home sits on top of a hill, I was able to see most of our county stretched out to the north before me. It was a perspective place for me—a vista that stirred in me a hunger for greater perspective of heart and mind. God's wisdom meets me to give me the gift of broader vision. Like that vista view, God grants us the capacity to see even further in our life when we might sometimes feel we have blinders on.

Decision places (where the paths meet). There are many crossroads at which I need wisdom. Will I live in God's love or linger in the places of fear? Will I be driven by anxieties and worries or be at home in God's peace? Will I live my life trusting in kingdom realities or live only by what I can take in by my senses? God's wisdom meets me to guide me as I make decisions at these crossroads in my spiritual journey.

Starting places (beside the gate). My life has had many beginning places. I've started new jobs, new initiatives, new projects. Every day can be a fresh starting place. Each morning greets us with new opportunities and prospects to live well with God.

. . . .

Which of these three places seem most familiar to you today? Wouldn't it be good to take a moment now to welcome God's wisdom to meet you right there?

GRACE AND DISCIPLINE: INVESTING OUR TIME

For everything there is a season, and a time for every matter under heaven:
a time to be born, and a time to die. (Ecclesiastes 3:1-2 ESV)

GOD INVITES US TO SHOW our love for him and for people by obeying and serving according to his loving call in our lives. He gives us the resources we will need as well as peace and grace.

Yet God's generous empowerment doesn't come to me as I sit around inactive and disengaged. The engine of grace requires the transmission of my engaged will. In prayer, for instance, I actively welcome grace into every relationship and activity of my life. As Reginald Somerset Ward says in *A Guide for Spiritual Directors*, we actively welcome grace into our life by spending the currency of our time:

> Grace requires for its use and fruition our cooperation, which is given by the soul through its authentic voice, the will, in the form of discipline. Discipline in prayer is expressed by paying the cost of receiving and developing the grace. If we search for the manner in which this cost must be paid, it would seem that there is only one universal currency common to all human beings in the world, and that is the amount of time between the present moment and the moment of our death.

Everything we involve ourselves in we pay for with the currency of time. What I do with my time determines the outcome of my life. I want to be a person who spends my time well and learn where I am spending it unwisely. I want every moment to be invested well. What am I investing my time in for the long term?

. . . .

Where do you see the difference between spending time and investing time in your life?

WHEN COMMUNITY OVERCOMES ISOLATION

Though one may be overpowered,
two can defend themselves.
A cord of three strands is not quickly broken. (Ecclesiastes 4:12)

SOLITUDE CAN BE GOOD—being alone in the loving presence of God. Isolation isn't so great—alone without friendship or help. The writer of Ecclesiastes explains how community is better than isolation.

First, he says that "two are better than one, because they have a good return for their labor" (Ecclesiastes 4:9). There is a synergy in collaboration that isn't possible in certain sorts of solitary work. Might this speak to American individualism? When we think about authorship of books, many assume that a book by one person is better than one by two or more authors. When we think of leadership in an organization, we tend to see one at the top, not two or more. We say, "I can do it myself." Ecclesiastes says it isn't always so.

One plus one can be greater than two. "If either of them falls down, one can help the other up" (Ecclesiastes 4:10). It is unfortunate when one who stumbles has no one help them up. When one person is in need, another person can help. If I seek to stand alone, I will also stumble alone, struggle alone, and fall alone.

It's hard to find encouragement or warmth alone. "If two lie down together, they will keep warm. But how can one keep warm alone?" (Ecclesiastes 4:11). This is when solitary communion can become lonely isolation. The coal that sits apart from the fire grows cold. The one who remains at a distance from others does, too.

. . . .

When have you been alone in a way that felt fruitless, vulnerable, or cold? Who might God have already given you to share this story with—to share this burden with?

DAY 71

A SHOUT OF PRAISE

Shout aloud and sing for joy, people of Zion,
for great is the Holy One of Israel among you. (Isaiah 12:6)

THESE LINES FROM ISAIAH shaped one day of an eight-day retreat. I was especially provoked by the invitation to shout aloud God's greatness. Since the retreat I was attending was silent, I was sure that the rest of the community would not be grateful for my obedience to this noisy command.

So I decided to take a walk to a nearby lighthouse that included a half-mile breakwater protecting the nearby harbor. As I walked I came upon signs that had turned me back the day before, indicating "Private Road" and "Members Only." If I was going to shout my praise from the lighthouse jetty, I was going to have to press past those warnings.

I finally realized the main road was public and, in fact, went all the way to the lighthouse. I continued walking nearly a half-mile out into the harbor on the rock jetty with waves crashing around me. They seemed to be challenging me to a shout-off. I saw the harbor front of the nearby town to the north and the Boston skyline to my southwest.

I don't shout very often, but God was urging me to offer shouts of joy his way. So I began to yell as loud as I could how awed I felt by God's creativity, God's great power, God's unfailing love for me, God's measureless goodness. The more I shouted, the more I felt holy energy filling my body, my mind, and my heart. How good to give praise to God with all the energy and volume God has given me.

. . . .

How and where might you freely shout your praise to God? Why not accept this holy invitation?

I AM NOT ANGRY

I guard it day and night
so that no one may harm it.
I am not angry. (Isaiah 27:3-4)

ON THE SAME RETREAT in which God used the words of Isaiah to invite me to shout my praise to him, the words above from Isaiah became a personal communication with God. God was speaking as "I" to me. "It" is his fruitful vineyard. I found myself changing "it" to "you."

"I am the Lord who watches over you. I bring refreshment to you. I guard you day and night to protect you from harm." But it was the last four words that awakened me: "I am not angry with you, Alan."

I grew up with a vision of God that seemed *very* angry with me. I had come to know Scriptures that reminded me God is slow to anger, but I still assumed God often had reason to be angry or disappointed with me.

When I read those words, I couldn't remember reading them before (though I had many times) or any like them. A general statement about God as slow to anger was frequent and familiar. God speaking personally to his people—to me—to say, "I am not angry" surprised me.

I thought about my shortcomings and offenses that I assumed provoked God's anger toward me, but God was wanting me to know that his bias is to keep his loving eye on me, to generously provide for me everything I need, to stand guard in my life to protect me from any lasting harm. Anger would do little to serve his purposes for me.

. . . .

Do you ever feel like God's posture toward you is anger or disappointment? How might these words of God through Isaiah brighten your vision of God's mercy and grace?

OVERCOMING FEAR

Fear not, for I am with you;
be not dismayed, for I am your God. (Isaiah 41:10 ESV)

THE COMMAND TO "FEAR NOT" appears hundreds of times in Scripture. God knows our human tendency to fear, or he wouldn't have offered such reassurance again and again and again.

But there is no simple switch to flip for sure obedience to this often-repeated command—at least, I haven't found one yet! Something I have found helpful, though, comes from spiritual director and pastor Reginald Somerset Ward. Hear his simple but potent insight from *A Guide for Spiritual Directors*:

> In considering fear, there is only one medicine which can produce an absolute cure; and that is a complete and overwhelming faith and simple trust in the love and power of God, in His will and ability to make of every happening in life a means of ultimate welfare and happiness.

Where faith is growing, fear diminishes. Trust—choosing to trust—in the reliable care and mighty capability of God leaves less and less room for fear that hinders, let alone fear that paralyzes. Trust in the love of God displaces fear. God really is working in everything—even our current circumstances—with an eye for our good and for the fulfilling of his good purposes.

What has it looked like in your life for you to respond in trust to God's love and power in places of fear? In what way might God be inviting you to a place of deeper, simpler trust?

GENTLE RESTORATION

He will not shout or cry out,
or raise his voice in the streets.
A bruised reed he will not break,
and a smoldering wick he will not snuff out. (Isaiah 42:2-3)

ISAIAH IS TALKING ABOUT "God's servant" here. He speaks in advance of what Messiah would be like. His righteousness is not a noisy crusade but a quiet, persistent pursuit. His kind of righteousness doesn't require a lot of shouting. He doesn't need to yell to get anyone's attention. He doesn't have to dominate to lead. He doesn't need to promote himself with impressive speech. He speaks truth with gentle persistence.

Isaiah uses two images to illustrate the gentle way of this Servant. First, he will not break a bruised reed. Isaiah's word for "bruised" is greater than a surface mark. The reed has been damaged. We don't tend to choose damaged goods. We prefer shiny new things. What good news, then, that Jesus is a master restorer. He is drawn to what has been bruised in us so that he can restore us.

Isaiah also talks about smoldering wicks. We don't want to work with something or someone who is almost extinguished. We want something new and exciting. But Jesus wants to tend that which barely smolders until it comes back to flame.

Don't you sometimes feel like you've been bruised or damaged along the way? Don't you sometimes feel like your life is barely alight? What good news that Jesus is drawn to you to renew, revive, and restore.

. . . .

Where have you felt damaged? When have you felt like your life was barely smoldering? Talk to Jesus about how he'd like to restore and revive you. Take a moment to listen for his gentle, strong shepherd's voice.

HE HOLDS YOUR HAND

I, the LORD, have called you in righteousness;
I will take hold of your hand. (Isaiah 42:6)

I CAN STILL REMEMBER the first time I reached over and held Gem's hand on one of our early dates. Suddenly the two of us knew that the relationship had reached a new level and that our roles might be redefined a bit. The amount of time we spent together grew. I began to think she might be more than my present girlfriend; she might be my future wife.

The everyday action of holding hands can also be a gift of safety and security. At a scary movie it is nice to have a hand to hold. When you are responsible for a child's safety, it is critical to hold hands in a crowd, in a parking lot, and when crossing a street. In reading these first lines of Isaiah 42:6, I imagine a good father taking hold of his young son's hand to guide him, protect him, encourage him, and be a companion to him.

Our heavenly Father has promised to take hold of our hand—to guide us, protect us, encourage us, and be a companion to us. May we be grateful when we sense—or when we choose to trust—that God has taken our hand today. After all, next to our heavenly Father, the Ancient of Days, each of us is indeed a little child.

· ·

Remember a time when God took hold of your hand. What difference did it make to your internal world? How did you feel as you reached back to take his hand?

I WILL KEEP YOU

I will keep you and will make you . . .
to open eyes that are blind,
to free captives from prison
and to release from the dungeon those who sit in darkness. (Isaiah 42:6-7)

THIS IS QUITE AN INVITATION God has for us, his people! As daunting as the details might be, notice the starting point: "I will keep you." Whatever aspect of God's invitation we are responding to, and whatever our anxieties and concerns, that promise can make all the difference.

The Lord will keep you—the Lord will keep me—and enable us to help those who don't yet know him. God will use us to love those who are spiritually blind and cause his love to shine through us so they can see him. God will use us to love those who are trapped in past sin and help them find the freedom of forgiveness, deliverance, and hope. God will use us to love those who sit in dark prisons—of their own making or made by others—and help them recognize the light of his truth.

We live in a time when many people in our sphere of influence are spiritually blind and imprisoned, even though they consider themselves completely sighted and free. God invites us to offer him our time, our energy, and our hearts for the good of those he brings into our lives. What a gift. What an honor.

. . . .

What if anything keeps you from responding more fully to your Good Shepherd so he can use you in his important kingdom work? What can and will you do to overcome those barriers?

DAY 78

STRONG TO SERVE

*And now the L*ORD *says—*
he who formed me in the womb to be his servant
to bring Jacob back to him. (Isaiah 49:5)

IN THIS VERSE, the Old Testament prophet Isaiah is talking about his calling, about his kingdom mission. In all that this calling has demanded from Isaiah, the prophet writes that God has been his strength.

In my own calling and kingdom mission, God has proven to be my strength as well (Isaiah 49:5). I am grateful for ways I am learning to rely on divine strength in my own felt sense of weakness. I long to work from this place of kingdom grace, gentleness, and humility. And the world around me needs whatever it is that God wishes to do through me. That could easily sound self-important, but this doesn't have a great deal to do with me. God is my strength. God is the one with the purpose, the ability to guide me, and the design to use me as he wishes.

I feel a connection to Isaiah's mission of bringing God's people back to him so that through them the entire world might come to know the true God. God called Isaiah to be a light to those who are not yet God's people so that they too might see how life in God is available to them and gives them a purpose for existence.

God is inviting you into this work as well. God will give you strength to fulfill this invitation if you want to respond to it.

· ·

In what ways does the calling to bring God's people back to him resonate with you? How would you describe your sense of calling from God? If you're not sure, make it a topic of prayer over the next few weeks. Ask God's Spirit to give you insight.

DAY 79

LISTENING WELL

The Sovereign LORD has given me a well-instructed tongue,
to know the word that sustains the weary.
He wakens me morning by morning . . .
to listen like one being instructed. (Isaiah 50:4)

THIS LINE OF SCRIPTURE has been part of my personal prayers for a very long time. Something in the spirit of it inspires and guides me as a teacher and preacher.

How do we grow in our ability to share good words well with others? How could we acquire what Isaiah calls "a well-instructed tongue"? How can we come to know how to speak to those who are exhausted in a way that refreshes and sustains them?

Isaiah suggests that this is a gift God gives. God has *given* him a well-instructed tongue. And the way God does this is by teaching Isaiah how to listen. Morning after morning Isaiah is awakened by God to listen well. But he isn't invited to listen like one getting ready to teach. He is awakened to listen like a student—an apprentice.

There is a difference between listening like one getting ready to teach and one open to being taught. I can listen like someone trying to prove my own opinions and perspectives, or I can listen like one willing to be enlightened and redirected. The best teachers are those who live in a lifelong posture of learning.

We learn how to speak words that help and bless others by learning to listen to the words of grace God speaks to us in our own need. Then we speak words of grace that have been tested in our experience rather than speaking words of theoretical grace.

. . . .

In what ways do you listen like one seeking to prove your current opinion? In what ways do you listen like one willing to be taught?

LAYING FOUNDATIONS

Enlarge the place of your tent,
stretch your tent curtains wide,
do not hold back. (Isaiah 54:2)

THESE WORDS BECAME PERSONAL for Gem and me in our early ministry when a trusted friend expressed his sense that God was inviting us to be open to an expansion of our scope of care and influence. We were serving in college ministry at a small local church at the time. His specific words, which we took to heart and still shape our work today, were that he saw us as "foundation layers" in the lives of others.

This became a prayer in the years to come: *Make us foundation layers in the lives of people who will go on to build more visible ministries than us.* We were being invited to an expansion of influence that would not necessarily result in greater visibility.

In that season our church staff invited someone known to be gifted in praying divine insight over others to pray for us. As we gathered, he shared that he had a vision of me as a servant, tireless and persistent. His vision moved to a scene in which I was standing in a deep trench.

This man's prayer rang true. Gem and I had been feeling like we were in a deep, dark pit. But then he said he believed that rather than a pit, this was the beginning of a foundation, and its size was not for a simple home but for a skyscraper.

Our sense was we were being invited to serve the visible and perhaps large ministries of others as foundation builders. Were we willing for our growing influence to be more invisible than visible?

· ·

How might God be increasing your influence in a way that doesn't involve increasing your visibility?

CHOSEN BEFORE I WAS FORMED

Before I formed you in the womb I knew you,
before you were born I set you apart;
I appointed you as a prophet to the nations. (Jeremiah 1:5)

GOD REMINDS JEREMIAH HERE that before he began to take shape in his mother's womb, God set him apart for a special purpose. It's hard for me to believe that I was formed in my mother's womb for a special purpose. My mother may not have been aware of God's purposes at the time in the way Mary clearly was about her son Jesus, but before I was even born, I had already been chosen . . . by God.

When I was four years old, anxious and fearful as so many little ones are, I was already chosen. When I was eleven and seeking to find some sense of meaning in a more and more perfect academic performance, I was already chosen. When I was thirteen and mercilessly teased by popular kids in junior high school, I was already chosen. When I was seventeen, desperately indulging in any pleasure I could find, I was already chosen. None of those bumps in my journey changed that I was chosen.

I feel humbled. I feel grateful. I also feel nervous, anxious, fearful, self-doubting, and insecure. As I experience these emotional echoes of something old, I am coming to trust and feel the honor of being chosen. I was wanted by God even before I was wanted by my own mother.

. . . .

Do you feel the honor of having been chosen by God? If so, how? If not, how might you enter into this fitting response to God's gracious act?

GOOD AND ANCIENT PATHS

Stand at the crossroads and look;
ask for the ancient paths,
ask where the good way is, and walk in it. (Jeremiah 6:16)

A CROSSROADS IS A MOMENT OF DECISION. We can move forward in more than one direction. Which path will we choose? Jeremiah invites us first to stand at crossroads in our lives. Resist the temptation to rush to a decision. At the crossroads, it helps to be still, to be receptive and . . .

Look. First, we must see the pathways before us. We can welcome the Spirit of discernment to enlighten us to what lies before us. We make a lot of hurried and therefore undiscerning decisions—choices that are often made not freely but on autopilot. It's much better when we stand and look. How will we understand what we see?

Ask for the ancient paths. There is goodness in the new thing God's Spirit does, but it will be in continuity with ancient wisdom. There are pathways of life and goodness that we've lost track of. We can ask for these ancient paths to be renewed for us. What is shaping our way of life these days? Are newcomers like social media and popular technology offering us good? We might find that there are better ways in the ancient past.

We know when we've found a good way when we walk in it and find rest for our souls (Jeremiah 6:16). When we find ourselves restless in our modern ways of living, we can ask if seeking more ancient ways might enable us to live and work more restfully.

. . . .

How does your way of life in the present feel restless? How do modern ways of interacting with others contribute to that restlessness? Why not ask God what ancient way might fit you better?

HOLINESS AND REST

Keep the Sabbath day holy
by not doing any work on it. (Jeremiah 17:24)

RESTING ONE DAY IN seven is a rhythm woven into the fabric of creation. It isn't just a rule to follow. It is how life works best. Jeremiah wants us to know that keeping a Sabbath is a matter of honoring what's holy. Holiness here isn't about being especially religious. Holiness is about prizing what is good.

Holiness doesn't mix things that don't belong together. If you open a carton of milk, you want only pure milk in there. You wouldn't like to see bits of grass or dirt inside the lid. We like our milk holy. Holiness is keeping things what they are meant to be.

So what is Sabbath meant to be? It's a day for resting—a day to enjoy life as a gift. The way we keep a Sabbath day holy is simple: we stop working. Work isn't bad, but we tend to worship at the altar of our own effort and activities. In Sabbath we learn to rest from our labors. We live in a restless world, and restlessness is usually honored more than resting. But God honors rest.

In resting we remember who we are. We rediscover our being at the center of our doing. It's an unholy thing to work on the Sabbath. God wants me to rest. Rest is holy before God. It is not laziness. It is not an evil to avoid. The evil to avoid is a lifestyle of constant work. All work and no rest are unhealthy.

. . . .

What does a day of rest look like for you? How are you tempted to work when you intend to rest? What keeps you moving when God's inviting you to stop?

REHEARSING COMPASSION

I remember my affliction and my wandering,
the bitterness and the gall. . . .
Yet this I call to mind and therefore I have hope. (Lamentations 3:19, 21)

JEREMIAH REMINDS ME OF the importance of what I choose to remember and rehearse. If it is my affliction, my wandering, the bitterness, and the gall (poison), the result is that my soul, my inner life, will be downcast with me. I love the little word "yet" that Jeremiah uses. It's an awakening word for me. What Jeremiah calls to mind is the Lord's great love, his unfailing compassions, and his great faithfulness (Lamentations 3:22).

It's not unusual for us to think about uncomfortable, distasteful, and painful things. Thoughts and memories like these have a way of capturing our attention. When I "well remember them," which is to say when I rehearse them or ruminate about them, they have a way of weighing down my soul.

It's taken me a while to realize that a noisy, negative thought that demands my attention does not obligate me to give it my attention. Anxiety may seek to engulf my thoughts, but I can choose to rehearse peace instead. Sadness may seek to overwhelm my soul, but I can remember that I also have reason to be joyful in God in the present moment.

The great news is that I do not have to rehearse everything that comes to mind. There is freedom when we realize we get to choose what we ruminate on. When we practice gratitude, we ruminate on grace. When we practice God's presence, we find ourselves more and more at home in his love.

· ·

When unpleasant or painful things come to your mind, what does it look like when you "well remember them"? What does it look like when you call God's compassion and faithfulness to mind?

COMPASSION MADE FRESH

Because of the LORD's great love we are not consumed,
for his compassions never fail.
They are new every morning;
great is your faithfulness. (Lamentations 3:22-23)

JEREMIAH WRITES THESE WORDS as a witness to the destruction of his city, Jerusalem, by the Babylonian empire. We would understand if Jeremiah was overwhelmed and undone in such painful and evil times. But Jeremiah somehow remembers God's love and compassion in this loveless, heartless moment in his life.

We sometimes experience pain and injustice. Horrible things happen in our lives. We may be tempted to see them as evidence that God's love has failed us. Jeremiah doesn't do this. He sees God present in love when love doesn't seem evident in the situation.

When I've faced hard times, it has helped me to begin my day remembering, even rehearsing, God's loving, compassionate presence. I'm tempted to first rehearse my wounds, my grief, my pain. Jeremiah would likely have found this easy to do as well, but he'd learned the reality of God's kind, generous presence amid an unkind, wounding season.

My pain and grief are often noisy and ever-present. I sometimes awake feeling anxious, fearful, or overwhelmed. It takes attentive seeking to turn my eyes toward the quiet, always-present God and to remember God's reliable care in my life. I can say to myself, "God, you are looking for new and fresh ways to show your love to me in this new day."

. . . .

What do you think and feel as you awaken to a new day? How might it help you to let yourself rest in the reality of God's creative expression of care for you in this moment?

A FULL PLATE

I say to myself, "The Lord is my portion;
therefore I will wait for him." (Lamentations 3:24)

I TALK TO MYSELF at times. Sometimes I use harsh words, but at other times I remind myself of good things. Jeremiah says he waits for God because God is his portion. A "portion" in the Scriptures is a share in something like an inheritance. God is that for me. The Lord is my hope for satisfaction. This is a good thing to remember.

Jeremiah reminds himself that he can safely wait for God because God will provide. God is the one who can fill my plate. I've often sat in the doctor's waiting room because I'm hopeful they will help me. I wait for a dentist because they are good at what they do. I can wait with peace and confidence when the one for whom I wait is worth the wait.

I'm willing to wait longer for something or someone I value more. I don't want to wait long in a fast-food line, but I've waited an hour or two to eat at a popular restaurant. I've waited in line (or online) for hours to get highly sought-after tickets to a show. My vision of God's great goodness expands my capacity to wait well.

How good that God is my portion. It's not so much that God gives me my portion, but God himself is all I need. God is the one who finally satisfies me. God piles my plate high with good things. I'll wait for God because God is my portion.

. . . .

For what have you found yourself waiting on God in your life lately? How might God be inviting you to turn your attention to waiting simply on him? Talk with God a bit about this.

DAY 88

A RIVER OF LIVING WATER

I will pour out my spirit on all flesh;
your sons and your daughters shall prophesy,
your old men shall dream dreams,
and your young men shall see visions. (Joel 2:28 NRSV)

THIS WORD THAT JOEL spoke for the Lord is fulfilled after the resurrection and ascension of Jesus on the day of Pentecost. And it is fulfilled for us today. Our bodies ("all flesh") become temples of God's Holy Spirit as we welcome Jesus' reign in our lives. And God's presence within us—his Spirit—enables us to see in a limited way from his divine and eternal perspective ("see visions"), to dream in line with God's heart and mind ("dream dreams"), and to speak words of blessing and truth to people on God's behalf ("prophesy").

This beautiful outcome is not limited merely to young men (as some might have assumed in that cultural setting). Sons *and* daughters will further God's kingdom in creative ways. The old will participate alongside the young. The socially low on the ladder ("servants," Joel 2:29) will have as much kingdom authority as any "somebody" does. God is not nearly as interested in our status in the world as we are.

Instead, it is God's design that every person receive so much of his poured-out Spirit that their winsomeness, grace, and love would be like a river of living water flowing from within them. God's Spirit can and does make this happen, and he does not use the same criteria for selecting candidates as we do.

. . . .

Who in your life embodies winsomeness, grace, and love? What does that person model for you?

YET I WILL REJOICE

Though the fig tree does not bud
and there are no grapes on the vines, . . .
yet I will rejoice in the LORD. (Habakkuk 3:17-18)

HABAKKUK USES THIS "THOUGH . . . YET" language to describe his life. "Though" is his disappointment with how his life has turned out. "Though" says he was expecting one thing but received another. "Though" says he made a large investment and got a small return. Everywhere Habakkuk looks, he sees another "though." The fig trees, grape vines, and olive trees haven't borne fruit. He talks about fields and herds that have disappointed.

I'm grateful that his "though" isn't a dead end. He continues with "yet I will rejoice in the LORD." "Yet" says his response is not determined by his meager circumstances. "Yet" says God is there when good returns aren't. Amid disappointing circumstances, "yet" looks to a good God who inspires joy.

What does Habakkuk see in God to raise the "yet" in his heart? What is it about God that inspires joy in discouraging circumstances? God is his *Savior* (Habakkuk 3:18). He rescues him in situations that have turned for the worse. God is *sovereign*. God is over all the "thoughs." They haven't surprised him. God is Lord over fruitless trees and fruitful ones, barren fields and those ripe for harvest.

Finally, God is his *strength* (Habakkuk 3:19). In this miserable place in Habakkuk's journey, God gives him strength. But for what does God strengthen him? What is he strengthened to be able to reach up on the heights? The difficult places of our lives can feel impossible. But the grace of God lifts us from low places into place of renewed perspective and hope.

. . . .

If you made a list of "thoughs" like Habakkuk's, what would be on it? What are the "yets" that give you hope?

QUIET IN GOD'S LOVE

[God] will rejoice over you with gladness;
he will quiet you by his love;
he will exult over you with loud singing. (Zephaniah 3:17 ESV)

THE GOD ZEPHANIAH DESCRIBES here is not hard to love. But he's not easy to love like a puppy either. This is a God we can love because of God's loving initiative. God loves us first. That's what I hear Zephaniah saying. Sometimes it helps me to hear words like this as though God were speaking to them to me personally:

"Alan, I am the Lord your God. I am always with you. What troubles you? What frightens you? What feels threatening? I am with you like a strong warrior. I will be with you to rescue you. You are always safe in my presence.

"You realize, don't you, Alan, that you delight me? I enjoy our friendship. I take pleasure in your development over the years. I find it easy to speak with joy about you. Though I've witnessed your stumbling and wandering, I continue to love you. You are becoming who I made you to be.

"In what ways are you worried, fearful, or unsettled? Let me quiet you in my love. Listen how I whisper words of encouragement and comfort in your ear like a loving parent speaks to her little one. Rest in my love. Sit in my loving presence and be secure. My love quiets you like your love quieted your sons when they were young. Remember how you used to sing over them when they cried? You learned that from me."

. . . .

What about Zephaniah's description of God here do you most needed to notice today? Take a moment to soak that in and express your heart to God.

PART TWO

FOLLOWING

OUR UNHURRIED

SAVIOR

THE ORIGINAL WORD

*In the beginning was the Word, and the Word was with God, and the
Word was God. He was with God in the beginning. (John 1:1-2)*

JESUS IS THE WORD from the beginning—with God as God. Jesus speaks
the world into existence. I am not the reference point of my life. Jesus precedes me and everything around me. John uses the word "was" four times to
affirm a past reality that foundations my present. "In the beginning" opens
and closes this scriptural sentence. This is my origin story. This is where everything begins for me.

My beginning isn't the day of my birth. It isn't the moment when my alarm
woke me this morning. My life was first a loving thought in the heart of God,
a thought finally spoken by Jesus to create me.

Jesus, the Word, was with God. This speaks of presence, of relationship, of
communion, of union. Jesus Christ was with God and was God. "Was" does
not imply he no longer is. Rather the opposite: he is now what he has always
been. John speaks of his own encounter with the human person of Jesus.
Jesus was more than a human person. He was God and was with God. And
so he is now.

I am living my life today in the presence of Jesus Christ, who was in the
beginning, who was with God and was God. And so he is now—he is with
God and is God now. I am not without help. I am not alone.

*May I find in you, Lord Jesus, all that I need to live well and work well today.
Grant me all of this and more from your abundance as God. Amen.*

. . . .

**Jesus is fully human and fully God. What does it mean to you today that
Jesus is "God-with-you"?**

DARKNESS CAN'T OVERCOME LIGHT

In him was life, and that life was the light of all mankind.
The light shines in the darkness,
and the darkness has not overcome it. (John 1:4-5)

"HIM" IS THE WORD, Jesus, whom John speaks of at the beginning of his Gospel. In Jesus was and is life. The very life of Jesus enlightens everyone who opens their eyes to look to him. The life of Jesus is the light of the world. And light overcomes darkness because light is something and darkness is nothing. It is an absence of something, and an absence of something doesn't win over the something that it isn't.

The life of Jesus shone out in the darkness of the Roman world. The goodness of his life was a bright sign for anyone who would look to him. Everyone who looked to and trusted him found their lives enlightened and brightened.

The life of Jesus shines in our lives today. The light of his life shines in us and through us now. The darkness in this world does not overcome the life of Christ in us. The darkness of despair cannot overcome hope. The darkness of anxiety will not overcome peace. The darkness of fear will not overcome love. The darkness of loneliness will not overcome presence. The darkness of insecurity will not overcome courage. Light wins over darkness.

Today, I welcome the light of Christ's life to shine in and through me. May the eyes of my heart and mind be opened to the reality of eternal living in a world full of deadness. And may the good light of God shine through me in a way that helps and blesses the world.

· ·

What forms has darkness taken in your circumstances, your thoughts, or your emotions these days? How might the light of Jesus' life shine in those very places?

DAY 94

A WITNESS OF LIGHT

There was a man sent from God whose name was John.
He came as a witness to testify concerning that light, so that
through him all might believe. He himself was not the light;
he came only as a witness to the light. (John 1:6-8)

I NOTICE SOMETHING IMPORTANT about how John's Gospel describes John the Baptizer. John is sent *from* God. Jesus *was* (and is) God and was *with* God. The gospel language about John the Baptizer is very different from its language about Jesus. Everything about John here shows that he is not an equal to Jesus. He is not the person in focus but a pointer to that person.

John saw the light of Christ and spoke as a witness. That's all any of us do. We are witnesses of what we have experienced in our encounter with God through Christ. He is the light of our lives. John came to believe that Jesus was who he said he was and was right when he described God's kingdom. He spoke of what he'd seen because he wanted everyone to understand the truth and see the light of Jesus.

John wasn't the light. It wasn't his job to shine as much as to point to the light of Christ. If we shine, it is only reflected light. We are not the focus of attention. We are pointers to the light of another who is with us.

Lord Jesus, open my eyes today to all the ways you are shining around us. And shine through us today by your Spirit in whatever way you wish. I welcome the light of your life in our lives today. I welcome the joy, the hope, the peace, and the love of your living light. Amen.

. . . .

Think about yourself as someone who is *from* God and sent by God into your world today. How might what you've seen of God shine through your life to bless others?

AT HOME AMONG US

The Word became flesh and made his dwelling among us. (John 1:14)

THE MESSAGE PARAPHRASE OF this passage is one of my favorites:

The Word became flesh and blood,
and moved into the neighborhood.
We saw the glory with our own eyes,
the one-of-a-kind glory,
like Father, like Son,
Generous inside and out,
true from start to finish.

The incarnation of Christ is such good news. The Word who is with God and was God is above us all. There is a vastness and a majesty in Jesus that inspires me and lifts my perspective. The Word became like us. We didn't have to keep wondering what a transcendent God was like. Jesus came to show us the Father.

Jesus Christ as flesh and blood was glorious with both a divine and a human glory. He displayed the glory of the Father, and he displayed the glory of humanity. Our lives shine as we reflect the beautiful light of Jesus into our world. When we try to shine on our own, there isn't any light.

The apostles, like John, had literally seen the glory of Jesus. They'd seen him shine on the Mount of Transfiguration. They'd seen him shine in his resurrection and ascension. And they'd seen him shine with love for the people who crossed his path. They were witnesses.

But so am I. I have not literally seen Jesus transfigured, but there have been moments when I witnessed the hand of Jesus in my life or around me that were glorious. I've seen Jesus shine. What an honor to speak as a witness of what I've seen in him.

. . . .

In what ways have you seen the light of Jesus shine around you recently?

LAYERS OF GRACE

Out of his fullness we have all received grace in
place of grace already given. (John 1:16)

JOHN THE BAPTIZER HAS just said Jesus surpassed him because he was before him (John 1:15). Now John is baptizing people and preaching before Jesus and his followers do so. But John knows that Jesus comes before him in priority because Jesus came before John in existence. He is more important than John because he came *before* John, even though he comes after John in this narrative.

It is good news that Jesus comes before me. He precedes me in every way. I act, knowing it or not, in response to his previous action. I enjoy good things he has provided. I have nothing I wasn't given.

This is the nature of grace. And John the Gospeler makes clear the grace upon grace we receive from his fullness. There is a piling on of grace. Grace after grace is ours from Jesus' abundance. He has more than we can imagine, so much so that hoarding it would be useless. He is not like us.

Out of Jesus' fullness we receive layer upon layer of generosity. Just when we think our lives couldn't be richer, he graces us even more. And his best graces aren't the things our culture assumes attract us. We are graciously loved. We are generously wanted. We are lavishly forgiven in our shortcomings.

We are blessed so richly that we have more than we can hold. We share this "more" with neighbors who live near us and cross our paths. Our lives become layered with grace.

. . . .

How has God already been gracious to you? In what way would you like to ask God to be even more generous to you, especially so your life can enrich others?

BOTH GRACE AND TRUTH

For the law was given through Moses; grace and truth
came through Jesus Christ. (John 1:17)

THE GIFT WE'RE GIVEN by Jesus is greater than the gift given through Moses. The Law, given through Moses, showed what life under God's kingdom was supposed to look like and how it was supposed to work. It gave requirements and standards for God's people. It gave a vision of what a good life might look like. But law did not enable or empower God's people to keep it.

The grace to live the truth has been given to us through Jesus. He empowers and enlightens us to live the sort of life the law of Moses describes. Jesus has seen God (John 1:18), so he can show God to us. And this is what Jesus came to do. When I hear what Jesus says, I hear how God speaks. When I see how Jesus responds to people, I see how God treats people. Jesus reveals God to me.

If my assumptions about the way God treats me don't look much like Jesus, they don't look much like God either. God isn't quick to anger. God isn't interested only in "important" people. What we see in Jesus is who God really is. This is what Jesus longs for us to know and believe.

No one is closer to the Father than the Son (John 1:18). No one is like the Father as is the Son. And Jesus came to draw us into that close relationship. He wants us to abide in the love he shares with the Father. This is where he wants us to make ourselves at home.

. . . .

What gut assumptions about God still linger in your imagination that are unlike the Jesus you read about in the Gospels?

WHO I AM NOT

Now this was John's testimony when the Jewish leaders in Jerusalem sent priests and Levites to ask him who he was. He did not fail to confess, but confessed freely, "I am not the Messiah." (John 1:19-20)

JOHN THE BAPTIZER IS asked by Jewish authorities who he is. His answer to them is, "This is who I am *not*."

First, he says, "I am not the Messiah." I am not the one who saves. I am not the one in focus here. John knows he's been sent to point to another. We don't draw attention to ourselves either. We are pointers of the way to Another.

John also says he is not Elijah (John 1:21). There is a sense in which John *is* the Elijah who Malachi said would come before the day of the Lord (Malachi 4:5). He came in the same spirit as Elijah.

John also does not claim to be "the Prophet" (John 1:21). The bottom line here is John has not come to talk about himself. He has come to bear witness of another. As he is questioned by leaders, he has less and less to say about himself.

When he finally responds to the question about his identity, he quotes the prophet Isaiah: "I am the voice of one calling in the wilderness, 'Make straight the way for the Lord'" (John 1:23; see Isaiah 40:3). He is on the outskirts calling out to anyone willing to listen: "Make way for the Lord's coming. Straighten up that which is crooked. Remove whatever may be in the way."

I am not the focus of attention. I don't save anyone. It is not my wisdom I've come to share. I am simply a voice crying out, inviting people to make way for the Lord's coming in their lives.

How does God invite you to follow John's example as a voice crying out in the wilderness?

DAY 100

AUTHORITY AND HUMILITY

"I baptize with water," John replied, "but among you stands one
you do not know. He is the one who comes after me, the straps
of whose sandals I am not worthy to untie." (John 1:26-27)

THE WORDS IN TODAY'S SCRIPTURE are John the Baptizer's response
to a question the Pharisees pose: "Why do you baptize if you aren't Messiah,
Elijah, or the Prophet?" The Pharisees are all about making sure everything
is done right. They don't think John has authority to baptize anyone if he
doesn't hold one of these offices.

The fact is that John's authority lies outside the frame acknowledged by
the Pharisees. John is authorized by God himself, not through their system,
structure, or tradition. This is tricky stuff. Plenty of people have asserted a
self-proclaimed authority that is little more than an expression of their own
imagination. The fruit of what they do tells the difference. The fruit of
John's life is humble service. He doesn't seek public acclaim (even though
it seeks him).

I love how John says only four words about himself before talking about
Jesus. "I baptize with water, *but* . . . " John doesn't want to talk about himself.
He wants to point to the Christ who has come to be among them.

Like John, I am not worthy even to take off Jesus' sandals. I am utterly
unworthy in myself. But Jesus reverses all of this by coming to wash *my*
feet—to serve *me*. I'm humbled and overwhelmed at such love. Jesus doesn't
want to talk about my unworthiness. He wants to treat me with serving love.
He is interested in relationship. He is interested in my being with him to work
with him.

. . . .

How does it strike you that the one John says he is utterly unworthy to
serve comes to serve us?

CLOSING THE GAP

The next day John saw Jesus coming toward him and said,
"Look, the Lamb of God, who takes away the sin of the world!" (John 1:29)

JOHN SEES JESUS AS the Lamb of God who comes to take away the sin of the world. He draws this imagery from the experience of sacrifices of lambs and other animals in the temple. They were offered as payment for the people's wrongdoings. I've sometimes heard these words in a way that sounded like Jesus coming to address my criminal record and secure for me a pardon.

There's truth there, but I need a broader vision of Jesus as Lamb of God. This means that if sin is relational separation, Jesus comes to take that away as well. Jesus comes to remove every barrier and gap between people and God. Jesus wants everyone to come to the Father. Jesus isn't just a good attorney. He's a good friend.

When I feel distant or even separate from God at times, Jesus comes to take away anything that creates such distance. When I may be tempted to focus on how I've stumbled or strayed, Jesus comes as the Lamb of God to address these realities in my life.

Our work on behalf of others is carried out in that same Spirit. When God gives us someone to share the goodness of Jesus as Lamb of God with, it's about helping them see him for themselves. Jesus wants to reveal himself to each of us as the one who brings us close to the Father. By the Spirit, Jesus offers himself as the one who reconnects us with God. He refreshes our religion and brings it back to life.

. . . .

How have you felt distant from God recently? Let yourself envision Jesus coming to close that gap and draw you in close.

COME SEE FOR YOURSELF

Turning around, Jesus saw [two disciples] following
and asked, "What do you want?"
They said, "Rabbi" (which means "Teacher"), "where are you staying?"
"Come," he replied, "and you will see." (John 1:38-39)

JOHN THE BAPTIZER HAS pointed two of his disciples to Jesus, the one he is announcing as the Lamb of God. They heard John describe Jesus this way, so they went to follow Jesus. Jesus speaks to these new followers and asks a simple question: "What do you want?"

They address him as teacher and ask where he is staying. It seems they'd like to have a visit with him. Jesus welcomes them to come and see. Later, we see they spent the rest of that day with Jesus.

Doesn't Jesus extend that same invitation to us? Spending a day with Jesus might involve getting away to a quiet, solitary place to enjoy his presence. But we can also spend a workday with Jesus. We can watch for his guidance and inspiration in each task, project, appointment.

I love the relationality of this Gospel vignette. The disciples seek out Jesus. He acknowledges their inquiry with an invitation to come spend the day together. We don't know exactly what they did, but they were together, and they enjoyed cultivating friendship with Jesus.

Andrew is one who spent the day with Jesus (John 1:40). This encounter has such an impact that he wants others to enjoy the same encounter with Jesus. Having come to Jesus, he wants to bring others to him as well. This is the nature of ministry. We make space to bring people into the presence of Jesus. We don't just talk with people about Jesus. We extend the invitation Jesus initiates—come see for yourself.

. . . .

How does your Christian life reflect friendship with Christ who invites you in? What might be his invitation to you today?

BRING THEM TO JESUS

*The first thing Andrew did was to find his brother Simon
and tell him, "We have found the Messiah" (that is, the
Christ). And he brought him to Jesus. (John 1:41-42)*

ANDREW IS ONE OF the two followers of John the Baptizer who heard
about Jesus as the Lamb of God and began to follow Jesus instead. When
Andrew experiences the presence and words of Jesus, he wants his brother,
Simon, to meet him as well.

I love the simplicity of the phrase, "And he brought him to Jesus." When
we experience Jesus in his love, wisdom, vitality, compassion, and fullness,
we want to bring others to him as well. I love the idea of bringing people to
Jesus. There are several ways I can do that.

I can bring people to Jesus in prayer. They may not realize I'm bringing
them into the presence of God with me when I pray for them, but they can
receive grace from God because of my praying. Sometimes I just say their
name before God. Sometimes a particular prayer comes to mind for them.
But mainly I bring them into the presence of Jesus.

I can bring people to Jesus by sharing my lived experience of the Scriptures.
When I engage with Christ in the reading and study of Scripture and then
share that encounter with others, it can be a way of bringing them to Jesus.

In my work, I often bring people to Jesus by providing reflection and retreat spaces in which they can encounter the Spirit of Jesus personally. The
Christian life is a life of deepening friendship and collaboration with Jesus.
He leads. I follow close. I'm so glad for those who brought me to Jesus a long
time ago.

**Whom has God used to bring you to Jesus? How might God use you to
bring others?**

WE'VE RUN OUT

On the third day a wedding took place at Cana in Galilee. . . .
When the wine was gone, Jesus' mother said to
him, "They have no more wine." (John 2:1, 3)

JESUS AND HIS DISCIPLES are invited to a wedding in Cana. Jesus' mother, Mary, is also invited. During the celebration, the unimaginable happens. The hosts run out of wine. Was it a failure in planning? Were there more guests than expected? Were people drinking more than they should have? Whatever the cause, this is a hospitality disaster.

It's a little surprising when the solution to the problem comes in a conversation between one guest and her son. Providing food and drink was probably not their responsibility. Perhaps the bride or groom was part of Mary's extended family, but Mary senses this may be an opportunity for Jesus to reveal himself.

Jesus often meets us when we've run out of something important. In this story, he meets the deficit with overwhelming abundance of remarkable quality. The miracle is transforming simple water into wine, but he doesn't make just a little. He makes perhaps 150 gallons of wine. And the banquet master immediately recognizes it's better than anything else they've served.

This is the way of Jesus. In the face of our shortcomings, he enjoys providing in abundance. In the face of our feeble efforts, he enjoys giving us the very best. I'm sometimes tempted to imagine Jesus making up a little bit of difference with something "good enough." But God is lavish in generosity. God is overwhelming in beauty and goodness. And, in love, God takes great pleasure in meeting our emptiness with plenty.

. . . .

Can you think of a time when you felt you'd run out of something you needed for life or work? What did (or might) it look like for Jesus to provide abundantly and richly in that place?

WATER INTO WINE

Jesus said to the servants, "Fill the jars with water";
so they filled them to the brim.
Then he told them, "Now draw some out and take it
to the master of the banquet." (John 2:7-8)

IN THESE LINES FROM Jesus' first miraculous sign in John's Gospel, I'm struck by these twenty- or thirty-gallon jars that are filled with water and turned to wine. What extravagance! This much wine might be as many as nine hundred bottles today. And that would have been on top of what the guests had already enjoyed. When did you last attend a wedding that provided that much wine?

The extravagance of Jesus does not stop at quantity. A first-century sommelier declares this the best wine of the night. Jesus comes to lead us into an extravagant life. This isn't measured in outward things like possessions or accomplishments. Jesus wants to transform the water of our offerings into much fine wine. There is a quantity and quality of peace, love, and joy that Jesus wants us to enjoy in him.

This moment in the story of Jesus arises when Mary sees that the wine provided for the celebration has run out. "They have no more wine," she says (John 2:3). Sometimes that's what my heart feels like. I've run out of energy, motivation, enthusiasm, or hope.

In such moments I imagine Jesus inviting me to fill the jars. He asks me to bring whatever water I have—common, everyday stuff—so he might transform it into fine wine. Today he invites us to "fill the jars" and then draw some out. Offer what you have to Jesus. Watch for how he will transform it into something remarkable that blesses many.

· ·

How might Jesus transform the simple water you bring him from your life into much fine wine? This would be a good question to ask him in prayer.

A SIGN OF GLORY

What Jesus did here in Cana of Galilee was the first of the signs through which he revealed his glory; and his disciples believed in him. After this he went down to Capernaum with his mother and brothers and his disciples. (John 2:11-12)

THIS WATER INTO WINE miracle was, as John puts it, the first of the signs that displayed Jesus' glory—his power, his authority, his abundant goodness, his holiness, his weightiness. Seeing Jesus do the work that only God could convinced the disciples he really was who he claimed to be. They trusted him. And they entrusted themselves to him.

John writes about something as mundane as Jesus' travel plans and social engagements. Cana would have been up in the mountains to the west of Galilee, while Capernaum was on the north shore of Galilee. It was probably a good part of a day's walk. It was, apparently, a place Jesus visited often.

Jesus lingered there for a few days with his mother, brothers, and followers. What would his brothers have thought about their eldest sibling leading a group of followers like a rabbi? He hadn't trained as a rabbi. What was he doing gathering disciples? In reality, his was an authority that arose from within—from who he was. His authority was given directly by God. It wasn't based on human standards, assessments, or processes.

As a follower of Jesus, I want to linger in his presence. I want to enjoy unhurried time like his family and followers would have enjoyed in Capernaum. I would love to visit, eat together, laugh together, enjoy one another's company. This is apparently something Jesus wanted then and still wants with us now. What a surprising gift to be wanted as a friend of Jesus.

. . . .

If you had been an early follower spending a few days with Jesus and his family, what might you have done together? Why not prayerfully imagine this?

SELF-CENTERED WORSHIP

*To those who sold doves [Jesus] said, "Get these out of here! Stop turning
my Father's house into a market!" His disciples remembered that it is
written: "Zeal for your house will consume me." (John 2:16-17)*

WITH THE APPROACH OF Passover, Jesus goes up to Jerusalem and enters
the temple courts. Passover is, of course, a time for remembering how an
animal's blood placed on the doorposts that night long ago in Egypt offered
protection from the Lord's judgment on Egypt. John the Baptizer has been
proclaiming Jesus as "the Lamb of God who takes away the sin of the world."
There's a clear Passover implication here.

As Jesus enters the temple courts, he sees merchants selling sacrificial
animals and others exchanging the worshipers' common money for special
holy money. Jesus reacts to them: "Stop turning my Father's house into a
market!" They have turned the temple from a place of worship and prayer—of
holy focus on his Father—to a place of personal gain.

It is possible to do this in our worship and devotion as well. Rather than
focusing on how we might encounter, worship, and commune with the living
God, we seek personal glory and gain in the form of attention or approval
from others.

The people selling animals for sacrifice or changing common money for
holy money would have said they were providing a necessary service. Jesus
doesn't see it that way. What he sees is that they aren't in his Father's house
to worship the Father. They're there to get something for themselves.

Our life in Christ, both personal and communal, is best lived in focus on
God, in communion with God, in humble worship of God.

. . . .

**When has your life of faith focused more on what you get from God than
what you offer? How would you like to express your worship to God in
this moment?**

THE TEMPLE OF OUR BODIES

But the temple [Jesus] had spoken of was his body. (John 2:21)

WHEN JESUS SAID, "Destroy this temple, and in three days I will raise it up" (John 2:19 NRSV), he was speaking about his body as a temple—and the Jews misunderstood. They heard these words while standing in the Jerusalem temple. Jesus, however, understood his own body to be a place of worship, of offering, of presence.

What would happen if I had a clearer vision of my body as a temple of the Lord? How might my moments be transformed if I remained awake to God with and in me? My physical disciplines tend to rise and fall with my sense of God with me and of who this God with me is.

Trusting the goodness of the God who is with me would enable me to experience the abundance such a good God gives. Fear rooted in a distorted image of God will keep me far from God and the actual goodness of his presence.

So what prompted Jesus to speak about his body as a temple? The sign of authority Jesus offered to the Jews was a cryptic comment about his coming death and resurrection. Jesus knew it was coming; his disciples did not.

My heart rises with this prayer: *Jesus, you were aware that the Holy Spirit fully indwelt you as you went about preaching, healing, and caring for people. I understand that the same is true of me as I live in you and you live in me. I want to follow your way in this. Strengthen my mind, my will, and my body to this end. Amen.*

. . . .

Since you are raised with Christ already, what impact does that have as you, a risen one, walk through your day?

POPULARITY AND PRIORITIES

But Jesus would not entrust himself to [the crowds],
for he knew all people. (John 2:24)

MANY OF US ARE HUNGRY to be popular. We'd like more people to see our social media posts. We'd like more people to say good things about us. But Jesus often did and said things that diminished his popularity. Listen to the words of Elton Trueblood, author of *Confronting Christ,* about how Jesus related to the crowd:

> Christ had no real hope in the crowds. . . . Their presence was no indication of a deep commitment. Consequently they could not be counted upon in a crisis. Crowds may be inevitable in a new redemptive movement, but it is not on the multitude that any movement can be built. Indeed, the passing popularity can be a genuine barrier. Christ deliberately tried to limit His popularity by warning those whom He helped against making the help known.

Much of my experience of church has focused on drawing a crowd and keeping them interested. This seems opposite the way of Jesus. After all, crowds don't really know what they want. They think they need excitement, but how much is enough? The answer, generally, is a bit more than last time.

Trueblood's assertion that "passing popularity can be a genuine barrier" is especially telling. Our world lives by the idea that all press is good press. Jesus knew better. Popularity may be the fruit of our culturally held values, but not everything the crowds get excited about plays well with the values of God's kingdom. We may find that what drives popularity is driving us in the wrong direction.

. . . .

What is your relationship to popularity? How might the perspective of Jesus help you deal with your perceived popularity (or unpopularity)?

BORN OF THE SPIRIT

Jesus replied, "Very truly I tell you, no one can see the kingdom
of God unless they are born again." (John 3:3)

JESUS SPEAKS TO NICODEMUS, a Pharisee who visits him at night.
Maybe Nicodemus doesn't want anyone to know about his visit. But he acknowledges the divine source of Jesus' words and deeds, so Jesus gives him
insight into the kingdom: "Be born again."

When I came to trust Jesus in my youth, I joined a community who described themselves as "born-again Christians." We saw ourselves as a special
category of Christians compared to others. We also liked to say we were
"Spirit-filled Christians." We sought to say something important about what
we'd discovered about life in God. In the end, though, phrases like these are
redundant. Jesus isn't talking about a special class of Christians. He tells Nicodemus that no one can even recognize the kingdom without a new birth.

Jesus wants Nicodemus to understand the nature of God's kingdom, but
Nicodemus can't get past the arresting image of an adult being birthed a
second time. Jesus tells him that being born of the Spirit, born into the
kingdom, shouldn't surprise him (John 3:7). Nicodemus is one of Israel's
teachers, after all (John 3:10). How can he provide spiritual leadership to
God's people if he doesn't understand how God's kingdom works?

Christian leadership begins with learning the ways of God's kingdom. We
can understand how to draw a crowd or build an organization, but Jesus
wants us to experience fresh perspective and a new vision in him. Jesus invites us, "See the kingdom. Enter the kingdom. Pay attention to the Spirit.
Watch for the movement of my Spirit today."

**How might Jesus refresh your awareness of God with you today? What
new thing might God wish to birth in you?**

REBIRTH REQUIRED

"How can someone be born when they are old?" Nicodemus asked.
"Surely they cannot enter a second time into their
mother's womb to be born!" (John 3:4)

NICODEMUS IS AN IMPORTANT person among his people. He's a member of the highly admired Pharisees and part of the highest ruling body of the Jews. Why didn't Jesus pick someone like him to be one of his disciples? Maybe someone who only wants to come at night isn't ready to be a follower. He may still see himself mainly as a leader.

The way Nicodemus affirms Jesus sounds more like a person in authority speaking to someone he sees as beneath him. "We know" (John 3:2) seems to say, "We're the authorities here, and we'll acknowledge that you have some sort of divine authority about you." His belief hasn't risen to the level of trust.

During this exchange Jesus throws Nicodemus a curve with his statement about how we must be reborn if we want to even see the kingdom of God. Nicodemus is willing to acknowledge that Jesus has some sort of kingdom-of-God authority, but Jesus implies he hasn't even *seen* the kingdom of God yet.

Poor Nicodemus just doesn't get it. He's so literal. He's trying to imagine how in the world he, an old man, can climb back into his mother's womb and be reborn. This kind of literalism always misses kingdom truth. The kingdom is a matter of Spirit, and we must be born of the Spirit if we want to discern the reality of the Spirit. This is our source of true authority. This is the way of the kingdom.

· ·

How is Jesus inviting you into a newness, even today, that is as radical as his invitation to Nicodemus to be reborn?

DON'T BE SURPRISED

You should not be surprised at my saying,
"You must be born again." (John 3:7)

EARLIER JESUS TALKED TO Nicodemus about seeing the kingdom (John 3:3). Now he talks about entering the kingdom. If we think of the kingdom of God as some future-day, somewhere-else place, we'll understand this very differently than if we understand it as something right here, right now among us.

I can enter the kingdom of God without moving an inch in space or a moment in time. I do so by being born in the Spirit. In the same way a human mother gives birth to a human child (flesh gives birth to flesh), so the Spirit gives birth to spiritual sons and daughters. We can enter into the mystery of God's kingdom here, but not here in the same way a local, state, or national government is here. It is really *more* present than these.

Nicodemus shouldn't have been surprised about this second birth or this birth from above. But his training had not included a sense of God's kingdom among us as much as it was about the Jewish kingdom of who's in charge and what's right.

Lord, thank you that I am born of your Spirit and may enter into the kingdom of God in which I am already at home. The kingdom of God is where I am. Anxiety isn't at home here. Peace is. Despair is not at home here. Hope is. Insecurity is not at home here. Confidence and courage are. May your kingdom come to reign in my mind, heart, actions, and relations today. Amen.

In what ways are you aware of the kingdom of God nearer to you than your own breath? How would you like this awareness to increase?

THE WIND AND THE SPIRIT

*The wind blows wherever it pleases. You hear its sound, but
you cannot tell where it comes from or where it is going.
So it is with everyone born of the Spirit. (John 3:8)*

SOME MORNINGS I SIT in my backyard enjoying the cool breeze. I pay
attention to how it feels on my skin. I remember wind is a metaphor Jesus
uses to help us understand the life of his Spirit. Just as a human body is alive
only if it is breathing, so we are alive inside as the Spirit breathes life into us.

In the creation story, humanity is dust until the Spirit animates us with his
breath. And that's how we are alive even today. I am truly alive only when
God is breathing his life in and out of me by his Spirit. But I've sometimes
forgotten this and imagined my life was sustained in other ways—by what I
eat, drink, accomplish, or acquire.

When I notice the morning breeze, I sometimes remember what Jesus says
about it. It blows where it wants. Unlike Jesus, I can't tell the wind to blow
somewhere else. It's the same with God's Spirit. We don't tell the Spirit where
or when to blow. Being God, the Spirit blows as he wishes, where he wishes,
and when he wishes. That's good news for us.

As a person born of the Spirit, I am like the wind. I can go wherever the
Spirit pleases to move me. Those who aren't alive in God's Spirit may not
understand where I come from or where I'm going and why. *May I learn how
to open the sails of my heart, mind, and spirit to be moved by the wind of your
Spirit, Lord.*

. . . .

**How alive do you feel these days? How might you welcome the wind of the
Spirit blowing in and through you?**

SEEING MYSTERY

"You are Israel's teacher," said Jesus, "and do you not understand these things?
Very truly I tell you, we speak of what we know, and we testify to what we
have seen, but still you people do not accept our testimony." (John 3:10-11)

NICODEMUS IS PUZZLED BY Jesus' language and the mystery of someone being born of the Spirit. Jesus, perhaps gently, asks him how he can call himself a teacher and be so unaware of the spiritual realities of his Father's kingdom.

Nicodemus is used to a delegated authority through human agency. He is accustomed to quoting and referring to the opinion and understanding of others. Jesus is talking about a reality he and his followers know as direct witnesses. They have seen the kingdom at work.

Jesus wants Nicodemus to understand he can experience eternal life if only he will trust him. Jesus wants him to experience the things he has believed his whole life. Jesus wants him to become a teacher who knows things and not merely quotes things. Jesus wants Nicodemus to know the kingdom of heaven as the dwelling place of God now among us, not just heaven as a future objective with little present effect.

Perhaps for Nicodemus, belief is professing something a group of fellow believers think about God. Jesus wants him to know it is trusting that what Jesus says about the kingdom of God is a real description of its nature and function. Jesus knows what the kingdom of God is and how it works. Like Nicodemus, we can trust him and experience eternal living in him.

Eternal life is relational and personal. It is with and in Jesus. This is how and where we enter the kingdom. *Lord Jesus, grant that our eyes today might be open to eternal life as real and present.*

. . . .

How might Jesus want to help you experience the reality of his life with and in you today?

THE GENEROSITY OF LOVE

For God so loved the world that he gave his one and only Son,
that whoever believes in him shall not perish but have eternal
life. For God did not send his Son into the world to condemn the
world, but to save the world through him. (John 3:16-17)

WHEN I WAS A YOUNG CHRISTIAN, there was no more familiar passage to me than this one. The challenge is not letting the familiar become stale. John here reminds us that God's basic orientation to this world in which we live is love. A primary way in which God engages this world in love is generosity—unique, holy generosity. He gives his *one and only* Son. If only we'd trust Jesus and take to heart how he lives and what he teaches, we'd experience eternal living.

We are mistaken if we imagine Jesus coming to criticize wrongdoers. He doesn't come to condemn. He comes to rescue, to help, to reveal to us the way to really live. We look in many places for the things we think we need in our lives, but it is in Jesus that we find what we truly need. Jesus comes close to me—into my neighborhood—to touch me and show me the way to the life I've sought in misguided ways.

When we trust Jesus deeply, we come to know and rely on his acceptance. When we don't trust Jesus but seek what we need in other ways or from other sources, we find a woeful life instead of a blessed one. We are often the cause of our own misery.

Like Jesus, I am not sent into the world to condemn the world, but to be a witness of the life and grace of Jesus to a world that needs him more than it realizes.

. . . .

When have you experienced Jesus coming to you to help and save you? When have you been tempted to envision him coming to shame or condemn you?

SEE NO EVIL

This is the verdict: Light has come into the world, but people loved darkness instead of light because their deeds were evil. (John 3:19)

JOHN USES THE WORD "verdict" just after saying God did not send Jesus to condemn the world. It's as though John is saying, "If you want to use the language of judgment, I can go there. Do you want a verdict? Here it is: Light has come into the world."

John is talking about everyday experience. People want to do what is wrong in the dark. They don't want a spotlight on their misdeeds. People are more likely to do wrong in secret than in public. The crime rate at 3 a.m. is different than at noon. Of course, there are those whose consciences are so seared that any hour is good for evil. They've ceased to care whether their deeds will be exposed.

But for most, remembering we are always in the light of God's presence is the best disinfectant for wayward impulses. And I'm not in the glaring light of an angry judge. That is not why he comes into the world and my life. I live in the healing light of a Great Physician who restores, renews, and frees me.

As I enter my day, grant that the gracious light of Your presence would shine brightly in and through me. May I bring into my encounters a sense of your presence with me in fresh and energizing ways. May I have eyes to see your light around me. Grant me wisdom to ask helpful questions that shine a light on the reality of our shared situations. Amen.

. . . .

How does it help you to remember that the light of God is always with you, and it is a gracious light rather than a condemning light?

POINTING TO ANOTHER

They came to John and said to him, "Rabbi, that man who was with you on the other side of the Jordan—the one you testified about—look, he is baptizing, and everyone is going to him." (John 3:26)

A FEW OF JOHN'S DISCIPLES are talking about how Jesus is essentially taking John's disciples from him. "Everyone is going to him," they say. They had been the "latest thing," but now their movement is dying. They don't feel they're the winning team anymore. People who used to come in droves to listen to John the Baptizer preach and to be baptized by him are now going to Jesus instead. They see this as bad news.

John wants them to widen their perspective. As this passage continues, John reminds them that their purpose was never to amass fame for themselves. John came as a witness of Another, not as the main one in focus.

John and his followers received a calling from heaven to prepare the way for Jesus. John's ministry was rooted in a gift. That's all any of us have. And if we're tempted to see it as not enough or if we see it diminishing, perhaps we need to widen the angle of our own lens.

John knows he is not the Messiah but sent ahead to announce his coming. So his purpose is to draw people to Jesus, not to himself. That's our purpose as well.

John summarizes his perspective with a simple, beautiful statement: "He must become greater; I must become less" (John 3:30). This is our mission. We aren't called to get more people excited about what we do. May God refresh that vision of pointing to Jesus today. May we find freedom in drawing attention to him.

. . . .

When have you been tempted to seek attention for yourself? How is it even better to point away from yourself toward the goodness of Jesus?

A POINTER OF THE WAY

He must become greater; I must become less. (John 3:30)

JOHN THE BAPTIZER ACKNOWLEDGES that Jesus will become greater while he becomes less. What a beautiful response! He's just been told people are leaving him to follow Jesus. He is losing his influence to Jesus. In my own life and service, am I willing to lose the attention of people to Jesus? Is my soul so needy that I am unable to point people to Jesus and away from myself?

Just before this statement, John speaks of how the bride belongs to the bridegroom (John 3:29). The bride is the people of God. The bridegroom is Jesus. The attendant is there to serve, not to draw attention. I am an attendant at this wedding between Jesus and his people. I am not here to draw attention to myself. How silly if a groomsman at a wedding were to voice disappointment at not receiving more attention than the groom did.

Forgive me, Lord Jesus, for when I have done exactly that. Forgive me for when I've played the false humility game and still drawn attention to myself. None of this kingdom business is supposed to point to me. It is about your people being united to you.

The goal of Christian leadership is not to promote myself—to aim at becoming greater myself. My aim is for Jesus to grow in the estimation of those I serve. I want them to focus on him, to walk with him, to work with him. It's very good news when he increases and I decrease.

. . . .

In what ways are you tempted to capture attention for yourself from others? What would it look like to follow John's example of pointing attention to Jesus instead?

A WITNESS OF THE SPIRIT

*The one who comes from above is above all; the one who is from the
earth belongs to the earth, and speaks as one from the earth. The
one who comes from heaven is above all. (John 3:31)*

JESUS COMES FROM ABOVE and therefore is above everyone, everything. John is from below and belongs to this world. Me too. I speak from
a human, earthbound perspective. I need the perspective from above that
Jesus gives me.

Unfortunately, not everyone who hears Jesus trusts Jesus. Some did not
believe he was speaking from experience because he contradicted long-held
traditions. Traditions are good when they resonate with kingdom reality.
They aren't as helpful when they are guarding thinner visions of reality. Jesus'
vision of reality is utterly true.

Jesus speaks on God's behalf to us—to me—today. God gives the Spirit
without limit to Jesus (John 3:34). Through Jesus, God gives the Spirit without
limit to me. The Father loves the Son and has placed everything in his hands.
And I am in his hands. The Father is quite fond of me. Jesus is too. The Father
loves the Son, and the Father and Son love me in the Spirit. What a rich,
inviting reality.

*Lord Jesus, you are above everything in and around me at this moment. You
came down to be among us and to reveal what we couldn't see on our own.
You came to tell us what you saw and heard. You spoke from wisdom. There are
moments when I speak with authority about truth you have shown me, and not
just good ideas that I've read or thought about. Thank you for ways that you
reveal yourself and your ways to me by your Spirit. I'm grateful.*

. . . .

**What truth do you think Jesus is wanting to speak into your life? What are
you hearing from him in today's reading?**

LIVING WATER

*Jesus answered her, "If you knew the gift of God and who it
is that asks you for a drink, you would have asked him and
he would have given you living water." (John 4:10)*

JESUS SPEAKS THESE WORDS to a woman he meets at a well in Samaria. He is sitting next to it in the heat of midday, weary from his morning's journey so far (John 4:6). Most Jews would have avoided a conversation with a Samaritan. They would have thought themselves above such a thing. But Jesus is not your average Jewish person.

Jesus begins his conversation with a question, not a statement: "Will you give me a drink?" (John 4:7). Jesus asks for help. He is honest about his thirst. I don't think he sees this woman as a servant but as a potential friend, so he asks for help.

The woman is surprised by the recognition implicit in Jesus' request. Jesus wants to bring her good news, and she seems to clearly need it. Midday isn't when most respectable people were coming for their daily water.

So what is this good news? Jesus says something like, "If you really knew the generosity of God, and knew that I have come to proclaim that generous grace, you'd be asking me for something more than the water that quenches physical thirst." Jesus has refreshment for her soul.

Today, Jesus wants us to know and trust in the gift of God. He brings this gift to us by the presence and power of his Spirit. He has living water that will refresh, restore, inspire, and energize us for our living and working today. Jesus himself is this Living Water.

. . . .

How do you find yourself thirsty these days? What are the deep, unsatisfied desires of your soul? How might Jesus himself be living water to quench that thirst today?

THIRST BECOMES A SPRING

*Jesus answered, "Everyone who drinks this water will be thirsty
again, but whoever drinks the water I give them will never
thirst. Indeed, the water I give them will become in them a
spring of water welling up to eternal life." (John 4:13-14)*

JESUS CONTINUES HIS CONVERSATION with the woman from Samaria. He wants her to know who the Father really is. He wants her to know the measureless generosity of his Father in heaven. She isn't getting it. Sometimes we don't either. We hear Jesus speak words to us, but we don't comprehend them. How good that he is patient to help us understand more.

Jesus wants this woman to realize that while well water quenches physical thirst, the living water he offers satisfies a thirsty soul. It wells up and over-flows to quench not just her thirst but that of many others. Jesus offers abundant life not just so we experience fullness but so we can offer the overflow of that goodness to others.

Jesus wants us to have a clearer vision of the life-giving abundance of friendship with God. It is like a well dug within us. Is like an artesian well of the soul rising to overflow for the good of those nearby. Our words can ex-press this divine richness. This is the reality of the kingdom of God in which we're invited to make ourselves at home.

Today, Lord Jesus, I open my soul to you. I welcome the gift of your life meeting me in my own places of thirst. May that thirst become like a spring that flows and overflows to bring goodness to everyone who crosses my path today. May I go from thirsty to satisfied to overflowing. Show me how to live for the good of others.

. . . .

What thirst might be quenched by the water Jesus offers you today? How can your growing satisfaction in what he provides become goodness you share with others?

REHEARSING REALITY

Yet a time is coming and has now come when the true worshipers
will worship the Father in the Spirit and in truth, for they are
the kind of worshipers the Father seeks. (John 4:23)

JESUS IS TELLING THE SAMARITAN WOMAN of a time in the future
when true worshipers of God will not have to travel to a specific geographical
location to worship. The Jewish person of Jesus' day would have envisioned
Jerusalem as the place to worship God. The Samaritans had a different destination for their worship.

Jesus inaugurated a time when the temple would become not a place but
a people. People would experience God's indwelling presence through their
trust in Jesus and their shared life in his Spirit.

That's the invitation Jesus extends to me today. Worship in this sense is
rehearsing reality in the presence of God. I acknowledge and express awe at
what is true in the kingdom of God, which is my actual present home. It's
good to remember and repeat this reality.

The woman Jesus met by the well believed worship needed to happen in a
certain place. Today some might assume the same, saying "this denomination"
or "that theological tradition" is the right place to worship God. This sounds
little like the Spirit of Jesus here.

God seeks those who will so align themselves with reality that they can
fully experience the generous grace of God's actual kingdom. Enriched in this
way, they are also able to extend that grace into all creation with authority
and power. What if what God seeks by way of true worshipers isn't for his
benefit but for ours?

- -

**What might it look like in this moment to express worship of God that is
rooted in the presence of the Spirit and an expression of truth—of
kingdom reality?**

NOURISHED IN COLLABORATION WITH GOD

"My food," said Jesus, "is to do the will of him who sent me and to finish his work." (John 4:34)

THE DISCIPLES LEAVE JESUS at the well where he meets and has a conversation with a woman. They know he doesn't have food since they've gone to town to get something. They are genuinely concerned for him. They want to provide for him. But Jesus surprises them.

Instead of the metaphor of water and thirst that shaped his conversation with the woman, he speaks of having food they don't know about (John 4:32). They take him literally and assume someone has come along and fed him in their absence. But that's not what Jesus is talking about.

Jesus is saying he is nourished by something more substantial than physical food. He is fed by being in union with the will of the Father and finishing what the Father started. He feels deep satisfaction and receives great energy from God even though his physical body has been without food for a while.

I remember hearing Dallas Willard observe that what God says feeds our bodies. He wasn't speaking in metaphor. He meant the life in what God says sustains our physical being. When we fast to feast on communion with God and what God says, we are actually nourished. It is different, but it is real.

I experienced this once when I felt drawn to drink only water for about ten days. While I felt slower physically, my sense of being alive and well inside was profound. Eternal life isn't just something for our souls but a gift for our whole being.

. . . .

When did God say something to you more nourishing than physical food? If you haven't experienced this, why not ask God to teach you about this kingdom reality?

RIPE FOR HARVEST

Don't you have a saying, "It's still four months until harvest"?
I tell you, open your eyes and look at the fields!
They are ripe for harvest. (John 4:35)

JESUS SPEAKS ETERNAL TRUTHS through everyday events. His listeners in this passage understood farming, since planting and harvesting were common among them. Jesus quotes a common saying acknowledging the typical four-month timeframe between planting and harvesting.

The disciples might have imagined they were just beginning to plant seeds of ministry that would take a long time to be ready for harvest. But Jesus knows others have already been planting. And there is a rich harvest ready right before their eyes. The woman of Samaria whom he'd met at the well was just one example of this.

Jesus affirms unknown sowers who have come before him. John the Baptizer, who planted for many months before Jesus came on the scene, is one obvious example. But there were many faithful prophets and rabbis who faithfully proclaimed the good news of God's kingdom in preparation for the coming of Jesus.

In my own work, I'm always benefiting from hard work others have done. The good fruit of my life is never the result of my work alone. This is true in any kind of productivity. This is humility in the face of productivity. Those who are rich must acknowledge all the privileges that were theirs before they began and all the hard work others have done that has benefited them.

Lord Jesus, please open my eyes to see the good fruit around me ready to be picked and enjoyed. May I learn to discern how the work of others has borne fruit that I'm privileged to harvest now.

What have been some fruitful experiences in your life lately? Who may have contributed to that harvest that you could acknowledge and thank?

HEARING FOR OURSELVES

They said to the woman, "We no longer believe just because of
what you said; now we have heard for ourselves, and we know
that this man really is the Savior of the world." (John 4:42)

MANY FROM THE REGION of Samaria came to trust in Jesus because of what the woman Jesus met at the well said about her encounter with him. A testimony is not an evangelistic technique so much as it is talking about a living encounter with Jesus. A testimony isn't a formula. It's a way of telling the story of how we've been touched, helped, enlightened, even transformed by Jesus.

The substance of the woman's testimony was, "He told me everything I ever did" (John 4:39). What had she done? She'd had five husbands and was now with a man who hadn't apparently become number six. What happened to the first five? Why hadn't she married number six? Maybe she did after her encounter with Jesus. Maybe not.

So when these Samaritans found the Jesus she'd told them about, they asked if he'd stay with them. Jesus stayed two days (John 4:40). They heard for themselves what he had to say. They now had their own testimony of who Jesus was and what he'd said to them. They witnessed his character. They found him to be trustworthy and wise. They believed him.

They didn't stop at believing the woman's testimony. They sought Jesus for themselves and came to trust him as Savior of the world as a result. He invites us to listen for ourselves and come to experience just how good and trustworthy he is. He invites us to share the story of our life-giving encounters so others might come, listen, and believe.

. . . .

When have you recently experienced something alive and real of Jesus in your life? How might you share that story with another?

HEALING OR MERE RELIEF?

When Jesus saw him lying there and learned that he had been in this condition
for a long time, he asked him, "Do you want to get well?" (John 5:6)

THE PARALYZED MAN IN this passage had been lying by the healing pool for a long time. In your own experience, maybe you understand something of how he must feel. In what way have you been disabled or unwell for a long time? Have you had—or do you now have—a specific idea about how you want God to heal you, free you, or restore you, but it hasn't happened yet? One reason we don't experience healing is implied in the question Jesus asks this man: "Do you want to get well?"

We would expect that anyone paralyzed for thirty-eight years would of course want—desperately and passionately—to be made well, but some people have learned a way of life that accommodates their unwellness. In such cases, getting well could mean having to learn a completely different way of living. Also, sometimes the pain of change feels greater than the pain of staying the way we are. Sometimes we say we want healing or wholeness, but what we really want is relief or accommodation.

Finding relief usually means a temporary reprieve from what hurts. Being healed means being changed, and sometimes change hurts more in the short term than the original pain. But the pathway of healing leads to a wellness and wholeness we never imagined possible.

. . . .

Are you open to the painful but fruitful journey of healing? How are you tempted to stop at the request for relief alone? Talk to God about this. If you find you want healing, ask God to lead you into the work of deep transformation that leads to lasting change.

HEALING COMMANDS

*Then Jesus said to him, "Get up! Pick up your mat and walk." At once
the man was cured; he picked up his mat and walked. (John 5:8-9)*

THIS MAN WHO LINGERS at the pool of Bethesda for decades but finds
no healing there finds it in Jesus. The man responds to the command to walk,
and he finds himself well. Might it be true that all the commands of Jesus are
meant to lead us to wellness, wholeness, and life?

Jesus doesn't issue commands designed to deprive or enslave us. Jesus
speaks words of strong guidance because he *is* life and wants life for us.
When Jesus speaks commands to us, they come in the spirit of "Be well!" or
"Be whole!" Jesus commands us in ways that resonate with our truest desires
and hopes.

But the Jewish leaders can only complain that the man is breaking the
Sabbath by carrying his mat (John 5:10). To them the Sabbath is a day for not
doing certain things. In obeying the command of Jesus that led to life, the
man is disregarding Jewish traditions about Sabbath. They have forgotten that
Sabbath was always about life and not just empty rule keeping.

Even today we can turn the commands of Jesus into oppressive rules rather
than pathways to life. We can distort the life-giving guidance of Jesus into a
kind of New Testament law that kills instead of giving life.

Authority for these Jewish leaders was a matter of rules and laws. Authority
as this healed man came to know it was a matter of power to accomplish
commands. How good when we learn to listen to Jesus and follow his
guidance into deeper, richer, fuller life.

. . . .

**In what ways does "obedience" sound limiting or constricting to you? How
can you come to see obedience as a pathway to wholeness?**

WORKING WITH THE FATHER

In his defense Jesus said to them, "My Father is always at his
work to this very day, and I too am working." (John 5:17)

HOW STRANGE THAT THE JEWISH LEADERS of Jesus' day believed
there was good that could not be done on a Sabbath day (John 5:16). They had
ceased to understand the gift of life that Sabbath was always meant to be.
They persecuted Jesus because he did good they hadn't authorized. They
thought they were serving God, but they didn't recognize God's messenger.

Jesus seems to respond, "You say no work can be done on a Sabbath. You've
missed the point of that command. My Father is working today, and so I am
working with him today." It's clear that Jesus was implying his equality with
God (John 5:18), and these leaders understood. If working on the Sabbath
weren't bad enough, this was blasphemy to their ears.

Everything Jesus did and said was true, and these leaders had a completely
distorted vision of him. Jesus was speaking the truth about his unique relationship with God the Father as God the Son. Calling God his *own* Father
was very different from a general fatherhood of God found in the Jewish
Scriptures. But they didn't feel free to speak of God as father anyway.

For me today, I am in you, Jesus, and you are in the Father. I am in your
presence as I live, move, have my being, and work. I am in the presence of
perfect love, perfect peace, abundant life, full joy, all present to energize, guide,
and strengthen me throughout this day. May I sense how I might join the Father
in the good work he does today.

. . . .

**What work lies ahead of you now? How might you enjoy the Father with
you as you do it?**

WE AREN'T WORKING ALONE

*Jesus gave them this answer: "Very truly I tell you, the Son can do
nothing by himself; he can do only what he sees his Father doing,
because whatever the Father does the Son also does." (John 5:19)*

LIKE JESUS, WE CAN LEARN how to do just what we see the Father doing.
Unlike Jesus, we mostly see what the Father is doing by watching the Son.
Jesus works with the Father and invites us to learn how to collaborate with
the Father and himself. This is the contemplative aspect of our work.

The Father loves the Son and shows him everything he is up to. And, re-
markably, the Son has invited us to be with him to watch what he does and
join him in these remarkable kingdom works. What work could be better
than that? I want to be about that work. I long to work more with Jesus than
for Jesus today.

These Jewish leaders kept claiming that Jesus was breaking the Sabbath,
but he wasn't breaking the Father's way of Sabbath. They persecuted Jesus
for violating their own rules. Jesus was working with God the Father while
these leaders were working against God. They had no idea that reality was
utterly opposite of their vision of it. What a terrible place to find oneself.
They were even willing to kill Jesus, violating a commandment they claimed
to hold dear.

It's tragic when those who claim to follow Jesus define that reality in their
own terms, then judge others against those terms instead of by the light of
God's real and present kingdom. They imagine Jesus would heartily affirm
their narrow, self-important vision. There can be no real peace, joy, or love
in such a confined space.

. . . .

**What is one thing Jesus might do if he had your life and your current
work? What might it look like for you to do that?**

TELLING THE TRUTH

If I testify about myself, my testimony is not true. There is another who testifies in my favor, and I know that his testimony about me is true. (John 5:31-32)

JESUS DOESN'T MEAN HERE that in testifying about himself he's being inaccurate or dishonest. Rather he seems to imply that no one accepts a person as their own witness. A person can say anything they want about themselves and, unless another witness verifies, it's hard to know if what they say is true.

I need to remember that my own "testimony" about myself is sometimes untrue. Too often my testimony about myself has been downplaying, devaluing, even self-condemning. I jump to the conclusion that my shortcomings and offenses are the main thing about me. But my testimony based on this negative focus is not the whole story. Jesus, on the other hand, always tells the truth about me.

Perhaps he says to me, "Alan, you come up short and are forgiven. You cross the line and are loved. You are a treasure because I made and value you. You didn't choose me. I chose you. I'm determined to work fruitfully in and through you in ways that last." Are these sentences perhaps truer than my own self-critical tendencies?

The other who testifies in Jesus' favor is John the Baptizer. Jesus wasn't desperate for John to say good things about him. He didn't "accept human testimony" (John 5:34). He didn't need people to tell him who he was. He had a Father who had testified from heaven, "This is my beloved Son" (Matthew 3:17 ESV). That Father speaks those same words to us. You are my beloved daughter, my beloved son. This is the testimony that matters. These are the words that count.

· ·

What do you tend to say about yourself? How does this compare with the good words God speaks of you?

RECEIVING SCRIPTURE

You study the Scriptures diligently because you think that in them
you have eternal life. These are the very Scriptures that testify about
me, yet you refuse to come to me to have life. (John 5:39-40)

JESUS SPEAKS THESE WORDS to Jewish leaders who see their authority as rooted in how they'd come to understand their Scriptures. They are diligent in their study of the Torah, the Writings, and the Prophets. They give such laser-focused attention to the written word of God that they are unable to recognize the living Word of God before them. They don't discern the person to whom their book is pointing. Authority is personal and relational. They think it is a matter of quoting the right words, but the Word is in their midst.

I've made the same mistake. Growing up in churches that highly valued the study and teaching of Scripture, I sometimes made the Bible the main thing. But Jesus is the main thing. God as Father, Son, and Holy Spirit is at the center of reality. In the end, this isn't a subtle distinction.

The Jewish leaders to whom Jesus speaks are utterly committed to the study of the Scriptures. They believe they will find eternal life in those words. They study the message of the Scriptures but fail to see their primary role of pointing to the Messiah. Jesus tells them the Scriptures are testifying about him. The Jewish leaders can't see or hear this. They refuse Jesus and so refuse life.

I'm glad for the attention given to the Bible in my own faith journey. Jesus clearly had vast stretches of the Scriptures committed to memory. How good to be able to listen to the voice of the living Word as I engage the written word day by day.

. . . .

How have you experienced the written Scriptures drawing you closer to Jesus, the Word made flesh?

TRUE GLORY

How can you believe since you accept glory from one another but do not seek the glory that comes from the only God? (John 5:44)

JESUS HAS TOLD THE JEWISH LEADERS who oppose him that he doesn't accept glory from other people (John 5:41). He's saying people don't have real glory of their own to offer him. When we glorify God, we return glory that God has already given us. Glorifying God is always reflecting glory. Christ is already glorious and does not need the approval of the people around him.

The Jewish leaders have a whole system of determining what matters, what's weighty, what shines. Jesus does not enter that system. They receive people based on human authority and glory, but they won't acknowledge the real authority and glory they are witnessing in Jesus.

They have this little, empty, self-referencing "glory" that they pass back and forth, like children trading shiny pennies. But they are completely detached from real glory that shines from God in Jesus. This is damning and they don't even realize it.

Any real glory in my life will not originate in the people around me. I can thank them for affirming comments but, in the end, substantial glory comes from God. It may reflect from people around me, but its source is God. I can simply say "thank you" for gracious words.

My true glory is reflected glory. God shines. God matters. And I can contemplate and mirror this glory. This is my calling. I want to be a good reflector of glory in everything I do. I'm grateful for the Spirit of God enabling me to live in such a way today.

. . . .

In what ways do you find yourself longing for the praise of those around you? How might Jesus speak glorious words that meet you in that place?

FOLLOWING JESUS: TWO OPTIONS

A large crowd kept following him, because they saw the signs
that he was doing for the sick. Jesus went up the mountain and
sat down there with his disciples. (John 6:2-3 NRSV)

THE APOSTLE JOHN IS straightforward about why the crowd was following Jesus. Rather than desiring to learn from this wise, compassionate rabbi to help others, the crowd wanted to see something exciting happen. They wanted to be there when Jesus did his next miracle. They wanted to be able to say they witnessed it.

Why do I follow Jesus? Maybe it's because of something exciting I expect him to do. Maybe there's something I feel I need or want from him. Or perhaps I follow him because he knows the way—because he actually is the way (John 14:6)—to life.

As I reflect on my reasons for coming to Jesus, is my motive closer to that of the crowd, or is my heart more like that of a disciple who sits with Jesus to learn from him to better follow him? Am I seeking benefits or transformation?

The crowd generally follows at a distance. Disciples follow Jesus closely.

. . . .

How closely are you following Jesus? In what ways are you wandering or even avoiding him? Reflect on your answer.

THE LIGHT OF HIS PRESENCE

*[Jesus] said this to test [Philip], for he himself knew
what he was going to do. (John 6:6 NRSV)*

JESUS HAD JUST ASKED PHILIP, "Where are we to buy bread for these people to eat?" (John 6:5 NRSV). From a human perspective, feeding such a huge crowd was an overwhelming, if not utterly impossible, task. How would the disciples come up with enough cash to feed thousands of people? Who nearby would even have that much food to sell?

In the back of my mind, I'm tempted to think Jesus said what he did as a kind of trick question for Philip. But Jesus isn't trying to trick us. He does test us, though. And testing brings to the surface dynamics that are present but perhaps unseen: in this case, does Philip trust Jesus? While the thought of being tested by Jesus may seem threatening, remember that whatever surfaces—a lack of faith, for instance—can be transformed once it is brought into the light of his presence.

Jesus knows what is going on in my life. When I feel he is testing me, I can be confident that he is not asking me trick questions. Instead, he wants me to be more mindful of our relationship and more aware of exactly who he is. He always does this from a motive of love. He wants to bring healing to what is unwell, restoration to what is broken, and cleansing to what has been dirtied.

. . . .

When, if ever, have you felt like God asked you a trick question? Now that you can look back at those circumstances, how might that moment have been a test designed to bring to the surface something in you that you needed to see?

GRACE MULTIPLIES SIMPLICITY

Jesus then took the loaves, gave thanks, and distributed to those who were
seated as much as they wanted. He did the same with the fish. (John 6:11)

TODAY'S PASSAGE COMES FROM the story of Jesus feeding the five thousand. I'm encouraged to remember that five small loaves and two tiny fish brought by a little boy were the starting point for this miracle. On its own, this meal might have stretched to help a friend or two, but it was obviously not going to help a crowd of thousands.

Jesus can take our unimpressive offerings and transform them into something that blesses hundreds and thousands of others. God does great work with our small gifts offered in love.

There is an intersection between the language John uses here about how Jesus receives and blesses this offering and his words in the upper room when he celebrates Passover with his inner circle. Luke, for example, shares that "he took bread, gave thanks and broke it, and gave it to them, saying, 'This is my body given for you; do this in remembrance of me'" (Luke 22:19).

Like he would later do in that last gathering of his close followers, Jesus stands among the thousands, takes the loaves, gives thanks for them, and distributes them to the people. Taken, blessed, given. It sounds like sacramental language. Jesus takes our little offerings, blesses them with gratitude to the Father, and, through us, gives them to bless the world.

Whatever little offering you have to offer others, bring it first to Jesus. Invite his blessing on it and trust him to multiply it to help many.

. . . .

Is there something in your life that feels like less than you wish it was?
What would it look like to offer it to Jesus and welcome his blessing of it
to help many?

DON'T BE AFRAID

But he said to them, "It is I; don't be afraid." Then they were
willing to take him into the boat, and immediately the boat
reached the shore where they were heading. (John 6:20-21)

WHEN JESUS WALKS ON the surface of the Sea of Galilee toward his disciples, they are terrified. They can't figure out what's happening. Perhaps they wonder if they are hallucinating. Jesus speaks to their reaction: "It's me. Don't be afraid."

In what fearful circumstances might I hear the voice of Jesus saying, "It's me. I'm here. Don't be afraid"? I'm fearful of rejection, abandonment, failure, incapacity. Might Jesus be present to me in these fears just as surely as he was present to his followers in the boat? Jesus doesn't pretend our fears don't exist. He acknowledges them. My fears are not unique to me. Many share the same fears I hold.

Jesus' answer to fear is presence. "I am with you." He is present to me as Protector when I fear danger. He is present to me as Friend when I fear abandonment. He is present in grace to strengthen me in my weakness. Presence is Jesus' fruitful response to my fears.

Jesus calms his followers with his presence and his confidence. The disciples take him into their boat, and they reach their destination. They are encouraged as they receive him. I pray that I'll have ears today to hear Jesus speak to my feelings of timidity: "I'm here. Don't be afraid. Let's do this together."

. . . .

What is a common fear in your life these days? When do you feel intimidated or threatened? Let yourself hear Jesus' words of loving presence to you in just this place.

WHAT WE WORK FOR

Do not work for food that spoils, but for food that endures to
eternal life, which the Son of Man will give you. For on him God
the Father has placed his seal of approval. (John 6:27)

WHAT DO I SEEK FROM GOD? Am I focused on what is temporary and fleeting or what is lasting and substantial? "Substantial" captures a key facet of what "eternal" is all about. It's more than duration. It's a quality of time and life.

Jesus invites the crowd, and he invites you and me, to expend our efforts in nourishment in eternal living. Jesus gives this food as a gift, but still requires effort to seek it.

What is this work? To what precisely does God invite us? Someone in the crowd asks just that question: "What must we do to do the works God requires?" Jesus defines the work of God as believing in the one he has sent (John 6:28-29).

Jesus invites us into the basics: "Work on trusting me." This is what we focus on and work toward. Everything good flows from there. We come to trust what Jesus says about his Father's kingdom. We share with others what we learn from Jesus about eternal living. We find ourselves well-fed, so much so that we share with others whose lives are hungry.

Something in me feels like that's not enough. Surely the work of God is much more than that. It is, but the work to which God invites us must grow in the atmosphere of trusting God. Overcoming my doubts about what Jesus says of himself and the kingdom is hard work. Being intentional about growing in this simple confidence isn't automatic.

. . . .

In what ways do you find yourself hungry these days? Where are you taking those hungers to seek satisfaction? What might it look like to find satisfaction in what Jesus is offering?

THE WORK OF GOD REDEFINED

The work of God is this: to believe in the one he has sent. (John 6:29)

WHAT COMES TO MIND when you hear the phrase "work of God"? When Jesus' disciples asked essentially that same question, Jesus didn't answer with a to-do list, an inventory of personal qualifications, or a set of required courses and specific accomplishments at the local synagogue. Instead, Jesus responded with an invitation to trust that he was indeed sent by God.

Often during Jesus' earthly ministry people asked for a sign to believe in; they wanted him to do something spectacular that only God could do. Jesus did plenty of healings, miracles, and other displays of power—and still not everyone believed. In this passage, and several times throughout the Gospels, Jesus did not give a checklist to potential followers. What Jesus did was invite them to believe in him and trust him. But this answer wasn't at all what everyone expected.

Doing God's work on this earth involves more fully trusting Jesus as our Savior, following him as our King, and loving him more and more with all that is in us. This is the point at which all true work for God begins. Jesus redefined the very nature of the work of God, and he invites us to join him in this very good work.

. . . .

Why is Jesus' call to simply believe in him such a challenge for some of us? Wherever you are on your journey with the Shepherd, how have you been learning to trust him?

BREAD FROM HEAVEN

Very truly I tell you, it is not Moses who has given you the bread from heaven,
but it is my Father who gives you the true bread from heaven. (John 6:32)

JESUS HAS BEEN SPEAKING to the crowd about seeking not only bread for their stomachs but bread that will nourish their forever life. They want to know what work God wants from them, and Jesus says, essentially, "The Father wants you to trust me because he sent me."

They pick up on the bread from heaven and assume Jesus is referring to the story of manna in the wilderness. They assume their ancestor, Moses, is the one to credit with this miracle, but Jesus reminds them that it was God, their Father, who provided for them long ago (John 6:30-32).

Our lives are not about mere human authority (like Moses) or provision (like manna). Our lives do not substantially improve through more achievements, acquisitions, or accolades. That which will sustain us and bring us alive comes through our communion with God in Christ. And God is very generous with us.

Jesus is the bread of God that comes from the presence of the Father and brings the possibility of eternal living to the world. We do not live by bread alone (Matthew 4:4). We truly live because Jesus nourishes our inner lives.

Let's welcome the continued work of God's Spirit that enables us to find life in friendship with Christ. Let's grow to live in a way more honoring to God in our bodies. Let's learn how to be nourished from the bread who comes from heaven.

. . . .

How do you find yourself hungry in soul these days? What would it look like to bring that hunger first to God? How might God meet you there and give you an eternal quality of joy in that very place?

NEVER HUNGERING

For the bread of God is the bread that comes down from heaven and gives life to the world. (John 6:33)

JESUS DESCRIBES HIMSELF AS the bread of God come down from heaven, but the listening crowd doesn't understand what he's offering. They seem to imagine some sort of miraculously multiplying bread that he's given them before. They've seen a few loaves become enough for thousands to eat and be satisfied. Perhaps they want a way to take that to go. If they could get their hands on bread that never ran out, they'd be set for life.

Don't we also sometimes want something from God that we can take along and be set? But God doesn't provide in a way that we can then leave him behind. God provides for us in relationship. Jesus is the bread. Every single day, he is the one who is feeding, nourishing, energizing, filling us. "I am the bread of life." We are nourished in relationship with him.

The way I learn to live so that my deepest hungers and thirsts are filled is not so much by partaking of something God gives but by enjoying God himself. If I try to take something from him and go on my way as though I no longer need him, I just might have the same experience as the Israelites had with the manna. Whatever they tried to save for later spoiled. Whatever I try to save for later spoils, too. There is a living immediacy about how Jesus provides for our souls. It is in contact with him that we remain fresh, alive, vital, encouraged.

. . . .

When has God's presence met you at your deepest places of hunger? What hunger would you like to bring to Jesus to see how he might meet you there today?

SOUL NOURISHMENT

I am the bread of life. Whoever comes to me will never be hungry
again. Whoever believes in me will never be thirsty. (John 6:35 NLT)

WHAT A BEAUTIFUL PROMISE the Shepherd makes to us, the sheep of
his flock!

Jesus is the one who truly satisfies our hunger and thirst. He was blunt in
proclaiming this truth: those who trust in him will never be hungry or thirsty
again. "Never" is confident language. These words sound a lot like the first
verse of Psalm 23 (ESV): "The LORD is my shepherd; I shall not want." We are
in the care of a Good Shepherd. We are watched over and lack nothing.

If I'm honest, since I began to trust in Jesus—and entrust myself to him—I
have experienced plenty of moments when I've felt hungry or thirsty in soul.
But that doesn't prove Jesus wrong. It simply says I'm still learning to fully
trust him. I know from experience that when I choose to trust Jesus and rest
in him, he thoroughly meets all my soul needs.

Jesus—and only Jesus—truly nourishes and satisfies a hungry and thirsty
soul. There are plenty of places to which I bring my hungers and thirsts that
don't satisfy me (because they can't). What about you? How do you long to
receive God's soul nourishment today more fully?

Think about what your soul gets hungry and thirsty for . . . and why Jesus
is the bread that meets those needs and satisfies your soul.

. . . .

**What keeps you from receiving the soul nourishment Jesus longs to
give you?**

THE BREAD OF LIFE

I am the living bread that came down from heaven. Whoever
eats of this bread will live forever; and the bread that I will give
for the life of the world is my flesh. (John 6:51 NRSV)

WHEN JESUS WAS TEMPTED by Satan in the wilderness, the enemy challenged him to turn stones into bread. Jesus responded, "Man shall not live on bread alone, but on every word that comes from the mouth of God" (Matthew 4:4).

In his ministry, Jesus—the Son of God, completely man and completely God—gave us words of life. Jesus himself feeds and nourishes me. He is the one from the heavens who gives himself to me so I might live an abundant life as I walk with him on this earth, as well as an eternal life of joy, freedom, and wholeness in heaven. Every other "good life" the world proposes is nothing compared to the goodness of life lived with Jesus.

But some people simply do not accept this idea. For example, some of the Jews who heard Jesus teach complained, "Is this not Jesus, the son of Joseph, whose father and mother we know? How can he now say, 'I came down from heaven'?" (John 6:42). They thought they knew Jesus because they had watched him grow up. They believed they knew exactly who Jesus was because they were familiar with the facts of his earthly life. They had eyes but failed to see.

Jesus is the living bread who came down from heaven. The life of Jesus nourishes us in deep and lasting ways. Jesus invites you to take in the good words he speaks so that your soul would be well-fed today.

. . . .

What two or three things have most surprised you as you have gotten to know Jesus better over time?

REAL FOOD

*For my flesh is real food and my blood is real drink. Whoever eats my flesh
and drinks my blood remains in me, and I in them. (John 6:55-56)*

JESUS SPEAKS THESE WORDS to Jews who don't know what to make of
them. Some recognize Jesus' habit of speaking in parables and realize he isn't
speaking literally. Others find what he says so offensive they don't reflect but
react to his words. They believe Jesus is being "unbiblical" in terms of the Law,
the Writings, and the Prophets.

What *is* Jesus saying here? These words have puzzled many over the centuries. Is he saying that if you regularly receive the Lord's Supper you'll live?
This sounds like magical thinking. I love when I receive, week by week, the
body and the blood of Jesus in the bread and the cup. But is there a way to
"eat his body" and "drink his blood" when I'm not gathered with God's people?
Might Jesus be inviting us into communion with the reality of his incarnation? Can I be nourished and refreshed by Jesus in my own day-to-day life
in prayerful conversation?

Jesus speaks of his body and blood as "real" food and drink. That is different from temporary food and drink. What goes in my mouth and eventually exits my body serves me for a time. Jesus nourishes and refreshes us in
a way that lasts. Jesus himself is my portion. He fills my plate. He fills the cup
of my life. Jesus is alive and present with me always. I can find life in him in
each moment. In him I can find zest, buoyancy, well-being, and energy for
all my life and work.

. . . .

**How would you like to offer your attention to Jesus in this moment? How
might your soul find its hungers and thirsts filled in this communion?**

EAT MY FLESH

Just as the living Father sent me, and I live because of the Father, so whoever eats me will live because of me. (John 6:57 NRSV)

JESUS IS AT THE HEART of this holy "just as" statement: according to the eternal plan of God, the Father sent Jesus the Son to live on this earth—and to die and live again on this earth. Jesus lived because of the Father's power on display in both the incarnation and the resurrection. Jesus uses the words "just as" about being sent by the living Father and living because of the Father. In the same way, those of us who eat and drink of Jesus live because of him, because of the truth he proclaimed, because of the immeasurable grace of God.

The Eucharist—also called Communion or the Lord's Table—is a corporate and visible experience of the reality that we are nourished and energized for God's work by eating and drinking of Jesus. But I am not limited to eating and drinking of Jesus only when I gather with other followers around bread and wine. I think the Twelve were eating and drinking of Jesus in those years of discipleship without once celebrating the Eucharist.

Again, I try to imagine being one of the Jewish leaders standing there hearing Jesus tell them to eat his body and drink his blood. I would have been puzzled, offended, incredulous. But Jesus was saying something important about the nature of eternal life: we enter in only through a vital, nourishing, life-giving, interactive relationship with Jesus.

. . . .

What does it mean to you that the disciples were eating and drinking of Jesus in those years of discipleship even though they didn't celebrate the Eucharist until that last night in the upper room?

THE SPIRIT GIVES LIFE

The Spirit gives life; the flesh counts for nothing. The words I have
spoken to you—they are full of the Spirit and life. (John 6:63)

WHAT IS THIS FLESH that counts for nothing? It appears to be human life apart from God. Jesus speaks similar words in the upper room: "Apart from me you can do nothing" (John 15:5).

Jesus speaks words full to the brim with Spirit and life. When I read the Gospels slowly, I find I feel connected to the story of Jesus. I sense the living voice of Jesus in this story. What a gift!

As this continues, Jesus asks Simon Peter if he feels like leaving when so many of his fellow disciples have. Peter responds, "Lord, to whom shall we go? You have the words of eternal life. We have come to believe and to know that you are the Holy One of God" (John 6:68-69).

The one who will temporarily betray Jesus on the evening of his arrest affirms his allegiance to Jesus at this moment. But he's right. Ceasing to follow Jesus as many did after this puzzling, difficult word about eating flesh and drinking blood would not be life-giving. Those who left Jesus left the one who speaks words of Spirit and life.

There is no one else to whom I might go either. I have come to believe and know that Jesus is the Holy One of God who speaks words of Spirit and life. That's been good for my soul over the years.

When I hear Jesus speak to me in Scripture, I come alive. That's what his words look like in my lived experience.

In what ways have you sensed the Spirit bringing you alive lately? In what ways do you desire the Spirit to do this where you've felt drained of life?

WHERE ELSE CAN WE GO?

Simon Peter answered him, "Lord, to whom shall we go? You
have the words of eternal life. We have come to believe and to
know that you are the Holy One of God." (John 6:68-69)

PETER SPEAKS THESE WORDS of devotion and faith in answer to a
question Jesus asks him and the other disciples: "You do not want to leave
too, do you?" (John 6:67). Several of Jesus' outer circle of disciples were offended or at least puzzled by his language about eating his body and drinking
his blood. Here Peter, as often is the case, speaks up for the group. These
words sound to my ear like stating the obvious: "Where else would we go?"

Who else would speak and live eternal life among them like Jesus had?
Like Peter, I have come to believe and know that Jesus is the Holy One of God.
I have come to believe that his is a vision of reality. When he speaks, I can
trust he is guiding me into a good and meaningful life. Jesus doesn't just offer
interesting opinions to which I give my assent. His words bring me life.
Lasting life. Real life. Vitality. Energy. Enthusiasm.

Over our lifetimes, as we test various voices crying out about the good life,
we discover that Jesus really is our life. Money is not life. Fame is not life.
Other places and people don't offer life. But communion with Jesus revives
me. Friendship with God in Christ refreshes and feeds me. I find more and
more life as I grow in deep trust and loving knowledge of God in Christ.
Where else would I go?

. . . .

Where else have you turned to find satisfaction or fulfillment? How have
you discovered in your own journey the life Jesus offers? What would you
like to say to God about this?

MAKING A NAME, RECEIVING A NAME

Jesus' brothers said to him, . . . "No one who wants to become a public figure acts in secret. Since you are doing these things, show yourself to the world." (John 7:3-4)

THOSE WHO ASPIRE TO BE public figures seek fame, reputation, or recognition. Jesus' brothers assume this is what motivates him—a name, visibility, popularity. They recommend he show himself to the world at the Festival of Tabernacles in Jerusalem. They imagine that Jesus wants the public spotlight because that's their own motivation. Instead, Jesus prefers to go to Jerusalem secretly.

How different from my own instincts. Now that I have written a few books, sometimes a desire arises in me to be a public figure. There is a practical hope more people will read what I've written. But sometimes there is also a secret hope more people will admire me. Jesus, however, wants to be seen only as the Father would reveal him to the world. He isn't looking to glorify himself but the Father who sent him.

This is freeing. Fame lacks meaningful substance. It comes and goes easily. I'm embarrassed at how strong my desire to be known can be. For example, I'm still tempted to base my sense of personal worth on whether people know me and value what I have to say.

I'm grateful, though, that the source of my worth never changes. My worth is still in who (and whose) I am. Writing books has not made me a different person. I am growing, but mostly I am the same person I was before I published anything. Popularity does not change who I really am. If I let the Father be the one to name me, the names given me by the crowd hold less power.

In what ways are you (or have you been) tempted to seek your value in the opinions of others?

TRY IT ON

Jesus answered, "My teaching is not my own.
It comes from the one who sent me. Anyone who chooses to do
the will of God will find out whether my teaching comes from
God or whether I speak on my own." (John 7:16-17)

INSTEAD OF THE AUTHORITY of the institution, Jesus had the authority of living communion with the Father. He lived in reality where others simply didn't. Jesus didn't receive authority like the rabbis did. His teaching was not an expression of rabbinical training. His teaching came directly from the one who sent him.

What beautiful confidence Jesus has in the teaching he brings, inviting anyone who wishes to try it on in their actual life to see how well it works. He says anyone willing to test what he says will discover he is speaking divine truth. He is speaking about reality. The best way to prove the truth of what Jesus says is not so much to argue, but to try it on. Test and see that Jesus' teaching works in real life. What Jesus says is from God and leads us to God if we'll follow.

Jesus was not speaking to impress. He was not seeking the admiration or respect of the crowd. He was not seeking to take anything away from the Jewish leaders of his day. He was seeking the glory of his Father in heaven. There was nothing false in this. And Jesus seeks to get their attention back on their own response and responsibility. They want to argue about the law of Moses but, as Jesus says, not one of those in the crowd is fully keeping that law. There is a pride in knowing the law that is betrayed by failure to keep the law.

. . . .

How would you like to respond to Jesus' invitation to act on his teaching to discover its truth? What teaching of Jesus is he inviting you to try on?

BREAKING THE LAW
TO KEEP THE LAW

Now if a boy can be circumcised on the Sabbath so that the law
of Moses may not be broken, why are you angry with me for
healing a man's whole body on the Sabbath? Stop judging by mere
appearances, but instead judge correctly. (John 7:23-24)

JESUS AND THE JEWISH leaders again come into conflict over the Sabbath. Jewish tradition had largely lost the unhurried gift that Sabbath was meant to be. Sabbath could have been a day of deep healing, but tradition considered healing work, and work wasn't allowed. There are times when well-intended human rules keep us from doing good that benefits others.

The example Jesus offers is their practice of circumcising a baby boy on the eighth day even if that ended up being the Sabbath. Circumcision would certainly qualify as work by their own definitions. Jesus suggests that if keeping this circumcision tradition is an acceptable way to bypass the Sabbath, then surely healing a man's whole body would also be good.

Jesus' assessment is that they are judging everything by outward appearances rather than judging correctly. This is also what happens when we turn faith in Jesus into a set of rules. We focus on rules about what to do or not do, what is allowed or not allowed, but disregard the inner realities those rules were meant to address. We seem more interested in looking good than in truly becoming people who live good, loving lives.

Rather than focusing on rules most of us have no trouble keeping, like "Don't murder," Jesus suggests a better focus: not to harbor anger against anyone (Matthew 5:21-22). The great commandment is living a life of love with God that touches every human relationship. If I pursue such a life, I'll find I don't need many rules.

Think of a rule about living well that is important to you. How might that rule be a facet of the deeper law to love?

TRANSFORMED THIRSTS

Let anyone who is thirsty come to me and drink. Whoever
believes in me, as Scripture has said, rivers of living water
will flow from within them. (John 7:37-38)

JESUS CRIES OUT AND invites us to bring our thirsts to him. Just as Jesus invited the woman at the well to do in John 4, we can drink living water and never thirst again. In fact, instead of thirst, we will come to find rivers of living water flowing from within us—by which Jesus means the fullness of God's Spirit flowing from within us. We can become not only temples (or vessels) of the Holy Spirit but conduits through which God's Spirit flows out into our relationships, our work, and our world.

The Greek phrase translated as "from within them" literally means "out of the belly"—the gut. Our places of deep feeling and passion can become profound expressions of the heart and passion of God's Spirit seeking to bring the world back to life in God through Christ. What we bring to God as a thirst can be transformed into a river. The key is to respond to Jesus' simple invitation, "Come to me. Trust in me. Drink of me." This is an invitation to stability, rootedness, and abundance.

. . . .

Let this prayer become your own today: *Lord, I am thirsty, but I take my thirsts to places other than you. I take them to places of distraction, to self-indulgence, to ways of numbing, to empty amusement, to driven accomplishment. Show me how to bring my deepest thirsts to you today. Show me the path to being a person of abundance for the good of others. Amen.*

TRUTH FREES US

To the Jews who had believed him, Jesus said, "If you hold to
my teaching, you are really my disciples. Then you will know
the truth, and the truth will set you free." (John 8:31-32)

JESUS IS HAVING A CONTENTIOUS CONVERSATION with Jews who have believed in him. But they have not yet been set free in the following of Jesus' teaching. Believers become free as they follow Jesus' teaching and experience freedom in their actual lives. Affirming ideas doesn't set us free. Living and practicing the truth Jesus teaches and models sets us free. Otherwise, like these believing Jews, we can end up agreeing with truth without entering the freedom of truth.

Knowing about truth does not set us free. Truth can be a burden if we don't submit to it and live into it. Jesus is inviting these Jews who believed him (and us as well) to three things:

First, hold to what Jesus teaches. Try it on. Follow his words and his ways. Second, follow Jesus as a disciple on the path by which we come to *know* the truth. On this path we come to know in our souls what we've agreed with as an idea. Truth then shapes us and becomes our home. Finally, on this journey of following Jesus as a disciple, be set free by his truth. Truth *will* set us free when we follow the One who calls himself Truth. This freedom is a relational reality.

When we follow the lead of our own wayward impulses, we become disciples of lust, anger, or greed, not of truth. What a gift to discover the freedom that comes when we follow the teaching and guidance of Jesus.

. . . .

In what way do you feel more like a slave than like a person living in freedom? Ask Jesus what it would look like to follow his teachings that lead to freedom.

EXAMINING OUR ASSUMPTIONS

Some of the Pharisees said, "This man is not from
God, for he does not keep the Sabbath."
But others asked, "How can a sinner perform such
signs?" So they were divided. (John 9:16)

THE PHARISEES ONCE AGAIN accuse Jesus of failing to faithfully represent God. We can do this today. We can become so attached to our frameworks or assumptions about God that we hold them more tightly than we do what Jesus does and says.

In our story, the blind man has been healed. It was as rare then as it would be today. His healing is undeniable. But some experience a disconnect between someone like Jesus disregarding their assumptions about God and doing miracles in the name of God. They have created a box for God that Jesus doesn't fit in. But God isn't in their little box any more than Jesus is.

Jesus invites us to look at the fruit of his life and work. What fruit did he bear? Does the fruit of his life reflect the character and work of God? Sometimes our preconceptions about God are stronger than our willingness to taste the fruit of what we witness.

When we are attached to our preconceptions of God, we're tempted to interpret all evidence in light of them. That's what the Pharisees did. They weren't interested in examining their assumptions in the light of reality they'd witnessed.

Lord Jesus, heal my blindness. Open my eyes to my own misguided assumptions and preconceptions. Loosen my grip on them so I might open my eyes to what you say is true and real. Free me from grasping at my little "truths" in ways that hinder me from abiding in Truth.

Why not ask Jesus if there are ways you are tempted to cling to mistaken preconceptions about him? Be still and listen. Wouldn't a little more freedom be good?

DO YOU BELIEVE?

Jesus heard that they had thrown him out, and when he found him, he said, "Do you believe in the Son of Man?" "Who is he, sir?" the man asked. "Tell me so that I may believe in him." (John 9:35-36)

JESUS SPEAKS TO THE BLIND MAN whom he'd healed. This caused a great uproar among the Jewish leaders because Jesus had again healed on the Sabbath day. The blind man knows that God has done something miraculous in his life. He's not sure who Jesus is, so Jesus asks him, "Do you believe in the Son of Man?" The formerly blind man is all ears, "Who is he? Please tell me."

The man is hungry to know the truth. He wants to trust in the one who has shown him so much power and grace. And he wants to be enabled to believe even if he doesn't at first understand. Understanding often *follows* trust. But it's always good to remember again what Jesus said: "Anyone who chooses to do the will of God will find out whether my teaching comes from God or whether I speak on my own" (John 7:17). Practicing Jesus' teachings leads us to understanding and knowledge.

Jesus' very presence was a judgment on the Pharisees who believed they were the ones who knew and saw truth. The Pharisees ask Jesus if he thinks they are blind (John 9:40). They "know" they aren't but are willing to humor Jesus' misguided expression of opinion. Jesus, having complete access to the Spirit of God, had the best chance of helping these Pharisees come to understand and embrace reality. They just wouldn't, and Jesus apparently couldn't overcome that. The blind man was healed and came to trust Jesus. The Jewish leaders rejected Jesus and proved their blindness.

. . . .

What has Jesus done in your life that has inspired you to trust him more?

WORSHIPING JESUS

Jesus said, "You have now seen him; in fact,
he is the one speaking with you."
Then the man said, "Lord, I believe,"
and he worshiped him. (John 9:37-38)

JUST BEFORE THIS, the blind man asks Jesus, "Who is he [the Son of Man], sir? . . . Tell me so that I may believe in him" (John 9:36). Our focus verses contain Jesus' answer to that question. The blind man knows he's been healed, but he does not yet know the identity of the one who has healed him. We often see kingdom benefits before we gain kingdom understanding. Grace often precedes (and enables) knowledge.

When it comes to our inner sight—something the Jewish leaders didn't have, which kept them inwardly blind—being *able* to see may not be as important as *who* we see. We need the Spirit of God to open the eyes of our heart so we see Jesus in his love, his grace, his power, his wisdom, his goodness. He is the one inviting us to trust him and to express our perception of his worth with words of worship. He wants us to see and respond to the reality of who he is. We need this more than he needs this.

· ·

Offer a prayer to Jesus in the spirit of this one: *Lord, today I believe. You took a blind man and gave him spiritual sight. I was utterly blind to you, your kingdom, and your living way, but you drew me to the Father. I believe you and am learning to trust you more. Thank you for your Spirit, which enables me to dwell in your presence throughout this day. Amen.*

LOOKING BUT NOT SEEING

For judgment I have come into this world, so that the blind
will see and those who see will become blind. (John 9:39)

JESUS MUST MEAN SOMETHING different here than he does elsewhere in John's Gospel, where he says he came *not* to condemn the world but to save it (John 3:17). Here he seems to say, "I came to see things and talk about things as they are."

If anyone in Jesus' day would have been considered wise and in touch with God, it would have been the Pharisees. They had an honored history. They were a respected movement. They were serious about God. But they were wrong. They were self-deceived. There are few things worse than that combination.

The longer we find ourselves following Jesus, the more tempting it can be to assume we're right about him all the time. But we just might be wrong at times. It is good to be humble in our knowing. It is good to remain a learner who can be corrected by the Scriptures and the Spirit. It is good to say to ourselves, "I *could* be wrong."

The irony is that if the Pharisees could have admitted their blindness, they would have found themselves on a path to being truly saved. They would not be guilty of what they could not see and knew they couldn't see. But because they made claims to see in their spiritual blindness, they were guilty. Lord, have mercy!

If I see anything today, it is not because of my amazing vision but because of God's amazing revelation. I see what God has shown me in Christ. This is always a gift. I was blind, but now I see.

. . . .

When have you realized you were wrong in some way about God? How did you respond in that moment?

THE SHEPHERD'S VOICE

The sheep listen to his voice. He calls his own sheep by name and leads them out. . . . And his sheep follow him because they know his voice. (John 10:3-4)

"THEY KNOW HIS VOICE." It's a simple phrase, but I find it especially touching: we are Jesus' sheep, and we know his voice. We learn to recognize the voice of another as we spend time with that person. If we spend enough time with them, we will at some point be able to pick their voice out of a crowd. When my wife, Gem, and I are at a large event, I know her voice, and I easily recognize her laugh from across the room.

So how do you and I come to know the voice of the Spirit that well? We don't want to miss him when he speaks in the depths of our souls. I've come to recognize his voice in large part because of my time reading the Scriptures. I've read and studied them long enough that I recognize that same voice when I hear it rising within my soul.

I've learned to recognize the voice of the Spirit in my heart and mind when I find myself surprised or challenged by some word that arises within me. God doesn't usually say the thing I expect God to say. I don't listen to the Spirit's voice as merely a recreational activity, though. What God says is life! I'm not following a stranger but a Friend. What's better than a conversation between good friends?

Wouldn't it be beautiful if more of Jesus' sheep came to fully recognize their Shepherd's voice?

. . . .

What are you doing to become more familiar with—and able to recognize— God's voice in your life?

THE GOOD LIFE

The thief comes only to steal and kill and destroy; I have come
that they may have life, and have it to the full. (John 10:10)

JESUS IS A VERY Good Shepherd. It's a metaphor most don't experience in daily life like his first listeners would have. Jesus is our guide. Jesus cares for us. Jesus leads us to good places. In these ways he shepherds us. I am one who is in his care. There are those who want only to take from me, but Jesus comes as a generous friend.

Sometimes voices arise that would lead me to emptiness and destruction. Jesus never leads me to such places. I need to discern the movements that arise in my mind and heart. In this Good Shepherd story, John calls Jesus the gate. He is my passageway to an abundant and good life. I live in freedom and make my way in and out of real life in him.

Why do I still struggle and instead listen to the voice of one who wants only to rob me? The thought that nudges me to fritter away time on a website may intend that I distract myself with things that are empty and meaningless. Instead of engaging my life, I avoid my life. The thought that suggests I eat food I don't need may be seeking to move me away from the bread of life. The temptation to do anything or go anywhere the Good Shepherd is not leading me is a path not of life but of loss. If I would listen to the Shepherd, I would hear words of good counsel leading me to abundant life.

· ·

Where have you felt emptiness more than abundance in your life lately? Ask Jesus how he would shepherd you from such places into a rich life with him.

COSTLY SHEPHERDING

I am the good shepherd. The good shepherd lays down his life for the sheep. The hired hand is not the shepherd and does not own the sheep. So when he sees the wolf coming, he abandons the sheep and runs away. (John 10:11-12)

JESUS IS OUR GOOD SHEPHERD. What he does is not for his own gain but comes from love. This is what good shepherding looks like. Good shepherds care for the flock. A hired hand is just doing a job for pay. If the job gets hard or dangerous, he's out of there. He's not being paid enough to endanger himself for the sake of the flock. But the sheep belong to the Good Shepherd, who will make any sacrifice necessary for them.

Today the Lord is my very Good Shepherd. Jesus is guiding my way and empowering my activities. I am being shepherded well by Jesus. He loves me and I belong to him. I'm learning to do my work together with Jesus.

I feel deeply humbled at such love and availability. Jesus is not far away in some distant heaven. He is near and heaven is near. He is here with me. I am not living light years from home. Heaven is my home.

I'm drawn to relationship with this Good Shepherd. It is rooted more in love more than research. I want to know truths, but even more I want to know Truth. I don't want to be a mere Bible scholar or theological expert. I want to know God in loving and reverent friendship. This is my hunger and thirst. Sometimes I forget this is what I hunger for and instead try to fill my soul with food, pleasures, achievements, or praise. But these come and go. What a good thing it is to be so well shepherded.

. . . .

How might Jesus want to shepherd you these days? How do you feel his guiding, caring hand with you?

KNOWN BY JESUS

I am the good shepherd; I know my sheep and my sheep know me—just as the Father knows me and I know the Father— and I lay down my life for the sheep. (John 10:14-15)

IN THIS VERY MOMENT Jesus is present to us as a Good Shepherd. That's a good thing to remember. It helps us when we let that reality sink in. If I let him, he will shepherd me to places of abundant life and fruitful work. When I don't stay close, I don't find my life or work nearly as fruitful.

How good it is to remember that Jesus knows me. My negative thoughts do not surprise him. My stumbles or struggles do not shock him. I am always with him. He is always with me. I know him, but even more remarkable is that he knows me intimately. He invites me to know him better (and not merely to know *about* him). This is a gift given me by God through Christ. The self-giving love of Christ has opened the way for me to make my home in the measureless love of Father and Son for one another.

Jesus invites his followers to listen for his voice. There is something present and alive about such an invitation. There is something spiritually real and vital here. What a difference it would make if all of us would listen first for his voice over any other voice. Sometimes we are listening more closely to certain political voices, or religious voices, or cultural voices over the voice of our Shepherd. The former divides us. The latter would unite us.

* *

How have you heard the voice of Jesus in this Good Shepherd image? What might it look like to keep an attentive ear open for his voice today?

OUR GOOD SHEPHERD

My sheep hear my voice. I know them,
and they follow me. (John 10:27 NRSV)

JESUS IS SO MATTER OF FACT HERE. His sheep hear his voice. He knows them and they know him. He leads them and they follow him. Similarly, when we hear the voice of our Good Shepherd—when we know him as Savior, as Lord, as Friend, and when we follow where he leads—he blesses us with eternal life. We will never perish. We will not experience the eternal death that is complete separation from God. We will never die. We are alive now and forever.

Not everyone who heard Jesus teach, however, understood his role as shepherd and their implied role as sheep. Many Jews wanted Jesus to use plain, straightforward language and tell them directly, "I am the Messiah you've been waiting for and seeking." Instead, Jesus essentially said, "I have told you what I want to say, and I have said it exactly the way I chose to say it. I know your hearts, though: I know you are determined not to believe me or to believe *in* me, even though what I do has all the marks of the Father's character, power, and love."

Like the Jews of Jesus' day, we might think plain words meeting our criteria are what we need. But Jesus gives us truth on his own terms. Rather than making demands of Jesus, we listen well so we can receive all the good he desires to give. He really is a *Good* Shepherd!

. . . .

What freedoms come with receiving Jesus as God's Son and living life with him by keeping his commands and following his example?

SECURITY IN OUR GOOD SHEPHERD

*I give them eternal life, and they will never perish. No one
will snatch them out of my hand. (John 10:28 NRSV)*

WRITING ABOUT JESUS AS Good Shepherd prompts gratitude deep within me. I feel honored to be a recipient of the Lord's friendship, wisdom, and love. The Jews of his day, however, weren't willing to believe Jesus when he called himself the bread of life, the Good Shepherd, the way to eternal life.

Instead they tried to access Jesus from a safe distance. They did not enter into the knowledge he was offering—namely, the knowledge of his friendship and of the generous grace that comes with following him. Jesus wanted to show the Jews how to *really* live as God's people: he wanted to welcome them into eternal life. But these religious people wanted to get their religious facts in order, and Jesus wasn't meeting them there.

Aren't we sometimes tempted to approach Jesus for our reasons rather than his? We may think we have the best ideas about what we need from God, but God would give us life that lasts if we would humbly listen to his counsel. He loves to lead us on paths that are just right for us.

Once we see—by God's grace—our need for this Good Shepherd, we experience the reality of security now and forever. The Good Shepherd protects us from thieves, robbers, and wolves. And we can rest in his promise that no one can snatch us out of his hand. Not now, not ever.

. . . .

How might Jesus want to be your Good Shepherd today? Is there something he wants to lead you out of? Is there something he wants to lead you more deeply into?

A DIVINE CLAIM

"We are not stoning you for any good work,"
they replied, "but for blasphemy, because you,
a mere man, claim to be God." (John 10:33)

THIS IS ONE OF THOSE MOMENTS when who Jesus is comes into focus. These Jewish opponents understood what Jesus was claiming about himself when he said, "I and the Father are one" (John 10:30). Any Jew making such a claim would be guilty of great blasphemy, and the penalty for such hubris would be stoning. Everyone knew that. Saying he was one with the Father was making a claim to divinity. (If Jesus was not divine, he would have vehemently denied their misunderstanding.)

They saw Jesus as a mere man. Surely the evidence of God's power at work in him should have exposed the unreality of calling Jesus a "mere" anything. They couldn't see who Jesus really was. How we see Jesus in our world and lives makes all the difference in how we respond to his message. If he's just a better teacher among many good teachers, we are free to take or leave his counsel. But if he made us and we belong to him, we are accountable to him in ways we wouldn't be to a merely good teacher.

I have come to believe that Jesus really is God. This has given foundation and framing to my life. When he gives instruction, he speaks as my wise Creator. He's the one who knows me best and knows what is truly good for me. I continue to look to Jesus to learn who God is and what God is inviting me to.

. . . .

How do you see Jesus? In what ways have you embraced the reality that Jesus really is our God? In what ways have you perhaps resisted this truth? Talk with God about this.

WHEN JESUS DELAYS

When he heard this, Jesus said,
"This sickness will not end in death. No, it is for God's glory
so that God's Son may be glorified through it." (John 11:4)

A MESSENGER FROM MARY and Martha has reached Jesus and told him Lazarus, their brother and his good friend, is sick. Jesus delays his journey to join them and declares Lazarus's sickness will not end in death. From our vantage point looking back, we know that this illness did not lead to permanent death. But for Mary and Martha, that's exactly what it did look like.

Jesus' words would have sounded cruel to Mary and Martha. They may have been tempted to think Jesus was mistaken, or worse—that he didn't care. Do I ever judge Jesus in light of what looks like lack of care rather than trusting in his care despite hard circumstances?

As Jesus prepares to begin his journey to Bethany, he says to his disciples, "Our friend Lazarus has fallen asleep; but I am going there to wake him up" (John 11:11).

Jesus speaks of Lazarus's condition with calm and peace. When Jesus speaks of sleep, the disciples understandably assume that Lazarus will wake up. Jesus speaks of a sleep from which no one naturally awakens. But Lazarus *does*!

We don't usually see death in the same peaceful, trusting light that Jesus does. We don't usually see hard things with the same calm that Jesus does. But Jesus is a master teacher and is willing to mentor us in just such a perspective. That's good news in our hard situations.

. . . .

Are you faced with unexpected hardship or loss that you're tempted to see as evidence of God's uncaring delay? Can you imagine a future in which God's faithfulness, care, and power will surprise you with a different perspective from the one you have now?

RESURRECTION LIFE

Jesus said to her, "I am the resurrection and the life. The one who believes in me will live, even though they die; and whoever lives by believing in me will never die. Do you believe this?" (John 11:25-26)

MARTHA'S BROTHER, LAZARUS, has died. Martha is barely able to hide her disappointment that her friend Jesus, who has healed so many, was not there in time to heal him (John 11:21-22). She does her best to put on a good face by acknowledging his favor with God and power to do whatever would honor God. But she's disappointed.

When Jesus tells her that her brother will rise again, she assumes a resurrection in the distant future ("the last day"), which she believes all faithful Jews will experience (John 11:23-24). Jesus is not talking about the future. He means to raise Lazarus now. Martha can't imagine this because it isn't something she's seen.

Jesus takes this opportunity to help her see resurrection is not some experience in the distant future but standing right in front of her. Jesus *is* the resurrection and the life (John 10:25). When Jesus says Lazarus will "never die," Martha must have wondered what he was talking about. Her brother has clearly already died. She knows and Jesus should know it.

To me today, Jesus says, "I am the resurrection and the life." He wants me to trust him in this. He invites me to live in the light of such a remarkable reality. "You will never die if you trust in me as your life. Do you believe this?" I find myself praying, *Lord, I believe what you say. Help me in every way where I let unbelief win. You really are life—a different kind of life—for me.*

. . . .

Is there anything in your life that feels like it's dead, never to rise again? How might Jesus bring life to this situation?

NEVER TOO LATE FOR RESURRECTION

When Mary reached the place where Jesus was and saw him, she fell at his feet and said, "Lord, if you had been here, my brother would not have died." (John 11:32)

MY HEART FEELS HEAVY when I read Mary's words, "Lord, if you had been here, my brother would not have died." I try to imagine the sadness and disappointment in her heart. She's tempted to imagine that Jesus could have shown a bit more care by arriving in time to help.

Mary is not wrong. Jesus certainly could have prevented Lazarus's death. He has that power. But there is a deeper truth Jesus wants Mary to experience. There is something about Jesus she doesn't know. He wants her to learn that not only can he prevent death, he can also conquer death. He wants her to encounter him as the Resurrection and the Life. Resurrection is a greater miracle than death prevention.

When we feel disappointed by what appears to be God's failure to show up, is it possible his intent might be to do something far greater for us than we could imagine? Might we learn something in the thirteenth hour, after God has seemingly failed to act on our behalf, that is greater than what we would learn if God arrived just in time to save us? The reality of resurrection requires the reality of death first.

. . . .

Have you ever experienced what seemed like God arriving too late, only to discover there was something more God wished to do? If so, what was that like? If not, how might you keep your eyes open to this possibility?

WORDS THAT RESURRECT

So they took away the stone. Then Jesus looked up and said,
"Father, I thank you that you have heard me." (John 11:41)

THIS IS THE PRAYER Jesus prays just before speaking three words that display the resurrection power of God: "Lazarus, come out!" Jesus is grateful to the Father for hearing him. He gives thanks for the sake of the crowd. They need to trust the truth about Jesus, that he really has been sent by God.

I feel awe as Jesus stands in front of Lazarus's tomb. Lazarus has been dead four days. In that climate decay has already done its work. But if Jesus can raise the dead, he can reverse the effects of death in Lazarus's body. And he does.

Jesus speaks to the old and dead places in me, parts of my soul that do not know life. This is my journey to greater fullness for the sake of others. When I was a child, I had religious experiences without living knowledge of God-with-us. As a junior higher, I felt nothing of the treasuring love of the Father during days of teasing and ridicule.

"Alan, come out!" Jesus says to those parts of me. "Come out of the tomb of self-accusation. Come out of the tomb of timidity and untruth. Come out of the tomb of hiding and avoiding. Step into the light." But this death has been at work far longer than four days. It's been years . . . decades. Even so, just as Jesus told the onlookers to unbind Lazarus and let him go (John 11:44), he says to me, "Come out! Be unbound and go free."

. . . .

Invite Jesus to speak words that will bring life out of death within you. Why not ask him to do for your soul what he did for Lazarus's body?

RELIGIOUS IDEAS AND KINGDOM REALITY

So the chief priests made plans to kill Lazarus as well, for on account of him
many of the Jews were going over to Jesus and believing in him. (John 12:10-11)

JESUS RAISED LAZARUS from the dead. Lazarus had been in the tomb for
four days, and countless witnesses knew he had died. A crowd of Jews came to
investigate for themselves. But not all were there to celebrate. Those in charge
of the temple had a different response. They had no interest in the reality confronting them but were committed only to defending their positions. Even in
the face of an undeniable miracle, they attacked reality to defend their beliefs.

The Jewish leaders refused to investigate the claims of Jesus, which were
supported by the work (and works) he did. Instead they felt compelled to
protect their religious system and their important place in it at any cost. This
makes me think of Elton Trueblood's words in *Confronting Christ*:

> If Amos had waited for some authorization of his preaching, he would
> have waited forever and in vain. Entrenched privilege, whether civil or
> ecclesiastic, does not arrange easily for its own destruction. Sometimes
> the barren tree must be uprooted and the only one with the courage to
> uproot it is the person who has the boldness which arises from the
> direct sense of God's leading.

"Entrenched privilege . . . does not arrange easily for its own destruction." But
the chief priests were more interested in their religious power than they were
in kingdom reality. Do we cling to beliefs at the expense of rejecting realities?

- -

Can you see examples around you of people clinging to beliefs without
regard to realities? Ask the Spirit of God to open your eyes to any ways in
which you are more tempted to cling to beliefs about God than to cling to
God himself.

LIVING IN THE LIGHT OF GLORY

His disciples did not understand these things at first; but when Jesus
was glorified, then they remembered that these things had been
written of him and had been done to him. (John 12:16 NRSV)

THE PHRASE "THESE THINGS" refers to the events surrounding Jesus'
entry into Jerusalem before he would be arrested, beaten, and crucified.
Shouts of "Hosanna!" would be replaced with shouts of "Crucify him!" While
the crowds were treating Jesus like a king coming into his kingdom, the disciples could never have envisioned how the day would end. Later, after Jesus
was raised from dead in the power of God's Spirit, they would have a fresh
perspective on all these things.

There are realities right in front of my eyes that I may not yet understand,
but a moment of encounter with Jesus and the reality of his glory may shed
light backward onto these things. I'm tempted to let my narrow perspective
in a challenging moment become my whole vision of the present and the
future. I need help to trust in the goodness of God and hope for what I cannot
yet see.

Just before he describes the disciples' struggle to understand, the apostle
John quotes the prophet Zechariah: "Do not be afraid, daughter of Zion.
Look, your king is coming, sitting on a donkey's colt!" (John 12:15 NRSV).
Jesus comes into Jerusalem humbly, riding on a young donkey rather than a
warhorse. Jesus may come into my situation humbly and gently rather than
with overwhelming power. I may not feel immediately secure in moments
like these, but there is power in this humble arrival. Jesus does not need to
yell to be heard. He does not need to overwhelm to have influence.

. . . .

How might the presence of Jesus, even coming gently and humbly, help
you find hope, courage, and peace in this moment? Talk to him about this.

SEEING JESUS

*[Some Greeks] came to Philip, who was from Bethsaida in Galilee, with
a request. "Sir," they said, "we would like to see Jesus." (John 12:21)*

I REMEMBER VISITING WHAT many archaeologists believe to be the
ruins of Bethsaida, just off the northeast shore of the Sea of Galilee. We saw
what some people had called "the fisherman's house," and it easily could have
been the home of Philip, one of Jesus' disciples who hailed from that village.

In John 12, some Greeks approach Philip while he is in Jerusalem for the
Passover feast. I love their request: "we would like to see Jesus." My desire
resonates with theirs. I want to see Jesus in the faces of my family, my friends,
and those I serve. I want to see Jesus in my relationships. I want to see Jesus in
my work. I want to see Jesus in the beauty of creation. I want to see Jesus
when circumstances are dark, discouraging, or overwhelming.

I feel that deep hunger to have a clearer and more intimate vision of Jesus
in every facet of my life. I get into the most trouble when my vision of
Jesus grows faint or blurry. Lord, open my eyes wider to see you more clearly.

. . . .

**When has seeing Jesus made a difference in your interaction with family
members, a friend, a neighbor, or someone in your workplace? What indicated to you that Jesus was present with you?**

PRESENCE FOR THE SAKE OF OTHERS

Whoever serves me must follow me, and where I am, there will my servant be also. Whoever serves me, the Father will honor. (John 12:26 NRSV)

THE SERVANT OF JESUS must be a follower of Jesus. That's what Jesus is saying here. There is no serving Jesus without following Jesus, but I have certainly tried at times.

Too often we may try to do good things for Jesus while, strangely, keeping our distance from him. How can we be part of his kingdom work without staying in close touch with the King? Imagine a self-proclaimed ambassador seeking to represent a nation without having so much as a conversation with its president. The ambassador might do amazing things, but who knows whether she is representing the president's purposes?

Service requires following *and* presence. And it's not hard both to know Jesus' presence and to follow him, our Good Shepherd, because Jesus wants that too. In fact, he promises it: "Where I am, there will my servant be also."

Think of how the Gospels show us the impact of Jesus' presence in the lives of those he teaches and heals, as he provides and cares for outcasts. With the very Spirit of Jesus residing in us, our presence in people's lives can also make a difference. We can express Jesus' sacrificial love by making time to be with a shut-in. We can heal broken hearts by loving the lonely and rejected. We can love those treated as outcasts by serving at a homeless shelter, suicide hotline, or neighborhood gathering.

Serving God means being in his presence for the sake of others.

. . . .

Where are you serving now? Think about formal ways you serve as well as informal ways. What difference will it make if you consider that Jesus is present in you and present to others through you?

THE HOLY IMPERFECT

Be perfect, therefore, as your heavenly Father is perfect. (Matthew 5:48)

PART OF ME IS TEMPTED to misread the intent of Jesus here. I might think this is a command to perfectionism, but Jesus is extending an invitation to holiness. These are very different understandings of what is "perfect."

Perfectionism puts pressure to find the best approach to a problem. Since there is always a better option than the one I've come up with, this is usually paralyzing. Instead of doing my best, I do little or nothing.

I've done this with spiritual disciplines. I have books and books of practices I might engage to grow in my life with God. But then I stress myself by asking, "Which of these is the very best one for me now?" This framework has a way of overwhelming me so that I keep waiting to figure out the best thing to do. Even if I decided on a practice that was less than the best and did it *now*, I'd probably gain far more waiting to figure out the perfect best.

"Holy perfection" is about growing in maturity. It isn't becoming flawless or without needs. The devil is lord of perfectionism. It serves his purposes far better than God's. Perfectionism is humanly impossible and a trap.

A better question in all of this is, "What is the good that lies right before me? What good might I actually do now?" Perfectionism makes me a paralyzed victim. Growing in wholeness, holiness, and maturity is an invitation to commune with the only one who is perfect.

. . . .

Have you ever found yourself paralyzed in the attempt to figure out the best way to approach something? What would it look like to simply do good now instead?

PRAYER AND HIDDENNESS

And when you pray, do not be like the hypocrites,
for they love to pray standing in the synagogues and on the
street corners to be seen by others. (Matthew 6:5)

THE KIND OF PRAYER that seeks the attention and admiration of others isn't communion with God. Jesus encourages us to a kind of holy secrecy when we pray. We are speaking with the unseen God. It's good for our souls to pray unseen.

Growing in prayer is more likely to move me in the direction of hiddenness than of publicity. The essence of our life is hidden with God in Christ (Colossians 3:3). This humble, unassuming reality of our true and inner life invites us deeper into conversational communion with God. We often think our life is somewhere else and requires a lot of self-promotion. But the self I promote bears little resemblance to the me made in God's image. A life of deepening prayer will increase my awareness that my eternal life is truly hidden in Christ.

Hidden in what way and from whom? True life is hidden from the wayward promises of advertising. Owning the latest tech or car does little to enliven my soul. Obsessing over the latest headlines doesn't generate joyful energy. The greatest accomplishments of the kingdom of heaven aren't likely to be front-page news.

In solitude, silence, and stillness, I can refresh my communion with the one who *is* life. I can listen to and speak to my Father who is unseen and secret. This is how I'll remember and refresh my experience of goodness in God. This is where I come alive.

. . . .

How do you feel about the counsel of Jesus to pray in secret? How does it sound inviting? What part of you resists this invitation?

SECRET PRAYER

But when you pray, go into your room, close the door and pray to your Father, who is unseen. Then your Father, who sees what is done in secret, will reward you. (Matthew 6:6)

TODAY'S READING WAS THE FOCUS of a one-day retreat I made at a local California mission. I had recently read something the desert father Abba Moses said about prayer: "Go to your cell and your cell will teach you everything." I sensed God saying, "Be. Don't escape. Don't distract yourself. Stay in the moment. Be silent. Be still. Listen."

I was seeking God's encouragement to overcome the anxieties and fears that tempt me to run or escape. Our Father in heaven sees what is done is secret. We can hear that as, "You can't hide from God," or hear it as, "God loves personal time with you."

I don't need to shout to get God's attention. I don't need to generate big emotions to feel God with me. I am not praying in front of God like he is an audience in the dark while I'm in the spotlight. I pray in conversation with God who is right there with me. My prayers aren't about impressing God but about being present with God.

As I lingered longer in that retreat setting, I sensed God saying something like, "Alan, just find a quiet, secluded place so you won't be tempted to role-play before me." I sometimes catch myself talking to the people around me rather than to God when I pray. Prayer is always communication with God. Praying in a secret place helps me remember this. Secret prayer is training for holy public prayer.

. . . .

The next time you come into the presence of God to pray, try being silent for a while before speaking. See if that helps you remember that God is near and wants to be with you.

TOO MUCH PRAYING?

And when you pray, do not keep on babbling like pagans, for they think
they will be heard because of their many words. (Matthew 6:7)

JESUS WANTS TO TEACH US how to live in conversational communion
with his Father in heaven. Jesus' life was rooted in just such a relationship
with his Father. And so he teaches us that the quality of our prayers is not
measured by the number of words they contain.

I have sometimes found myself praying and I hardly knew what I was
saying. I'd begun speaking words in familiar patterns and had little sense of
a heart alert to the one I was addressing. In the end I was babbling instead of
praying. I was saying words in an autopilot mode that didn't reflect my actual
thoughts or hopes.

When I remember this tendency, I've found it good to be quiet when I
begin to pray, even if only for a few seconds. Whether I am praying in private
or in a public setting, a moment of silence to offer God my attention helps
me remember what I'm doing. Beginning with a listening heart rather than
a mouth quick to speak has proven fruitful.

Before I pray, it's good to remember that God already cares about what I
need. God is interested and aware. I'm not trying to convince God to care. I
am coming into the presence of love when I pray. My prayer does not inform
God of something he did not know. Prayer is a chance to be with God amid
the needs I feel. Prayer is more about presence than it is speaking sentences
and paragraphs.

. . . .

Have you, like me, ever caught yourself babbling in prayer? Experiment
with a moment of quiet, listening presence with God before you speak. See
if that helps.

THE UNWELCOME UNEXPECTED

Can any one of you by worrying
add a single hour to your life? (Matthew 6:27)

I DON'T LIKE SURPRISES. I suppose there are exceptions, but my most common response to the unexpected is anxiety. I am still learning that surprises are not automatically threats. As I draft these words, I just got news that someone I was counting on for an upcoming event cannot participate. I felt their contribution was key, and now I'll have to pick up the slack. My knee-jerk, unwilled reaction is to worry.

Lord Jesus, you've said anxiety does nothing to help me or my situation. You've said worry will not add an inch to my stature or a day to my life. Anxiety does not enhance my life. It diminishes my life—my creativity, my vision, my joy, my hope, my energy. Anxiety is draining—even destructive.

So when surprises jump out and startle me, I can do what you encouraged other worriers to do: focus my attention first on God's goodness and God's reign in my life and in my world. Unwelcome surprises cannot rob me of the faithful care and provision of God. That which overwhelms me in moments when I'm stunned by the unexpected is overwhelmed by the mighty, caring presence of God-with-us.

Instead of letting my autopilot anxiety response take the steering wheel of my will, and therefore my day, I can see my concerns against the backdrop of God's gracious, powerful, peaceful presence. God is bigger than unwelcome surprises.

. . . .

How do you respond to unwelcome surprises? What happens in your thoughts, your emotions, even your body? In what ways do you respond with anxiety? How might you entrust your worries to God now?

SEEKING FIRST

Seek the Kingdom of God above all else, and live righteously, and
he will give you everything you need. (Matthew 6:33 NLT)

I ONCE HEARD A PASTOR say the choices between good and bad are often easy to see, but the choices between good and better are more difficult. I've thought about that often. It's easy for me to decide to go to church on Sunday morning instead of staying home and watching television. It's harder to know whether I should read a good book or look for an opportunity to serve a neighbor in need.

Every day we face choices between good and bad as well as choices between good and better. Jesus' words in Matthew 6:33 can help us deal with both types of decisions: "Seek the Kingdom of God above all else."

It can be easy to spend big blocks of time and enormous energy on secondary things when we approach them as though they were primary. What is primary? Jesus calls us to love God with all we are and to love our neighbors as ourselves (Matthew 22:37-39). In today's verse he calls us to seek God's kingdom above all else. The two ideas are related, and both require us to make our relationship with God primary. Only then can we live and influence out of being filled by God's love. That's just what everyone needs.

. . . .

Consider a typical day or week in your life. What minors are you tempted to major on? In other words, how are you living (or not living) in keeping with the priority of loving God and loving your neighbor? What changes do you wish to make? How might a mentor help?

THE UNHOLY NARROWS

Enter through the narrow gate. For wide is the gate and broad is the road that leads to destruction, and many enter through it. But small is the gate and narrow the road that leads to life, and only a few find it. (Matthew 7:13-14)

I'M AMAZED AT THOSE who assume the small gate and narrow road coincide with their small, narrow ideas about God and God's ways. To me, their definition of "narrow" does not look like an abundant life. They seem more often to live pinched, cramped lives with little joy, peace, or love and a lot of anger and judgment.

A person can live in a narrow way that is empty of life and full of destruction. The reason few people find the narrow way of God's kingdom has nothing to do with whether they attend a particular church or participate in a specific denomination. They don't find it because they don't want to surrender and fully entrust themselves to the mystery and majesty of who God is. They want a God they have full control over, a God who fits in their tiny box with its narrow definitions, a God they think they understand perfectly. These are the unholy narrows.

The narrow way Jesus defines will challenge everyone. We will all experience a certain discomfort when we encounter that way. It will squeeze out of us everything that is not life. It will squeeze out pride, conceit, self-satisfaction, and judgment of others. If I feel comfortable with my own definition of narrow, then likely I have missed its true meaning.

. . . .

In what ways has the narrow way of Jesus challenged you and drawn you to places of surrender? In what ways have you been tempted to define "narrow" in a way that made you feel more comfortable?

A MEAL WITH SINNERS

While Jesus was having dinner at Matthew's house, many tax collectors
and sinners came and ate with him and his disciples.
When the Pharisees saw this, they asked his disciples, "Why does
your teacher eat with tax collectors and sinners?" (Matthew 9:10-11)

JESUS AND THE PHARISEES had very different perspectives about those the culture labeled as misfits or, worse, transgressors. The Pharisees saw such people as morally contagious. Being near them just might rub off. Jesus saw those who were broken or spiritually unwell the way a doctor sees a sick patient—as someone needing care. Jesus' response to the Pharisees' questions, in fact, was, "It is not the healthy who need a doctor, but the sick" (Matthew 9:12).

"Tax collectors and sinners" were those who lived outside the moral code of the Jewish religion. Tax collectors were often fellow Jews who served the Roman government and their own self-interest more than the broader Jewish interests. Sinners were those who were cast out from Jewish society. They did not observe the traditions. Such people were rejected and condemned by Jewish leaders.

But in the presence of Jesus, they were welcome. He wanted to show them that real life in the kingdom of his Father was far better than the "good life" they were pursuing. How do I respond to those who are social outcasts, especially because of their choices in life? Would such a person feel as welcome in my presence as they would have felt at dinner with Jesus? Do I see myself being in moral danger in the presence of the wayward or in a position to serve their well-being in God's good and beautiful kingdom?

. . . .

Who are the "tax collectors and sinners" in your part of the world? How can you join Jesus in being with them to serve their good? What's a next step you could take?

THE TEMPTATION OF RELIGIOUS JEALOUSY

Then John's disciples came and asked him, "How is it that we and the Pharisees fast often, but your disciples do not fast?" (Matthew 9:14)

FATHER, I'M SOMETIMES TEMPTED to jealousy when other disciples seem to have it easier. Protect me from resenting the spiritual disciplines you lead me to, which can seem more challenging than those others face. I don't know their journey with you, and I don't understand their challenges. You aren't robbing me of peace or joy. You are training me for them. Your discipline is leading me into places of greater freedom even if they feel like greater limitation now. Help me see present discomfort and self-denial as steps on my journey to abundant life. That's what they are. You are training me because you love me.

Enable me to stay awake and responsive to the new things you are doing in and around me. I don't want to be like an old garment that can't be restored by the new thing you are doing. I don't ever want to become so inflexible and rigid that I can't welcome the present restoring work of your Spirit. As I age, I find myself tempted to remember "the old days." Those were good days full of grace, but your grace for me is now. I am alive today.

Sometimes I come to places in the journey when something seems no longer possible. I feel weary, discouraged, even hopeless. But you are the one who raises the dead. Impossible isn't your way. You do easily what I cannot imagine. Do the work only you can: raise us from depression into joy, from anxiety into peace, from anger into patience. Renew me.

. . . .

Where has your spiritual journey felt challenging lately? How might this be evidence of God's loving training of you rather than empty hardship?

MORE THAN A SPARROW

Are not two sparrows sold for a penny? Yet not one of them will fall
to the ground outside your Father's care. . . . So don't be afraid; you
are worth more than many sparrows. (Matthew 10:29, 31)

I'VE COME TO LOVE the birds that visit our backyard feeders. I enjoy the sparkling, red-breasted hummingbirds. I'm pleased at the bright yellow orioles who visit us in spring and summer. But most of the birds are more like sparrows. No bright colors. No impressive hovering at the feeder. In Jesus' time sparrows were only a half-cent each. (Why would anyone buy a sparrow then anyway? There can't be much meat on a sparrow. I don't recall any "sparrow offerings" in Leviticus.)

When the common house finches in our yard eat most of the seed I put out in our feeders, I'm tempted to wish for visits from more exciting birds and fewer boring ones. But that might be Jesus' point. Those things we are tempted to overlook or devalue are a great treasure to their Maker. He is a witness to the birth and death of every sparrow.

And I don't have to be impressive or exciting to be loved. God cares for me for his own reasons. I don't have to be afraid that God is going to change his mind about me. In other words, I can remember how much God cares for me, thinks of me, and watches over my life when I am tempted to feel afraid.

Father, I will not be afraid today because you care so well for me. You want my good. You like me. You are glad I am your son. I'm grateful for these things. Amen.

. . . .

Take a moment to step outside and notice the birds in your neighborhood. What do you see and hear? Reflect on God's creative care for each one of these.

EXPECTATIONS: WHEN JESUS LOOKS PAST OURS

When John, who was in prison, heard about the deeds of the Messiah, he sent his disciples to ask him, "Are you the one who is to come, or should we expect someone else?" (Matthew 11:2-3)

WHAT IS JOHN ASKING FOR? John wants verbal confirmation that Jesus actually is the Messiah, or he wants Jesus to tell him to wait for someone else. Maybe John thinks Jesus is merely another forerunner of the actual Messiah, like himself. Perhaps John is looking for some sign that Jesus is going to deliver the Jews from Roman oppression. He hasn't seen any evidence of that yet.

What does Jesus give him in response? He responds not with a verbal affirmation but a declaration of visible evidence of the kingdom coming among those in need (Matthew 11:4-5). He is a Messiah (King) who is doing the very things Isaiah said Messiah would do. But most people who were looking for Messiah had forgotten about the prophet's words. They expected ruling political power, but Jesus came in the power of kingdom compassion.

Since Jesus is not fulfilling the vision and understanding of the Jews (including John, apparently) about the role of Messiah, they are offended.

We too can be quite attached to our expectations. Jesus reminds us that our expectations are not lord. He is.

- -

When have you had expectations of Jesus that left you feeling disappointed? When did you want Jesus to say something, clarify something, change something, or do something and he didn't respond as you hoped or expected? How have you responded? How would you like to respond?

A RESTFUL PRESENCE

Come to me, all you who are weary and burdened, and
I will give you rest. (Matthew 11:28)

JESUS HAS SOMETHING TO SAY to all who find themselves exhausted and overwhelmed. His invitation is simply to come to him. Jesus is a refreshing presence for the weary. Jesus is a helpful presence to the burdened.

We tend think of rest as something to be earned. "You deserve a break today." "You've earned yourself a good rest." The problem is that rest doesn't work that way. Rest is a gift from the hand of God. Rest is the soil from which good work grows rather than a place to collapse on the other side of a finish line.

When I think of rest as something earned, I often find it hard not to remain in the earning orientation that got me there. I keep measuring myself by productivity even when I am trying to rest. I can fill a moment of rest with just as much activity as I do a moment of work.

Jesus will give rest to the weary. This is what he wishes to do. Our work is to be receptive to Jesus. The challenge is that when I'm weary, I'm sometimes too tired to receive rest. I sometimes numb myself through media or busy myself with personal chores rather than sinking into the refreshing, renewing presence of Jesus.

When we come to Jesus, he is not always handing out assignments. He certainly invites us to join him in his work, but Jesus also gives the gift of rest to those who find themselves weighed down by their life and work.

. . . .

What do you do when you find yourself overwhelmed? How might you embrace this invitation of Jesus to find rest in friendship with him?

LEARNING HOW TO REST

Take my yoke upon you and learn from me, for I am gentle and humble in heart, and you will find rest for your souls. (Matthew 11:29)

JESUS HAS JUST EXTENDED an invitation to the weary and burdened to receive the gift of rest from him. How does this work? Jesus' primary strategy to give us rest is to offer his yoke. That might have surprised his first listeners. A yoke was how they did work. A yoke enabled them to pull a cart or a plow. They might have struggled to understand how an implement of work would help them find rest.

Jesus was inviting them to take *his* yoke. They knew what the yoke of Roman oppression felt like. They were familiar with the heavy yoke of religious rules. Taking Jesus' yoke meant becoming his student. He was claiming to offer a way that was gentle rather than harsh, humble rather than overbearing.

Many Jews would have used a yoke of oxen to accomplish the hard work of carrying a great load or plowing a field. A yoke harnessed two animals to work together. I have imagined taking the yoke of Jesus meant he handed over a yoke that I then carried away alone. Doesn't it make more sense that he invites us to join him in his yoke?

The yoke of Jesus is restful for our souls because we aren't alone in it. His yoke keeps us close to him, even when we are joining him in the work he comes to do. It is also restful because between Jesus and me, I am not the one carrying the heavy end. Jesus is the primary laborer, and I am his colaborer.

. . . .

Can you imagine yourself being in a yoke next to Jesus? What might make it feel light and well-fitting for you?

THE EASY YOKE

For my yoke is easy and my burden is light. (Matthew 11:30)

THERE ARE WAYS OF living that are hard on people. Workaholism and addictive ways of life diminish us rather than increasing our joy. There are ways of practicing religion that make people's lives harder. The Pharisees had a way of making the Jewish law burdensome rather than life-giving.

The yoke of Jesus is well-fitting, and it sits easily on our shoulders. It does not demand more than we can give. It does not rub us the wrong way. It is a yoke of life and joy rather than of demands and exhaustion. The guidance of Jesus is meant to bring freedom and vitality. John, one of his first followers, says living in the love of God is a matter of keeping his commands—and those commands are no burden (1 John 5:3).

Learning to live close to Jesus makes our lives easier to live. His yoke is how we learn to make our way through difficult times in our lives. As I've made my way through hard seasons, I've had a great sense that Jesus is making them a bit easier and lighter.

I want to keep learning how the way of Jesus is the one that fits my life best. The yoke of making everyone happy is far heavier. The yoke of perfectionism has proven unbearable to me. The yoke of guilt has sometimes overwhelmed me. But the yoke of Jesus is a place where I learn holy security, freely given forgiveness, great mercy, and deep grace. His yoke really is easy, and his burden really is light.

. . . .

When has your way of living felt burdensome? How might the yoke of relationship and collaboration with Jesus lighten your load?

A PLAYFUL GOD

The angel said to the women, "Do not be afraid, for I know that you are looking for Jesus, who was crucified. He is not here; he has risen, just as he said. Come and see the place where he lay." (Matthew 28:5-6)

I HAD A UNIQUE EXPERIENCE of God-with-us one Easter morning. It was a season when my tendency to self-accusation was especially strong. In such seasons, I carry in my gut an untrue image of a God who lets me come to him but is mostly disappointed with my failures. I find it easy to talk with others about a Jesus who is joyful and gracious, but sometimes I struggle to remember this for myself.

When I rose to my alarm at five o'clock that morning, it was still dark. As I walked from my side of the bed to the bathroom, I heard a strong inner voice that said, "Ah, he is risen!" It had the same sound and feel as other times when I sensed the Spirit speaking. My first response was to think, *"He is risen" makes perfect sense on Easter. Christ* is *risen.*

Eventually, it dawned on me that perhaps God was being playful. He was using the familiar Easter language of resurrection to describe getting out of bed. The voice didn't come with any tone of sarcasm. It sounded like the teasing of a friend. God seemed to be acknowledging me with affection.

But I had a hard time embracing this and imagining Jesus being playful on this day when we celebrate his resurrection. I was the one who should have said those words to him. But I came to experience that the new life of Jesus is playful, even lighthearted. "He is risen" is not just a historical fact but a living, breathing reality. I am risen with Christ.

. . . .

How might the phrase "He is risen" be a meeting place for you and Jesus today?

GOD'S KINGDOM IS GOOD NEWS

The time is fulfilled, and the kingdom of God has come near;
repent, and believe in the good news. (Mark 1:15 NRSV)

IT WON'T COME AS a surprise to anyone reading this that the word *gospel* means "good news." What is the "good news of God" Jesus is proclaiming? To what degree does the good news Jesus proclaims sound like the good news often proclaimed by North American Christians?

Jesus puts it simply: "The time is now. God's kingdom is near. Repent. Believe in this good news." The time is now, and the kingdom is near because Jesus came into the world at a specific time and place. The kingdom is near in him. The good news is personal in him.

Jesus is close to us, and we are close to him when we are following him and heeding his counsel, abiding in him in loving and humble obedience, and resisting impulses that take us away from him in empty acts. This is the spirit of his invitation to repent. It is both a turning away from and a turning toward. It's not just a matter of morality but a matter of loving allegiance to Jesus.

The good news for me today is that God's good reign is near in Jesus. I can allow the good, pleasing, and perfect reign of God to hold sway in my life now. The desires that reign over so many don't lead to real goodness. The reign of God in our lives blesses us. The reign of unholy impulses drains and damages us. The way of Jesus' reign in our lives really is good news. Let's turn ourselves to fully embrace it.

. . . .

In what way might God be inviting you to turn away from something you're chasing so you can fully embrace his leadership today?

CALLED AND WANTED

Jesus went up on a mountainside and called to him those he wanted, and they came to him. He appointed twelve that they might be with him. (Mark 3:13-14)

JESUS CALLS TO HIMSELF those he wants. His choosing is not some theological technicality. He has chosen us because he wants us with him. Luke's telling of this story has Jesus spending the night on a mountainside praying, then choosing the Twelve the next morning (Luke 6:12-13). I would love to have listened in on the conversation between the Father and the Son that night. What did Jesus say to the Father about those he was drawn to choose? How did the Father share his heart with his Son as he prepared to make this critical decision?

When it comes to our own life of prayer, it would help us to remember how wanted we are when we come. I've sometimes been tempted to imagine that God is willing to hear my prayers only reluctantly. Or I've imagined that my prayers are an imposition on the God who has all of creation on his mind. I'm not sure why I've assumed this at times, but I have.

The Father, the Son, and the Spirit enjoy our presence. God desires our fellowship. God takes pleasure in our prayerful conversation. Like the Twelve who come to him that morning after his night of prayer, we come to him because he wants us and chooses us. When I come into the presence of God who is always with me, whether I am quiet or have something to say, I can be confident that God has been looking forward to my time in his presence.

. . . .

How do you imagine God feeling when you come into his presence to pray? How wanted do you feel? How wanted do you think God wants you to feel?

PULLING WEEDS

Still others, like seed sown among thorns, hear the word; but the worries
of this life, the deceitfulness of wealth and the desires for other things
come in and choke the word, making it unfruitful. (Mark 4:18-19)

WHEN I HEAR GOD speak to me, a seed is planted in the soil of my heart. Whether or not it will grow to fruitfulness within me has much to do with the condition of that soil. Are there seeds of anxiety, greed, or lust already planted and growing like weeds? If I've let those seeds grow in my heart, then what God has to say isn't going to be nearly as fruitful and free in me. The condition of my heart soil is unfavorable.

Am I anxious about what I will eat and drink, or about whether my family's financial needs will be met instead of seeking first his kingdom and his righteousness? Then there are weeds that can be pulled. *Lord, I would be glad if you would pull them.*

Am I living under the illusion that I would have joy, pleasure, satisfaction, or peace if I had just a little more money, had this or that possession, or was able to afford to go there or do that? Is my heart content or discontent? Discontentment is a weed that crowds the space where God's words could take root in me and bear fruit.

Might spiritual practices be a way of cooperating with God in the weeding of the soil of my heart? Simplicity, solitude, silence, and fasting can be a gardening tool to uproot and remove such weeds from my heart.

. . . .

Take some time to talk with God about weeds that may be growing in your heart. How might this be a pathway toward a more fruitful relationship with God today?

ALONE WITH GOD TOGETHER

*[Jesus] said to them, "Come with me by yourselves to a
quiet place and get some rest." (Mark 6:31)*

BY THEMSELVES. A SOLITARY place. Jesus invites his disciples to be
alone together. Obviously, they will be alone together *with Jesus*, but I also
believe that alone *with God* is implied.

I'm an introvert. I like to be alone. But this sense of being alone together
with others happens less often in my life. I love opportunities when Gem
and I can take a retreat together. We'll go to a nearby monastery and book
two rooms. We are together over meals but alone with God the rest of the
twenty-four hours.

I have led retreats where most of the time is spent alone with God, but the
attendees are in community together. I've been on eight-day silent retreats
where I'm quiet before God in the presence of a few dozen. We don't talk,
even if we eat meals at the same table. We are there together to be in the
presence of God.

What are we doing? I believe we are responding to Jesus' invitation, one
he still extends: "Come with me by yourselves to a quiet place and get some
rest." Jesus takes the initiative ("come"). Jesus wants our company ("with me").
Jesus wants to curate moments for us to be alone with the Father as he has
modeled ("by yourselves"). Jesus leads us, like the Good Shepherd he is, to a
quiet place. Jesus gives us the gift of rest. Do you hear his words of invitation
to you today?

. . . .

**What would it look like for you to follow Jesus to a quiet place where you
can find rest for your soul? Why not plan an extended time alone with
Jesus so that you can accept his invitation?**

COMPASSION EMPOWERS US

So they went away by themselves in a boat to a solitary place. But many who saw them leaving recognized them and ran on foot from all the towns and got there ahead of them. When Jesus landed and saw a large crowd, he had compassion on them. (Mark 6:32-34)

JESUS AND HIS DISCIPLES take action to obey his words of invitation: "Come with me by yourselves to a quiet place and get some rest" (Mark 6:31). But while they are in the boat on their way, a crowd runs ahead of them and meets them on the other shore. When Jesus sees them, his emphasis on the importance of rest is superseded by his shepherd's heart for the crowd.

Jesus often rose each morning before anyone else to get away and be alone in the presence of the Father. But, at least in this case, compassion trumps his plans to withdraw. Sometimes the need of the moment supersedes my own needs.

But if I never withdraw to the lonely places, if I always defer to the needs of others and make myself continuously available, I may find I don't have much to offer. I must learn how to keep the cup of my life full to overflowing so that I can fruitfully serve those who cross my path.

Jesus, the Good Shepherd, is moved to service by the needs he sees in the crowd. We are his followers. As we witness the priorities of Jesus, they can become our priorities as well. And we can remember that Jesus continued to withdraw to lonely places to pray. There is a holy and dynamic tension between solitude and community, between prayer and ministry, between contemplation and action. May God's Spirit be the one to guide us as we navigate that tension.

. . . .

How would you describe the relationship between solitude and service in your life these days? Does one get more attention and energy than the other?

TESTING JESUS OR FOLLOWING HIM?

Why does this generation ask for a sign? (Mark 8:12)

IN JESUS' DAY, PEOPLE sought signs that would prove his identity. We also live in a generation that wants a sign, that seems more interested in exciting happenings than in walking in relationship with Jesus. Yet Jesus' own life—his actions, his interactions, his character—are more than enough evidence of his identity as God's Son. The way Jesus lived, what he did, how and what he taught—they all point to the truth that he is God's Son.

Yet the Pharisees approached Jesus "asking him for a sign from heaven, to test him" (Mark 8:11 NRSV). The Pharisees were experts in the Torah as well as the oral tradition around it. They put great emphasis on following both the law and tradition. They weren't interested in trusting Jesus or following him. They wanted to stand at a distance, test, and assess him.

They were unwilling to come, listen, and learn whether he could be trusted. With hard hearts and closed minds they tested Jesus, and they saw only what they wanted to see. It's always helpful for me to ask myself graciously and gently, "Why am I coming to God right now? Am I coming in response to his invitation, or am I coming with some personal agenda?" God cares about our concerns and welcomes us to bring them to him, but he also wants us to embrace his trustworthy purposes with a receptive, attentive heart.

. . . .

When we are talking with people whose hearts are hard and whose minds are closed, how can we talk about our faith in Jesus, our relationship with him, his role as Good Shepherd in a way that is inviting to them?

A FAITH JESUS DOESN'T WANT

But when Jesus turned and looked at his disciples, he rebuked
Peter. "Get behind me, Satan!" he said. "You do not have in mind
the concerns of God, but merely human concerns." (Mark 8:33)

IN MARK 8:32, PETER contradicts everything Jesus has just told the disciples about the Son of Man suffering and being rejected by the Jewish leaders before dying and rising again. Suffering, rejection, and death are not part of Peter's vision for the Messiah. This is not the sort of leadership he's hoping Jesus will exercise. He envisions Messiah as a political and military leader against imperial Rome and religious Jerusalem.

Peter wants Jesus to win, but Jesus calls him "Satan," which means "adversary." I'm sure Peter saw himself on Jesus' side, but Jesus declares Peter is against everything the Messiah stands for. Peter's vision is merely human. He does not understand God's concerns.

This is where we get trapped. We often look at our lives, families, or work from a human perspective. But as Christ-followers we live, relate, and work within the kingdom of God, which has a divine economy that functions differently from the without-God world. There is abundance rather than scarcity. There is selfless love rather than self-seeking individualism. There is holy hope rather than deep desperation. This is the kingdom Jesus sought first and Peter had overlooked.

When we pray, are we bringing only our concerns to God, expecting him to address them quickly in the way we prefer? Or are we learning how to pray with the concerns of God in mind? When it comes to the person or situation I'm praying over, am I learning to ask what might be on God's heart?

. . . .

What or whom are you concerned about right now? Take a moment to ask God what is on his heart about this, then be still and listen for God's response.

THE SURPRISING GRACE OF INSECURITY

It is easier for a camel to go through the eye of a needle than for someone who is rich to enter the kingdom of God. (Mark 10:25)

THESE WORDS OF JESUS baffled and astounded his first-century listeners. Wealth was assumed to be a sign of God's blessing! By implication, those people were near—if not already in—the Lord's kingdom. What was Jesus saying?

Jesus was commenting on the very real power of money and possessions to give us a false sense of security and self-sufficiency. Ironically, God's abundant blessings can make people think they don't need him.

Elton Trueblood writes the following in *Confronting Christ:*

Security is itself a barrier to spiritual growth. The broken and the needy are far closer to the Kingdom than are those who feel adequate and successful. God reaches us most easily when there is a crack in our armor. The barriers of our own making, which effectively exclude us from the Kingdom, are real and in some cases almost insurmountable, but with God all is possible.

Trueblood's words make me think of the man who asked Mother Teresa to pray that he would find clarity. Her response was, essentially, "You don't need clarity. What you need is trust."

Security works the same way. We don't need security so much as we need trust. It is hard for the rich to enter God's kingdom because, trusting in money, they don't feel any need for the kingdom or the King. They may not even want the kingdom or want to know the King. How sad to think about what they are missing.

. . . .

What is keeping you from trusting God and entrusting yourself to God today? Take a moment to acknowledge the first three examples of God's faithfulness that come to mind—and let those encourage you to trust him this day.

TWO LITTLE COINS

A poor widow came and put in two very small copper
coins, worth only a few cents. (Mark 12:42)

"IT IS TRUE THAT it is only within our power to give two mites, our time and our desire," writes Reginald Somerset Ward in *A Guide for Spiritual Directors,* "but the Son of God held that the gift of the widow, though it was worth less than a farthing, was the best of the offerings made to God, since it was all that she had."

These words resonate in my soul. Ward suggests that the currency we invest in our spiritual progress is our time and our desire. Maybe we feel that our time and desire are small, like the widow's two small coins. But Jesus sees and values our little offering. He knows its value because he knows our hearts and our intentions when we pray.

When I'm praying, what am I intending? I may be trying to fulfill some religious duty I believe a Christian should satisfy. I might be acting out of empty habit. Perhaps I'm on autopilot, going through the motions and unable to remember the last time my prayer was a time of Jesus filling my heart and touching my soul.

Instead, I can respond to God from love rather than duty. I can pray from a whole heart. I can offer honest words to the God who is present—my love, my praise, my affection, and my grateful acknowledgment of God's grace.

What do you do—or might you do—to keep prayer alive, to approach it as a life-giving conversation with God and not a mere duty?

GOD OVERCOMES OUR ENEMIES

Praise be to the Lord, the God of Israel,
because he has come to his people and redeemed them. . . .
He has raised up . . . salvation from our enemies. (Luke 1:68, 71)

WHEN THE PEOPLE OF Israel in Jesus' day dreamed and prayed about God rescuing them, their focus was on the oppressive rule of Rome. They felt their lack of freedom under Roman authority, and they pleaded for God to overcome their enemy. That's the kind of salvation they were seeking.

I wonder if we're any different today. Aren't our prayers often focused on asking God to vanquish our outward enemies? We are in debt and want God to rescue us financially. We are in a difficult relationship and want God to change that other person. We are in a difficult job and want God to give us a new one. These are all perfectly reasonable prayers, and God cares about what concerns us.

But sometimes our greatest problems are not *out there* but *in here*. Sometimes our troubles are the fruit of something within us that we are unaware of. Enemies like anxiety, fear, anger, and lust do great harm to us and those around us. So when God doesn't seem to answer our prayers about outward enemies, we fear he isn't interested in them. But perhaps when God seems to disregard what most concerns us, he is actually focused on something that will bring us a greater degree of true freedom. Sometimes God answers the prayers we don't know to pray.

God knows our true enemies better than we do. He knows we are sometimes our own worst enemies, and he seeks to restore his kingdom purposes in our hearts.

. . . .

How have you become a kind of enemy to yourself? How might the loving power of God overcome this inner conflict? How might you cooperate with God's work?

SINNERS LOVE HIM

The Pharisee . . . said to himself, "If this man were a prophet, he would have known who and what kind of woman this is who is touching him—that she is a sinner." (Luke 7:39 NRSV)

JESUS AND SOME FRIENDS have accepted a Pharisee's invitation to dine with him in his house. What does the Pharisee see that raises such a judgmental reaction in him? As they are at the table eating, a woman of bad reputation enters the house and comes to Jesus, weeping, then actually washes his feet with her tears and dries them with her hair (Luke 7:38). She kisses his feet and anoints them with some ointment she has brought with her.

What humility and love! But that isn't what the Pharisee sees. He doesn't see this woman's heart. He can notice only how notorious her life is. Whatever she was known for—perhaps adultery or prostitution—must have made her a public outcast. The Pharisee assumes that Jesus is unaware of her status. He also assumes that this woman will somehow pollute Jesus and that he ought to know better than to let her touch him.

The Pharisee believes in the classic "outside-in" approach to morality—something the Pharisees were famous for. But Jesus comes as a physician for those who need healing. Physicians must be up close and personal with all kinds of illness and brokenness to be able to help. And so instead of being polluted by the woman, Jesus brings healing and forgiveness to her. She doesn't pollute him. He saves her.

. . . .

Do you ever fear that something dirty "out there" will make you unclean? How might you bring the holiness and goodness of Christ with you wherever you go, helping heal the world rather than being polluted by it? Talk to God about these things for a bit.

FORGIVEN LITTLE, LOVING LITTLE

Therefore, I tell you, her sins, which were many, have been
forgiven; hence she has shown great love. But the one to
whom little is forgiven, loves little. (Luke 7:47 NRSV)

JESUS ISN'T DENYING THAT the woman who has washed his feet with her tears and dried them with her hair has a notorious reputation. He even says her sins are many. But is Jesus really saying some people need forgiveness for greater amounts of sin and other (good) people (like us?) have nearly no sin? I wonder if Jesus' statement is more a matter of awareness than anything else.

We all fall short in countless ways. The Pharisees were quick to see sin in the lives of others and quick to put a holy face on themselves for anyone who was looking. They failed to see the sins, which were many, in their white-washed hearts. They did not realize their own need for forgiveness.

Then Jesus makes this remarkable equation: the more we understand ourselves to be forgiven, the more love we embrace and share with others. If I feel I have hardly anything to be forgiven, I will have little gratitude, humility, and care for others. I will tend to judge others rather than love them.

Jesus says this woman's kisses and anointing have shown him more love than the Pharisee host has. No other Jewish leader would have seen it that way. What the Pharisee sees as dishonoring, Jesus sees as honoring. What the Pharisee sees as polluting, Jesus sees as blessing. This is Jesus' way of truth, mercy, and love.

. . . .

When are you tempted to judge another? What is it that tempts you to look down on them? Might this be the place in your own life where you need to receive the mercy of Jesus? Take a few moments to reflect on this idea prayerfully.

GRACE-INSPIRED GENEROSITY

Soon afterward he went on through cities and villages, proclaiming and bringing the good news of the kingdom of God. And the twelve were with him, and also some women who had been healed of evil spirits and infirmities . . . who provided for them out of their means. (Luke 8:1-3 ESV)

DID YOU NOTICE THE LAST PHRASE of this passage? "Who provided for them out of their means." Yes, Jesus and the Twelve relied on the support of people who were committed to following him and learning from him. Many of their primary supporters were women who had benefited from Jesus' healing ministry and now traveled with him and the disciples.

Blessed by God's gracious healing, these women provided financial support so that others would benefit from Jesus' healing, teaching, and grace. Even today, people who partner with a kingdom ministry are often those who have benefited from the grace of that ministry. We have experienced that in Unhurried Living. We have seen that when people are blessed by God through what we offer them, they often partner with us to further the reach of our ministry.

In other words, our ministry partners receive before they give. We give what we have of kingdom grace, and they give what they have, including financial support. We do indeed serve God and his people together.

Jesus freely gave what he had, and some people freely gave back what they had.

. . . .

God blesses us, his people, so that we can be a blessing to others (see Genesis 12:2-3). In what ways have you been able to be a blessing because of God's blessings to you? What additional blessings did you experience because of giving?

BEARING GOOD FRUIT

*The knowledge of the secrets of the kingdom of God has been
given to you, but to others I speak in parables. (Luke 8:10)*

JESUS SHARED HIS KINGDOM secrets with those who followed him, but
he spoke less plainly to those who were seeking only to get something from
him. Jesus wanted to share everything he had with those who would be his
friends and followers.

What Jesus had to share was too powerful and priceless to be given to
those who were merely curious. He was seeking those who would commit
themselves to the fruitful narrow path taken by all who would listen to his
counsel and follow his lead.

In the parables these disciples were asking about, Jesus talked about a
farmer sowing seed. Some fell along the path, some on rocky ground, some
among thorns, and some on good soil. Except for the seed that landed on
good soil, the farmer's seed was eaten by birds, withered once it sprouted, and
was choked out by thorns.

I want to be good soil. I want very much to be a person who, when I hear
what Jesus says to me, holds it close to my heart with honesty, openness, and
good intentions, and who then acts on what Jesus said. I want to persevere
with patient endurance until God enables me to bear kingdom fruit in my
life, my relationships, and my work. Doesn't that sound inviting?

**Look again at the description of good soil above. In what way is God
nudging you to become more receptive and responsive to his guidance?
Take some time in prayer to ask God to show you what weeds he wants to
pull out and how you might cooperate with him in this.**

A FAMILY RESEMBLANCE

My mother and my brothers are those who hear
the word of God and do it. (Luke 8:21 ESV)

SOME PEOPLE ARE BETTER than others at recognizing family resemblances. To be honest, when looking at a newborn, I often can't say whose nose he has. But some family resemblances simply can't be missed—and I'm not just talking about identical twins. At times I can see, without a doubt, which parent's nose or eyes or hair a baby has!

We can also detect resemblances that go beyond physical features. For instance, a mother and daughter might speak in the same unique cadence and tone of voice, or a father and son may laugh the same way or walk with the same gait.

Family resemblances can be uncanny and even unexpected. Consider that Jesus acknowledged as family those who were following his counsel and embodying his love. That kind of behavior is what makes for a family-of-God resemblance in you and in me. To the degree that I am living according to Jesus' counsel and commands, he would say, "Alan is my brother." I'm stunned by that sentence: "Alan is my brother." But the converse is also true. I am not living as Jesus' brother if I live my life or conduct myself in ways that do not honor him.

Think about what character traits and regular actions reveal the reality that you are a child of God—and which traits and actions don't express this reality.

. . . .

Put your name in the blank as you imagine Jesus saying, "_____ is my brother/sister." Read the sentence silently as well as aloud, noting your emotions. What do you feel?

WHO IS THIS?

[Jesus said to his disciples], "Where is your faith?" They were afraid and amazed, and said to one another, "Who then is this, that he commands even the winds and the water, and they obey him?" (Luke 8:25 NRSV)

HAVE YOU SENSED JESUS asking you at one time or another, "Where is your faith?" He asks with kindness and grace, but still he asks. Life can shake our faith. The unexpected, the injustices, the diagnosis, the disarray, the consequences of sin (our own and those others commit against us), the low bank account, the high expectations—many things can cause storms in our lives. And yes, our faith is often shaken and sometimes feels completely blown away.

But maybe, like the disciples, you've seen Jesus calm a storm in your life. Maybe you also have been prompted to ask, "Who is this?" This is the incarnate Lord and Creator of everything, able to walk the ground of his own creation and be present with those who call him Savior.

As today unfolds, let's be alert for situations that are actually invitations to rest in Jesus. Let's receive challenging circumstances as opportunities to gently trust in him. When we do, we will find peace from the internal storm, if not from the external circumstances. May we sense Jesus' companionship throughout the day.

. . . .

Consider a past storm that you saw Jesus calm. If you didn't see his hand in the moment, maybe you can see it more clearly looking back. What were the circumstances? What was the resolution? What impact did this experience have on your faith?

FINANCIAL FARMING

Go! I am sending you out like lambs among wolves. Do not take a purse
or bag or sandals . . . for the worker deserves his wages. (Luke 10:3-4, 7)

EARLY IN HIS MINISTRY, Jesus spoke these words to about seventy of his
followers as he sent them into the surrounding towns and villages. Clearly,
such ministry would require them to trust God. Then Jesus added a little
twist. They weren't to take any food or money with them. They were to trust
God not only for ministry opportunities and changed lives, but also for food,
water, and a place to sleep.

Later, however, on the last night of their earthly time together, Jesus said
something different:

> He said to them, "When I sent you out without a purse, bag, or sandals,
> did you lack anything?" They said, "No, not a thing." He said to them,
> "But now, the one who has a purse must take it, and likewise a bag.
> And the one who has no sword must sell his cloak and buy one."
> (Luke 22:35-36 NRSV)

In ministry, for many years I went where God called without carrying
along obvious stores of funding—and I never lacked anything. Later in my
ministry, I came to believe that God was inviting us to greater intentionality
and initiative in managing our finances. I sensed it was a movement toward
maturity in my way of working with God in life and ministry.

Perhaps this is a season for you in which it's time for traveling light and
trusting God's provision moment to moment. Or maybe it's a time for strategic initiatives and wise investments to provide for your present and
your future.

. . . .

Stewardship is caring for resources belonging to another. Reflect on this
idea of stewardship in your own experience. How has this idea affected
your financial farming through the years?

WORRIED AND UPSET

"Martha, Martha," the Lord answered, "you are worried and upset about many things, but few things are needed—or indeed only one." (Luke 10:41-42)

THE STORY OF MARY and Martha has been used to contrast contemplatives and actives, prayerful people and hard workers. While there is truth in these comparisons, I am drawn to the compassionate words Jesus speaks to his good friend Martha. I recognize familiar symptoms of hurry that I've seen in my own life.

Martha is distracted by all the preparations that need to be made to provide hospitality to Jesus. Preparation can be a way of failing to be in the present. Instead of merely making good plans for a future opportunity, we can become engrossed with all the possible troubles that might arise in an unknown future. Distraction is not our best frame of mind, but it's a common feature of the hurried mind.

Martha feels unloved and alone. She says, "Don't you care that my sister has left me to do the work myself?" (Luke 10:40). She seems to accuse Jesus of a lack of empathy for her situation. Frantic hurry has a way of disconnecting us from nearby people could care for us. Of course Jesus cared for his friend Martha.

Finally, Jesus sees that she is "worried and upset" about many things. She is anxious, and she's frustrated. She's afraid her hospitality will be harmed by the lack of Mary's help. She's frustrated that she's left with all the work herself.

But, always, what Jesus wants most from us is not our service, but our friendship. He wants who we are more than what we do.

. . . .

Which signs of soul hurry in Martha's life sound the most familiar to you? How might Jesus speak with the same compassion to you that he does with Martha?

JESUS SHARES HIS PRAYER

One day Jesus was praying in a certain place. When he
finished, one of his disciples said to him, "Lord, teach us to
pray, just as John taught his disciples." (Luke 11:1)

THE DISCIPLES NOTICE JESUS' life of prayer. They are so affected by what they've seen they ask him to teach them how to pray. What comes next in Luke's Gospel is what we commonly call "the Lord's Prayer" (Luke 11:2-4).

This pattern of prayer Jesus recommends shows up in his own way of praying. Notice Jesus' prayer in the Garden of Gethsemane. Twice he urges his disciples to pray not to fall into temptation (Luke 22:40, 46), just as he suggests in this model.

In the garden, Jesus addresses God as Father (Luke 22:42), just as he begins this prayer with, "Our Father in heaven." The substance of Jesus' prayer in Gethsemane is, "If you are willing, take this cup from me; yet not my will, but yours be done" (Luke 22:42). I'm sure you hear the echoes of, "Your kingdom come; your will be done, on earth as it is in heaven" (Matthew 6:10).

Both in his own life and in his encouragement to his disciples, it seems that the pattern of prayer Jesus taught was his own. When I reflect on the Lord's Prayer, it seems a comprehensive way of thinking about the main things I want to talk with God about day to day.

What a beautiful, fruitful gift this prayer is! What a wise guide to help us live our lives in conversational communion with our Father in heaven.

. . . .

Take a moment to slowly pray the Lord's Prayer. If you don't have it memorized, simply pray it from your Bible in Luke 11:2-4. Let each phrase intersect with your life as you find it in this moment. Let this prayer be an unhurried encounter with God.

MATERIALISM: A SOUL ACCELERATOR

Watch out! Be on your guard against all kinds of greed; life does not consist in an abundance of possessions. (Luke 12:15)

WE LIVE IN A WORLD that assumes that the good life is measured mostly by what fills your portfolio, wallet, garage, or closet. But Jesus says the opposite. He wants us to realize that "the drive to possess is an engine for hurry" (*An Unhurried Life*).

Materialism makes our lives more hurried by having more things. The pervading culture makes an implicit promise to us: buy more things and you'll have more joy and well-being. I'm not suggesting that poverty is virtuous, but there comes a point when having more things means having more worries, unsatisfied desires, or envy of those who have more things than you do.

Measuring the fullness of our lives by the abundance of our possessions is subject to the law of diminishing returns. The answer to the question, "How many things must I possess to be finally and fully satisfied?" is inevitably, "Just a little more than I have now." I believe I need more things to have more joy, so I must earn more money to buy those things. A hurried soul is one of the many taxes levied by a materialistic lifestyle.

What if I already have the most valuable abundance in the gift of communion with God through Christ? What if instead of frantically seeking abundance in outward ways, I could find contentment in the abundance that is already mine in God? What if I could live out of that abundance rather than living to get more of something I don't yet have?

. . . .

Is there something you've come to believe you must have to be truly happy? Can you envision experiencing joy now in the absence of that thing?

A HEALING JOURNEY

When he saw them, he said, "Go, show yourselves to the priests."
And as they went, they were cleansed. (Luke 17:14)

THIS VERSE COMES FROM the story of Jesus healing ten lepers. Many healings in the Gospels are immediate. This healing is a process of Jesus urging them to act, and when they do, they experience healing.

Emotional healing in my experience is usually more of a process than a momentary experience. Many of the healings in the Gospels were of a human condition that was then impossible to cure by human means. Jesus healed the blind, paralyzed, demon-possessed. Jesus raised the dead. Jesus exercised his power to do for people what no one else could.

Why doesn't Jesus heal our emotional wounds in the same way? Why wouldn't Jesus heal our inner wounds or disabilities as quickly as he did those physical needs? Why does transformation take time?

I wonder if God heals our emotions more often as a process because it takes time to learn how to live differently. We might not know how if our emotions were healed in a moment with the same coping habits in place. God seems to heal our hearts at the pace of transformation.

Being unblinded or resurrected isn't a process in the Gospel story. You are either blind or you can see. You are either dead or alive. And Jesus gave the gift of sight or life as a miraculous gift. I am grateful Jesus gives the gift of emotional healing at the pace we can receive it . . . and no faster. Inner healing is usually unhurried.

. . . .

In what ways are you hungry for God to bring healing to your inner life? How would you like to talk with God about that? What would you like to ask him for?

WALKING IN TRUTH OR WINNING ARGUMENTS

"Tell us by what authority you are doing these things,"
they said. "Who gave you this authority?"
[Jesus] replied, "I will also ask you a question. Tell me: John's
baptism—was it from heaven, or of human origin?" (Luke 20:2-3)

THIS IS ONE OF MANY STORIES in the Gospels illustrating the conflict between Jesus and the Jewish leaders. Jesus came to announce truth—to describe reality. The Jewish leaders were more interested in being right than in being real. They wanted to win their argument more than they wanted to walk in truth. They had a position on divine reality they were only seeking to prove.

What a dangerous place to find ourselves! How many believe themselves to be engaged in the work of "defending the truth" but end up doing the same things as these Jewish leaders? Do some people win arguments at the cost of their own soul?

I want to be open to reality as it is—as you've created it. I want to live in harmony with the ways of your kingdom rather than by my own current assumptions. But I'm attached to the vision of reality I've come to believe. It would be hard to discover that there are things about you or the world you've made about which I've been wrong. But if I'm not willing to change my mind about something like that, I'm not really a student. I'm only seeking to reinforce my existing perspectives and assumptions.

Father, may I always remain a learner in your presence. May I hold my arguments loosely so I'm ready to be corrected or redirected by you. Protect me from defending my own positions or convictions when they conflict with divine reality. Amen.

. . . .

Are you a person of strong convictions? In what ways? Are you learning the art of holding your convictions loosely enough to let Jesus counsel and teach you? Talk to him about this.

DAILY PRACTICE

*Each day Jesus was teaching at the temple, and each evening he went out
to spend the night on the hill called the Mount of Olives. (Luke 21:37)*

LUKE HERE IS DESCRIBING a rhythm in the life of Jesus in his last days
on earth. Day by day he taught at the temple. A lot of people were there to
hear him. Night by night he went back to the Mount of Olives, perhaps the
garden at Gethsemane.

The rhythms in Jesus' life continued even in what would be the most tu-
multuous day of his earthly life. Jesus' prayer in Gethsemane was not a one-
time crisis but an ongoing pattern. Spiritual practices are rarely best as
one-time big events. They are usually better as ongoing processes.

This is the nature of our formation. Individual moments may catalyze
something in our journey, but it is ongoing processes that transform us
over time.

Luke seems to suggest that Jesus' prayer at Gethsemane was not a single
night of wrestling but a process that took place over many nights before the
Father in prayer. When wrestling with a sense of something difficult God is
asking of me, I may need to spend many episodes of extended solitude and
prayer before coming to a place where I can abandon myself to God's will in
love rather than thin resignation.

We are on a journey with Christ. We are learning to live our lives as a
continuous walk with God in the real circumstances of our day-to-day lives.
Jesus models this for us.

. . . .

**To what ongoing practices have you sensed Jesus inviting you recently?
They are best begun simply, so how would you like to begin (or continue)
such practices?**

AUTHORITY THAT SERVES

The kings of the Gentiles lord it over them; and those who exercise authority over them call themselves Benefactors. But you are not to be like that. Instead, the greatest among you should be like the youngest, and the one who rules like the one who serves. (Luke 22:25-26)

HUMAN RULERS WHO DO NOT serve under the kingdom of God demand attention, expect special and exceptional treatment, and require their will to be obeyed without question. They do not come to serve but to be served. They want to be admired and respected, if not fawned over. Jesus says none of this should mark the character of servants in his kingdom.

In contrast, King Jesus invites his servants—you and me—to give attention to the needs of others. He wants God's purpose and love to be our focus. In fact, in Jesus' kingdom, his people—you and I—are called to practice service. We may be tempted to think of ourselves as above others, whether consciously or subconsciously. We might try to serve others from this perceived elevated place, but God wants us to remember that we are all people in need of grace.

In kingdom service we don't seek anyone's admiration or accolades. We learn to point to Jesus in all we do so the people we serve in his name will admire him and not us.

. . . .

Can you think of an act of service (your own or another's) where the focus was on God's presence and not on the person serving? What did that look like? What did it feel like?

REPENTANCE IS GOOD NEWS

*And he said to them, "Thus it is written, that the Messiah is to suffer
and to rise from the dead on the third day, and that repentance
and forgiveness of sins is to be proclaimed in his name to all
nations, beginning from Jerusalem." (Luke 24:46-47 NRSV)*

"THUS IT IS WRITTEN." The writings of the Old Testament pointed ahead to a Messiah who, instead of coming as a heroic conqueror, would suffer and die. He would then rise on the third day to conquer an even greater enemy than Rome. He would conquer death. Here in Luke 24, Jesus is speaking to his inner circle after his resurrection. He is reminding them of what the Law, the Prophets, and the Writings had said about him.

The message that is to be proclaimed around the world in the light of this victory is one of repentance and forgiveness of sins in the name of Jesus. Forgiveness is good news. How good it is to know that God prefers to put our shortcomings and line crossings behind him. God delights in mercy. He longs to forgive us more than we long to be forgiven.

But repentance is good news too. Many people assume repentance is about limitation, legalism, or judgment. Repentance reminds us that necessary changes are possible. Aren't there realities about your present inner life you would like to change? Aren't there ways you'd like to be more free, more whole, more fully healed and restored?

Repentance says this freedom and healing are available if we turn toward the God who frees us and heals us. Repentance is turning away from that which harms us, enslaves us, and even poisons us. Repentance is turning our heart, mind, and body toward the one who heals, rescues, and restores us. Good news, right?

· ·

**What would it look like right now to turn toward the God who loves you
and desires your freedom, wholeness, and healing even more than you do?**

A GOD WHO SERVES

Jesus knew that the Father had put all things under his power, and that he had come from God and was returning to God; so he got up from the meal, took off his outer clothing, and wrapped a towel around his waist. (John 13:3-4)

GOD IN FLESH WASHED the feet of his students. What a powerful moment of humble courage. Jesus shows great strength in this service of his followers.

"Jesus knew that the Father had put all things under his power." This moment of servanthood is an expression of power, not powerlessness. Being a gracious servant of others requires far more strength than being served by others. Jesus serves in the knowledge of his God-given authority over all. Kingdom power is always given, never taken.

"Jesus knew . . . that he had come from God." The Father is the source of Jesus' life. Jesus knows where he comes from and where his roots are planted. He doesn't need something from those he serves. Jesus sees his present in the clear vision of his past. Sometimes I see my past as liability because I fail to envision God's good intentions that gave birth to me.

"Jesus knew . . . that he was returning to God." Jesus knows where his path is leading him. He is confident about the God-given goal of his life. The suffering that would soon enter his life was not the end of his story. Sometimes I create goals for myself that are well-intended but not eternal. I can find my deepest purpose in the reality that I am returning to God.

God gives us the gift of authority, identity, and purpose. In this we can enter our world as servants with plenty to give.

· ·

Which of John's three phrases that provide the foundation for Jesus' act of love and service feels most timely for you? Reflect on how what Jesus knows about himself is also true for you.

THE COURAGE OF SERVANTHOOD

Now that I, your Lord and Teacher, have washed your feet, you
also should wash one another's feet. I have set you an example
that you should do as I have done for you. (John 13:14-15)

SERVING OTHERS IS EMPOWERED by the confidence of secure provision and holy belonging. Jesus served from a place of abundance and confidence. His service was an expression of strength, not weakness. Holy service is like that.

Although not one of the disciples had humbled himself and taken on this servant's task, Jesus got on his knees to wash twenty-four dusty feet. When he got to Peter, the former fisherman objected to the Rabbi washing his feet. But Jesus was firm: "Unless I wash you, you have no part with me" (John 13:8).

I empathize with Peter. It would feel absolutely wrong for Jesus to wash my feet. If anyone should be washing feet, that person should be me and the feet should be his.

But Jesus reminds me that his humble act of serving is relational, not just functional. Peter's impulsive reaction, "You will never wash my feet," is really him saying no to the wishes and will of Jesus. Jesus wants Peter to have a heart willing to trust that he has good reason for what he's doing.

Jesus comes to you today, serving you from a place of loving authority. He stoops to wash your feet. His service is a way for you to become his follower in the service of others. What does that look like today?

. . . .

When were you faced with a task that felt too messy, too difficult, or too humiliating for you to take on? How did you respond? Would you respond differently now if the same opportunity arose for you?

AN UNTROUBLED HEART

Do not let your hearts be troubled. You believe
in God; believe also in me. (John 14:1)

JESUS SPEAKS GOOD WORDS to me in troubling times. He encourages me not to let outward trouble sink into my inner world. I don't have to let my heart become troubled in troubling circumstances. I can trust Christ amid uncertainties and difficulties.

But I'm tempted to see troubles as the largest reality in my life. I let them dwarf my awareness of a substantial, eternal kingdom in which I'm presently at home. Troubles often shock and overwhelm me. When I rehearse the trustworthy presence of Jesus, it helps. I have a home for my soul more reliable and far less troubling than this world in which I presently live.

Jesus invites me to trust in a substantial (if invisible) reality that is greater than my visible circumstances. This takes practice. And the way to this spiritual reality is not a technique. It is not a strategy. The way to my untroubling home with the Father is a Person. Jesus says he is the way, the truth, and the life (John 14:6). I am learning how to make myself more at home in this reality. I am welcome and wanted in the Father's presence because Jesus brings me with him there.

There is a place of trusting Jesus that enables us to live and work like Jesus. Jesus lives in full dependence on the Father in the power of the Spirit. We are welcome in this same place. *Lord Jesus, enable me to find my heart at home and at rest in your presence.*

. . . .

What has been troubling your heart lately? How would it help to see Jesus filling the horizon of your perspective rather than your troubles?

EVEN MORE HELP

If you love me, keep my commands. And I will ask the Father,
and he will give you another advocate to help you and be
with you forever—the Spirit of truth. (John 14:15-17)

I HAVE SOMETIMES HEARD this first line as, "If you love me, prove it!" It has sounded like Jesus is skeptical about my love for him. But this is not the character of the one who served the disciples by washing their feet. Jesus has given us every reason to be confident in his love for us.

Jesus helps us understand what it looks like to be truly at home in his love. When we know ourselves to be perfectly loved, we are free to follow the goodness of Jesus' counsel. We experience his guidance as full of grace and kingdom benefit. Jesus gives us commands designed to bring us more deeply into the goodness, beauty, and reality of his kingdom.

I have not only the help of Jesus in learning the ways of his kingdom. Jesus has asked the Father to send the Spirit to stay with me—even in me—to help me. Jesus wants us to have all the help we need to enter his kingdom of grace and truth. It is an invisible kingdom, so we need invisible help—the help of his Spirit—to cultivate this way of living well.

Love and obedience live in union. Obedience is not the path to being loved. Obedience is the reality of being at home in love. Disobedience creates distance. Disobedience resists love and chooses its own empty way. Why wouldn't I want to live at the living heart of all reality? Why wouldn't I want to make myself at home where love reigns?

. . . .

How has the reliable love of Jesus been inspiring you to follow him more closely? How might it continue to do so even more?

OUR SPIRITUAL GUIDE

*But the Advocate, the Holy Spirit, whom the Father will
send in my name, will teach you all things and will remind
you of everything I have said to you. (John 14:26)*

JESUS REMINDS HIS FOLLOWERS of the help of his Spirit hours before
he will be arrested. He knows they are going to feel alone and helpless. But
he is already letting them know they won't be abandoned. The Father will
send the Spirit. And the Spirit comes in the name—in the same character—
of Jesus.

The Spirit teaches us everything and reminds us what Jesus has said. This
is more than human teaching, which in Jesus' day focused on teachers quoting
and arguing with one another about minor matters. Jesus taught with authority because he listened to the Father. Thanks to the presence of his Spirit,
we can listen to the Father and learn to speak the words we hear him say.

This happens in a place of peace. Jesus says, "Peace I leave with you;
my peace I give you. I do not give to you as the world gives" (John 14:27). Such
peace doesn't result from outward resolution. It is a kingdom peace. It is
peace on a different and divine level. Divine peace is different from the peace
of this world in that way.

The peace Jesus gives us is not a commodity we can take with us somewhere else. It is Jesus' own peace. In the kingdom of heaven, peace is a Person.
He gives peace to us because he gives us himself. He is with us through the
empowering, guiding presence of the Spirit. His presence *is* our peace.

In what ways do you find yourself looking for peace that is the fruit of
something changing "out there"? How might you discover peace that is
the fruit of friendship with Christ in you?

EVEN MORE FRUITFUL

I am the true vine, and my Father is the gardener. He cuts off every branch in me that bears no fruit, while every branch that does bear fruit he prunes so that it will be even more fruitful. (John 15:1-2)

JESUS ALONE IS THE TRUE VINE. Every other vine I attach myself to ends up draining me. A true vine gives life to a branch. A false vine sucks life from a branch. When I feel my life is empty, I may well be abiding in a false vine. What a gift, though, to awaken to this reality and to have the freedom and power to choose to abide in the true vine, and to be well-tended by my Father in heaven, who is the gardener.

It has been suggested by a few that "cuts off" could also be translated "lifted up." The metaphor then is that branches that don't bear fruit are lifted off the ground so they can get more light, air, and space to be fruitful. The Father works to restore unfruitful branches and prunes fruitful ones to lead to greater productivity. Pruning cuts away good branches so better ones can grow.

We become engrossed in many things in our lives. We spread ourselves thin, as Bilbo says in *The Hobbit*, like butter scraped over too much bread. We become unfocused, so the Father works to prune our lives so our energy and effort can be directed to that which is most fruitful. In the moment it is painful to lose what gets pruned, but when I look back from the place of greater fruitfulness, I have gratitude.

. . . .

When have you experienced the fruitfulness of abiding in Jesus as the true vine? When have you experience a draining of life when you've connected to some false vine? Where do you find yourself today?

EMPOWERED TO ABIDE

I am the vine; you are the branches. If you remain in me and I in you,
you will bear much fruit; apart from me you can do nothing. (John 15:5)

I'VE SOMETIMES READ THIS VERSE as talking about my responsibility to abide in Christ. Understandable. But the vine precedes and gives birth to the branch. I love how Andrew Murray describes this reality in *Abide in Christ*:

> Let me listen and believe, until my whole being cries out, "Jesus is indeed to me the True Vine, bearing me, nourishing me, supplying me, using me, and filling me to the full to make me bring forth fruit abundantly." Then shall I not fear to say, "I am indeed a branch to Jesus, the True Vine, abiding in Him, resting on Him, waiting for Him, serving Him, and living only that through me, too, He may show forth the riches of His grace, and give His fruit to a perishing world."

Murray first focuses on what the vine does before focusing on what the branch does. Likewise, my first focus is not on my abiding activity but on the work of God in caring and providing for me so well. My abiding doesn't cause something as much as it receives something.

As the vine, Jesus carries me, provides for me, gives me what I need, uses me for his purposes, and fills me with every good thing. Because he has first loved me, I am then able to be a branch that abides in the vine, rests in him, waits for him, serves him, and lives my whole life in communion with him. In this way I can bear good and abundant fruit that truly lasts.

. . . .

Rather than a burdensome responsibility or unreachable standard, how might this command to abide become an empowering invitation to you instead?

AT HOME IN LOVE

As the Father has loved me, so have I loved you. Now
remain in my love. (John 15:9)

JESUS HAS LOVED ME in the same way that the Father has loved him. Fully. Deeply. Consistently. Selflessly. This is how loved we are in this very moment. The love of the Father and Son for me right now is the foundation of my sense of who I am. This is how I come to find myself at home in God.

Remaining in the love of Christ looks like obedience. But obedience is more about a listening relationship than it is about following rules. The great commandment we are invited to follow is simply the command to be loved, love God back, and share this love. This is how Jesus lived (and lives). This is what Jesus models and invites us to follow. Jesus abides in the Father and remains in union with his love. We can, too.

Jesus means all of this to be an experience of rich and deep joy (John 15:11). He is not burdening us with onerous and irrelevant rules. Jesus knows the joy we'll experience as we align ourselves more closely with the ways of his Father's kingdom. We find energy and strength in this joy. Excitement rooted in outward stimulus sustains only if that input lasts. Joy is sustainable kingdom energy.

Whatever love Jesus experiences from his Father he shares with us. He gives us the affection the Father expresses to him. He speaks to us the words of delight the Father speaks to him. Just as the Father loves Jesus, Jesus is loving us. Here and now.

. . . .

Reflect on a particular way the Father has expressed his love for the Son. How might Jesus be showing that love to you in this moment?

TWO DIFFERENT WORLDS

If the world hates you, keep in mind that it hated me first. If you
belonged to the world, it would love you as its own. (John 15:18-19)

THE WORLD. MY EARLY EXPERIENCE in conservative churches gave
me a very strong sense of a world in which we did not belong. But sometimes
that sensibility was more about our narrow values than it was about two
different kingdoms.

We had unknowingly baptized many of our North American values to feel
a little more Christian to us. We baptized greed and imagined it was the
abundant life. We baptized contempt and imagined it was fighting the good
fight against the enemies of the faith. But the kinds of upside-down values
Jesus taught and lived were far from us. So we didn't love our enemies. We
fought our enemies and branded them as evil.

Whatever the world is that Jesus says hates us, it hates us for the very
reasons it hated and resisted him. It was the ways in which Jesus stood against
the values and priorities of this world that made him its enemy.

We would sing hymns like, "This world is not my home. I'm just passing
through." But we were unclear about whether we were talking about a value
system or about people we disagreed with. We weren't interested in learning
to love these "enemies" for whom Christ gave himself.

Ironically, the "world" that hates true followers of Christ are often the religious ones who measure everything by their own standards rather than by
the values of Christ's kingdom. They hated him, and they'll hate anyone else
who decide to make their home in that upside-down kingdom.

**Who feels like an enemy to you these days? What is one loving thing you
could do for their good that would be in the Spirit of Jesus?**

DIVINE HUMILITY

When the Advocate comes, whom I will send to you from the Father—the Spirit of truth who goes out from the Father—he will testify about me. (John 15:26)

THE HOLY SPIRIT IS among us to speak about Jesus. Jesus came to show us the Father. The Father is happy to send Jesus and the Spirit to us. Father, Son, and Spirit are in mutually affirming relationship. They do not focus on themselves but on the others. Humility is the divine reality that lies at the center of creation. Our self-centered, self-serving, self-focused world is a distortion of this beautiful reality.

When God invites us to humility, it is an invitation into kingdom reality. Pride is what is unreal. Rather than highlighting ourselves, we point to another.

We testify about Jesus. The Spirit enlightens and empowers us to this end. This is real living. We do this in hope that the Father is honored and sought by many.

John reminds us that the Spirit of truth guides us into all truth (John 16:13). He doesn't speak on his own. He speaks only what he hears from the Father and Son. We learn that our lives are a gift given by God. Our words and work are a gift as well. Humility is acknowledging the good in our life is given and the fruit of our lives is rooted in the life of God.

The Spirit guides us into a deeper appreciation for the kingdom reality of humility. The Spirit speaks what he hears from the Son. The Son speaks what he hears from the Father. God speaks with one voice in three persons. This is a relationship in which we'll grow for the rest of our lives.

. . . .

In what ways does humility feel negative to you? How might humility be inviting as we gaze on our humble God?

AN ETERNAL LIFE

Now this is eternal life: that they know you, the only true
God, and Jesus Christ, whom you have sent. (John 17:3)

FOR THE LONGEST TIME I imagined that eternal life would be real to me after I died. It was a heavenly reality, but heaven wasn't yet. In his prayer Jesus says eternal life is not an everlasting stretch of time but a loving relationship with God that lasts.

It is not just a guarantee for the future. It is God's gift to us in the present. Loving knowledge of the God we see in the face of Christ is a way of life that lasts. It is sustainable. Better, it is ever-increasing. It is more than knowing about God in biblical facts, doctrinal affirmations, or theological structures. These are like bricks in the foundation of our home in loving knowledge of God.

Jesus' description of eternal life comes in words of prayer he speaks to his Father. This is what Jesus wants us to know more fully, so he speaks to his Father about it. Jesus wants our experience to echo his own human experience of the Father. This is what it means to be truly alive.

In each moment of our lived experience, Jesus is speaking with the Father for our good. And our best "good" is growing in loving knowledge of God. It is knowing ourselves to be a delight to God because he made us and we belong with him. I imagine Jesus asking the Father to refresh our awareness of his love for us. I really live when I remember I'm already loved by God right now and will be forever.

. . . .

What are some ways you've understood eternal life? How does Jesus' way of talking about eternal living speak to you in this moment?

MUTUAL SUBMISSION

All I have is yours, and all you have is mine. And glory
has come to me through them. (John 17:10)

THERE IS COMPLETE UNITY between Father and Son. There is no "mine" and "yours" but only "ours" in the Trinity. So it doesn't fit for there to be a selfish "mine" among God's people either. God wants the mutual generosity of Father, Son, and Spirit to be multiplied among us. When we love and serve one another, God's glorious selflessness shines in us and brings him honor. Jesus prays that this unity would be protected (John 17:11).

Our unity is not merely agreeing on doctrinal distinctions. It is not merely sharing a set of common beliefs. It is an organic, relational unity rooted in a life we share together with Father, Son, and Spirit.

Jesus talks about these things because he knows we'll discover the depths of his joy in unified life (John 17:13). Deep joy is not the fruit of a self-serving life but of mutual submission expressed in lived unity. Unity is the fruit of our common life in God. He is the one who knits very different individuals into a single community. There is no human commonness strong enough to do that.

Joy is the fruit of awakening to the reality of God as mutually generous and us as united with him. There is a lightness of heart and strength in this union with God we share. We find ourselves weak and burdened when we fight for personal causes against one another. Jesus prays this would change among us. Let's allow that prayer to be realized.

. . . .

When do you last remember having a disagreement with a fellow Christian? Did it lead to disunity, or were you able to love despite your difference? Talk with God about this.

JESUS' SINGULAR PRAYER

My prayer is not for them alone. I pray also for those who will
believe in me through their message, that all of them may be one,
Father, just as you are in me and I am in you. (John 17:20-21)

HERE JESUS IS PRAYING specifically for you and me. He prays for those
of us who have come to trust him through the message of those first disciples
passed down to us. I can imagine him looking into future centuries and envisioning you and me in loving relationship with him. I'm part of that lineage.
What a gift!

So when Jesus prays for us, what does he want for us? He asks the Father
that we would be one with each other the way the Father and the Son are one.
Jesus asks for complete unity, not a mere unity of religious policies or clones
of a strong personality. It's a holy unity rooted in the reality of love. And Jesus
prays for it because we can't achieve it without his gracious assistance.

What's remarkable is that Jesus says this union is how the whole world will
realize God sent Jesus to love us in the same way Father and Son love one
another in the Spirit. True unity is our greatest form of influence in this world.
But we seek lesser unions. We feel more comfortable if everyone shares our
perspective. Instead of discovering how Jesus might be the center around
which we unite, we see ourselves as the reference point of this union. Then it
shouldn't be a surprise that such an attempt leads to alienation among us.

This world will believe that Jesus is the one sent by the Father to proclaim
ultimate reality when we are united with him together in love.

. . . .

In what ways have you sought a unity that was more opinion-focused or
position-focused? What might a unity that is Jesus-focused look like?

AN UNEXPECTED KING

*Pilate then went back inside the palace, summoned Jesus and
asked him, "Are you the king of the Jews?" (John 18:33)*

PILATE WENT OUTSIDE HIS PALACE to talk with the Jewish leaders
because they would have been unclean if they'd gone inside. They wanted to
enjoy their Passover even while they were plotting the death of Jesus. Religious observations aren't always connected with real values. Sometimes they
are self-centered instead of God-centered.

Pilate, the Roman governor, has a conversation with one he believes to be
a religious figure. He has no idea he is speaking with the ruler of all. Pilate
would not have thought of himself as a king. That was the Caesar in Rome,
Tiberius. But Pilate presumes to be over Jesus as one of his subjects.

Pilate gets to the heart of the charge from these Jewish leaders: Jesus has
claimed to be King of the Jews. That puts him at odds with Caesar and Rome.
Jesus answers his question with a question of his own. "Is this your idea, or
have you heard about me from others?"

Pilate wants no part of a Jewish squabble and says as much. But Jesus won't
be drawn into this squabble or Pilate's curiosity. His kingdom is not one based
in human authorities or armies. His kingdom is "from another place." That's
putting it mildly. The kingdom of Jesus is from the place above all places—the
presence of God. His is a kingdom that will continue long after Pilate's reign.

I am part of a kingdom that is bigger than noisy political bickering. The
kingdom of God precedes and surpasses any other rule. I have been given
authority in this kingdom.

. . . .

**How might remembering that Jesus is King over every kingdom—
especially over political tensions—be life-giving for you?**

RECOGNIZING RESURRECTION

Early on the first day of the week, while it was still dark,
Mary Magdalene went to the tomb and saw that the stone
had been removed from the entrance. (John 20:1)

THIS IS THE RESURRECTION story I've heard so many times. I'm not sure if I ever noticed that it was in the predawn hours when Mary Magdalene went to the tomb of Jesus. What woke her? What was her intention? What did she expect to find? She would have assumed she would not be able to get into the tomb because of the huge rock in front of the entrance, let alone the Roman soldiers on guard.

Instead, she finds no stone and no soldiers. There is an open tomb and no Jesus inside. Her first assumption is the one I might have made: Someone has stolen his body. Where have they taken it?

Mary Magdalene doesn't recognize resurrection when she sees it. She doesn't realize that's what she is witnessing. There is a reason for the absence of the body she cannot imagine. He is alive again. He has risen into his kingdom. She will see him next in his risen body. So Mary runs to where Peter and John are staying to report what she's seen. Is it still dark? Does she wake them up?

I wonder if I recognize resurrection when it comes to me. I have experienced moments that felt like dying—pain, hardship, loss. Might resurrection puzzle me when it first crosses my path? Might I be looking for it in one way and it arrives in another? Resurrection is an unexpected form of life that arises out of death. May God's Spirit grant us insight to recognize it.

. . . .

When have you recently experienced a kind of death—loss, hardship, pain? What might resurrection look like in this situation? Speak with God about this.

JESUS UNRECOGNIZED

"They have taken my Lord away," she said, "and I don't know where they have put him." At this, she turned around and saw Jesus standing there, but she did not realize that it was Jesus. (John 20:13-14)

MARY MAGDALENE GOES BACK to the tomb as Peter and John run off to investigate her report. Jesus is still gone. She is grieving. She looks inside the tomb again to see where Jesus should have been. But instead of emptiness, she encounters two angels in white seated where Jesus' body has lain.

I don't know that she's ever seen an angel before. They ask her a simple question, "Woman, why are you crying?" (The "woman" address is not belittling. It is simply a way of acknowledging her.)

Mary again says some unknown "they" have stolen Jesus' body. She wants to know where they have put him so she can continue to grieve and care for him. In answer to her grief, Jesus appears, but she does not recognize him. Perhaps this is because she is not expecting him. Perhaps it is also because he is in his kingdom body, one that can appear wherever he wishes.

This Jesus, present but unrecognized, is a theme for me as well. Jesus is always with me. He promises he'll never leave me or forsake me. But I forget and fail to recognize his presence. I feel his apparent absence even when he promises he'll never be absent.

May the Spirit of God enable me to know and recognize the presence of Christ in this day. May I trust even if I do not feel he is with me. May I sense his companionship in each encounter and each engagement.

. . . .

Can you think of a time when you felt abandoned or forgotten by Jesus? Why not pray, asking that Jesus would help you recognize his presence with you even then?

CALLED BY NAME

[Jesus] asked her, "Woman, why are you crying?
Who is it you are looking for?" . . .
Jesus said to her, "Mary."
She turned toward him and cried out in Aramaic, "Rabboni!"
(which means "Teacher"). (John 20:15-16)

JESUS SPEAKS TO HIS GOOD FRIEND, Mary Magdalene, but she still doesn't realize him. When he says her name, she awakens. She suddenly knows him and calls him by her favorite address, "Rabbi!"

When Jesus speaks our name, we recognize him. When Jesus comes to us personally we wake up to his presence with us, the presence of a kingdom drenched in love. In seasons when I find it hard to discern how God is with me in my frustrations and failures, he calls me by name, and I remember. I am simply, purely, fully loved today. This is my great reality.

Jesus tells Mary to go "to my brothers" (John 20:17). What an intimate way to talk about his Eleven. He wants her to tell them he is ascending to "my Father and your Father, to my God and your God." Jesus shares God and Father with us. We are family. The posture of Jesus today is, "I am with my Father and your Father, my God and your God. You have a home in us. You belong. You are for you, your good and your fruitfulness."

Lord Jesus, grant me a vision of what that might look like today. I know there is much good to which you are calling me, but I struggle to see it and engage it. Open my eyes, my ears, my heart. Sharpen and strengthen my intentions. Grant me a vision of you that will reflect itself in the form of a vision for and with you. Amen.

. . . .

Be silent for a few moments, inviting Jesus to call you by name. Can you envision him doing for you what he does for Mary?

SENT FORTH IN PEACE

Jesus said, "Peace be with you!
As the Father has sent me, I am sending you."
And with that he breathed on them and said,
"Receive the Holy Spirit." (John 20:21-22)

JESUS WANTS YOU AND ME to have his peace when he sends us out into a world that knows little of true peace. At best, peace in this world is mostly about the absence of obvious conflict in our hearts and relationships. At worst, a lack of peace means people are at odds with one another in heartbreaking ways.

It would appear that the means by which Jesus gives his peace to his followers is by breathing his own breath onto them: Jesus gives us his Holy Spirit. My body breathes in air and lives. My soul breathes in God's Spirit and lives.

Our physical breathing is involuntary. We have more of a choice when it comes to our spiritual breathing: Will we acknowledge Jesus as our Lord and thereby receive (inhale) his Spirit? And when we are following Jesus, will we yield to him every morning, breathing in his Holy Spirit in fresh ways and asking him, the Good Shepherd, to lead us through the day for the Father's purposes? Living in the power and energy of God's Spirit brings us into a life of joyful service that has eternal value.

· ·

Reflect on a time when you experienced the power and energy of God's Spirit being breathed into and through you. Thank him for making a difference and spend some time enjoying his presence with you now.

COME HAVE BREAKFAST

*Jesus said to them, "Come and have breakfast." None of the disciples dared
ask him, "Who are you?" They knew it was the Lord. (John 21:12)*

JOHN TELLS US A LITTLE STORY about an encounter between the risen
Christ and a few of his disciples.

Simon Peter decided he needed to do something, so he did what he
knew—he went fishing. And six other disciples joined him. But it was an
empty night of effort. In the morning, they noticed an unfamiliar stranger
who called from shore. After conversation, this stranger suggested they try
throwing their net out on the other side of the boat. Peter had heard this one
before; he had been given advice from an apparent amateur once, and it re-
sulted in one of his best fishing trips ever. And now, again, they caught more
fish than they could bring in, and John immediately recognized Jesus.

What a beautiful and holy moment! What I love is the simple invitation of
Jesus to his apprentices: "Come and have breakfast." Jesus cares for our practical needs. Jesus blesses us by meeting our most basic requirements. He
shows us love in tangible, simple ways. Blessing us in places of hunger blesses
him. It is yet another way for him to show us he loves us.

How humbling that the Lord of the universe would take time to make a
fire and cook up breakfast for his friends. Can you imagine Jesus rising before
you in the morning, going to your kitchen, and making a delicious breakfast
because he loves you? Jesus is still serving his disciples after he's risen, because it is the nature of love to bless, help, and serve others.

. . . .

**Ask God's Spirit to show you a simple way in which Jesus recently showed
you love that you might not have noticed. Offer thanks as you remember.**

HOW THEY DID CHURCH

*They devoted themselves to the apostles' teaching and to fellowship,
to the breaking of bread and to prayer. (Acts 2:42)*

I WONDER IF WE HEAR this line from Acts and imagine these early Jesus-followers faithfully going to Bible study, church meetings, potlucks, and an occasional prayer meeting here or there. Maybe we see the hardcore few attending a midweek prayer meeting.

This verse is saying much more.

First, the apostles were speaking from their eyewitness experiences and their living relationship with the risen Christ, Jesus of Nazareth. They weren't simply talking about Jesus; these witnesses to the resurrected Lord were sharing Jesus' life with other followers.

Also, the details of their fellowship are revealed in this passage, which points to much more than simple meeting attendance: "All the believers were together and had everything in common. They sold property and possessions to give to anyone who had need. Every day they continued to meet together in the temple courts" (Acts 2:44-46).

These early followers of Jesus were together and shared what they had with one another. Some even sold their property or possessions to meet the needs of their brothers and sisters. There was little sense of "mine and yours" and a much greater sense of "ours."

Also, the "breaking of bread" was more than eating meals together. It was sharing a time of being spiritually nourished at the table Christ gave us: "They broke bread in their homes and ate together with glad and sincere hearts" (Acts 2:46). What a beautiful family photo!

. . . .

In what ways does your community in Christ reflect the early church's way of living together in Christ? How might you all take new steps together?

THE GOSPEL IN WORD AND DEED

*As for us, we cannot help speaking about what we
have seen and heard. (Acts 4:20)*

ELTON TRUEBLOOD IN *CONFRONTING CHRIST* writes, "There are people who say they do not need to make a vocal witness, because, as they express it, they 'just let their lives speak.' This appears as humility, but is really self-righteousness. No person's life is good enough to speak with any adequacy."

This sounds a bit like the line sometimes attributed to Francis of Assisi: "Preach the gospel at all times. If necessary use words." But Trueblood exposes the presumption that underlies such a statement. How will someone who knows nothing of the gospel figure out that our kindness, care, and goodness are fruits of communion with Christ without words that bear witness to this reality?

Of course, my way of life needs to harmonize with my verbal witness to the goodness, beauty, and truth of God's kingdom. But even at my best, the witness of my life doesn't say much about the good I do being fruit of God's kingdom. The life of Jesus was perfectly good, but still he proclaimed the good news of the kingdom in both word and deed. He invites us to bear witness to what we have seen and heard in him.

I want my life to speak well, but without words of witness, there isn't a way for others to attribute that goodness to anyone but me. Acknowledging the fruitful work of Christ in me is an act of humility and worship. This requires words—good words, public words, praising words, thanking words.

. . . .

How would you like to speak about the goodness of what God has been doing in you so others will understand and sense his invitation?

SCRIPTURE SURPRISES US

Paul went into the synagogue, and on three Sabbath days he reasoned
with them from the Scriptures, explaining and proving that the
Messiah had to suffer and rise from the dead. (Acts 17:2-3)

ONE WAY WE KNOW we're listening well to the Scriptures is if they continue to surprise us. If we find they always say something we already expect, if there no longer seem to be any mysteries, we might be in trouble. Consider Paul's custom here of speaking to Jews in the synagogue about Jesus, for example.

The common Jewish vision of Messiah in Paul's day would not have been of a suffering, dying, and rising Servant but of a conquering king who would overthrow Roman rule. But this was not actually the whole vision of their own Scriptures. Paul opened their eyes to a truer vision directly from the Scriptures they held dear. He gave them insight and evidence about the true nature of the Messiah.

There are many times when I feel I must, like Paul, help those who would call themselves God's people today see the true nature of Messiah. As in Paul's day, we have often revised our vision of Messiah to fit more easily within our cultural assumptions. We, too, want a triumphant Messiah who is mostly on our side promoting our agenda.

Doesn't this speak to the current climate in any age? We assume the job of the Messiah is to bless and fulfill our expectations. I'm hungry to learn how to reason from the Scriptures not for *my* vision of life, but for the reality of what Jesus intended and, therefore, intends now. I want to continue to let myself be truly surprised by the truth of Jesus in these pages.

· ·

When do you recall something in Scripture surprising you? How did the Scriptures highlight something in your assumptions or expectations that needed revising?

HOW TO BE BIBLICAL

The Berean Jews were of more noble character than those in Thessalonica,
for they received the message with great eagerness and examined the
Scriptures every day to see if what Paul said was true. (Acts 17:11)

IN MY EARLY YEARS as a Christian, this passage was held up to extol the virtues of passionate, daily Bible study. I still think that's a good idea. The Thessalonian Jews were unwilling to examine their assumptions about God in the Scriptures. They assumed they already had an accurate view of the Scriptures.

The angry assertions of the Thessalonian Jews (Acts 17:5-7) powered over the simple truth of what Paul was declaring, explaining, and even proving. Evidence meant nothing to them. They had to defend their pre-existing beliefs, which had the weight of tradition behind them, even if it was misguided tradition.

In defense of their vision of God, these Jews in Thessalonica completely disregarded the counsel of God. They were not learners. The Bereans were. At whatever personal cost, they were willing to listen and search the Scriptures for a vision of God's person and God's way that would end up contradicting much of what they currently believed.

This is not easy for any of us. We are all tempted to be more like the Thessalonians. We've believed certain things about God's ways for years, and then someone comes along to say our vision of God may have been misguided. Are we more invested in our present opinions than we are in our willingness to learn from Jesus?

Let's be Bereans. Let's allow the Scriptures to test us, try us, teach us. And let's not be too quick to assume something unfamiliar is automatically wrong. The Bereans didn't.

. . . .

How might you respond if your study of the Scriptures struck at the core of your current assumptions about God and God's ways? How Berean would you be willing to be?

LIGHT OVERCOMES DARKNESS

The light shines in the darkness,
and the darkness has not overcome it. (John 1:5)

JESUS IS THE LIGHT for all people and not just for me. That light shines into every darkness and cannot be overcome. The light of Jesus shines into the world and the darkness in it does not overcome that light.

But when it comes to my own dark thoughts or emotions, the light of Christ shines there too. Rather than being overwhelmed by such darkness, I can find freedom in the light of Christ. My dark thoughts and emotions often feel strong but are quite weak in the light of Christ's shining presence. What I've often needed (and learned to ask for) is the help of God's Spirit to open my heart's eyes and turn them toward the shining presence of Christ.

Light shining into me becomes the light that shines through me. As I learn to walk in the light of God's presence, I learn to walk as light in my world. Christ does not shine a blinding light onto my path or into my heart, so my way of being light in this world will be as merciful and gracious as the way in which Christ is a light in this world.

So when I sense the invitation of God's Spirit to allow the light of truth shining in the face of Christ to shine into my mind and heart, I welcome it not only for my enlightenment, but because I believe that God wishes to shine through me for the good of my world.

. . . .

Where might Christ want to shine the light of mercy and grace into your life? How can this become a gracious light that then shines through you for the good of others?

LIVING IN GOD'S LIGHT

If we walk in the light, as he is in the light, we have fellowship with one another, and the blood of Jesus, his Son, purifies us from all sin. (1 John 1:7)

WE CAN ENJOY FELLOWSHIP with God only if we remain where he is. There is no darkness in God. If we hide in the darkness of pretending, avoiding, or play-acting, then there isn't a real "me" there to enjoy communion. I can't hide myself and abide in God.

I used to think "walking in the light" referred to some sort of eventual moral perfection. I've been in recovery from this sort of unreachable standard for a while now. I've come to believe walking in the light is walking in humble honesty about my offenses in light of God's healing mercy and restoring grace.

In that light, anything in me that isn't what it was meant to be is cleansed. In this gracious light, I find others like myself who also walk in this gracious light. In this place together—being known by God and growing close to him together—we enjoy true friendship with one another. We see ourselves and each other as we are, in our true beauty and actual brokenness.

Rather than walking in the darkness of trying to deceive others, ourselves, and God, I learn everything in my life is perfectly safe to bring into the presence of God's healing, restoring grace. I walk in the light. When I wake to ways I've been hiding, this is a moment to step back into the light of confession and humble prayer.

. . . .

When have you been tempted to put on a good face in prayer? What has it looked like to pray words that didn't ring true to what was happening in you? How is God inviting you into the light of honest confession and receiving of grace?

ALIVE IN CHRIST

This is how we know we are in him: Whoever claims to
live in him must live as Jesus did. (1 John 2:5-6)

I OFTEN FIND IT helpful to pray a passage in my own words. Here is my paraphrase of 1 John 2:3-11.

"Alan, you can be confident you really know me if you live in my counsel. Anyone who claims to be close to me but wanders in disobedience is deceiving themselves instead of living. But if you keep close to me by doing the kinds of things I do, then the love of God is made more whole in you. Again, Alan, since you claim to live in me, actually live *in* me—whatever you see in me as you read the Gospels, let that shape who you are and what you do.

"You are my friend, and I'm not telling you anything surprising or unusual. This is what I've been saying from the beginning. And yet I came to show you the scope of this central reality—love. You saw what love could become in me. My love was the light that shone in a dark world, then and now.

"So if anyone claims to live in the light of love but treats others hatefully, they are wandering in the dark. But if you let my love overflow your life for the good of your neighbor, you are living in love. And love helps you keep your footing. Love makes your way sure. You wander when you forget you are loved, and then you wander in your relationships with others. You live like a blind man when I have given you clear vision."

. . . .

Was there a particular line in this prayerful paraphrase that seemed especially timely for you? Why not read it again and speak with God about it?

THE WISDOM OF LOVING GOD

I am writing to you, fathers,
because you know him who is from the beginning. (1 John 2:13)

THE BEST SPIRITUAL FATHERS and mothers are the ones who are mature, seasoned, and willing to care for the interests of others more than their own. John has a message for these parents because they are the ones who know the eternal God. John does not acknowledge them for their business success or impressiveness. He speaks to them because they know God.

Spiritual parents are those who have learned anything that disregards the God who created the world is an empty promise. This is how John puts it: "For everything in the world—the lust of the flesh, the lust of the eyes, and the pride of life—comes not from the Father but from the world. The world and its desires pass away, but whoever does the will of God lives forever" (1 John 2:16-17).

Spiritual parents are those who recognize that what this world promotes as high-value is short-lived. They are those who have an unhurried vision of goodness. Immature men and women are those who spend their lives seeking not the kingdom but the satisfaction of bodily cravings and fulfillment of visions of personal success.

Fathers and mothers in the faith have learned seeking life in the promises of this world and seeking life in God are very different paths. John isn't saying I shouldn't have a great affection for the beauty and goodness of what God has made. In this verse, "world" refers to a universe that has decided to seek life apart from the living God. May I continue becoming a mature parent in the kingdom of heaven.

. . . .

How do you find yourself growing in your journey of loving and trusting God?

ENJOYING THE UNPLANNED TOGETHER

*As for you, the anointing you received from him remains in you,
and you do not need anyone to teach you. (1 John 2:27)*

WE ARE NOT DESPERATELY dependent on human teachers, but we can receive what God's Spirit wishes to teach us through them. I love the way Thomas Merton speaks of such things in a letter to a friend who was coming to visit (published in *The Hidden Ground of Love*):

> I look forward to seeing you and John H. and a few others in October but let's make it purposeless and freewheeling and a vacation for all and let the Holy Spirit suggest anything that needs to be suggested. Let's be Quakers and the heck with projects. I am so sick, fed up and ready to vomit with projects and hopes and expectations.

Merton was looking forward to an informal visit from a few close friends who would be visiting his monastery. Perhaps he suspected that his friends would feel pressure to "make the most of the time." Perhaps he was reacting to what felt like oppressive planning of projects in his monastic community. As a monk, Merton led a fairly scheduled life, one that perhaps left less time than he wished for purposeless freewheeling.

I am sometimes the one who saddles myself with plans and pressures. Recently I've been learning to trust God's guidance. Often my tendency to be organized and structured has been more about control than simply seeking to be responsible. Perhaps, like Merton, I'm becoming a bit more Quaker-like as I age.

. . . .

Do you tend to be a more structured person or a more freewheeling, spontaneous person? What happens when circumstances move against the direction of your preferred mode?

OUR FATHER'S RESOURCES

See what great love the Father has lavished on us, that we should be called children of God! And that is what we are! (1 John 3:1)

I'M STILL LEARNING HOW to access the abundance of God as a child of God. As a son of my heavenly Father, I have access to all the grace and goodness he provides. I know this and am growing to rely on the abundance my Good Shepherd provides.

Prompted by that thought I recently wondered, *What if I pray? What if I ask the Father plainly and trustingly for what I need right now? Isn't this what Jesus has told us to do?*

Jesus did indeed teach this, and he did so with a vivid word picture—an analogy—that even those who aren't parents can appreciate:

> Is there anyone among you who, if your child asks for bread, will give a stone? Or if the child asks for a fish, will give a snake? If you then, who are evil, know how to give good gifts to your children, how much more will your Father in heaven give good things to those who ask him! (Matthew 7:9-11 NRSV)

Ask. Search. Knock. These are words Jesus uses to talk about praying. My Father in heaven will not be stingier with me, his child, than I have been with my own sons. In fact, Jesus promised that our Father in heaven will give good gifts to those who ask him. Prayer is a relational encounter with a loving Father. It is asking. It is searching. It is knocking. And, thankfully, prayer leads us to places of receiving, finding, and entering in.

. . . .

Rather than thinking about how you want God to change your situation, what might he give you, in your own soul, that would help you in this situation?

SETTING OUR HEARTS AT REST

If our hearts condemn us, we know that God is greater than
our hearts, and he knows everything. (1 John 3:20)

WHEN OUR OWN HEARTS speak against us, John wants us to know how to find rest in God's presence (1 John 3:19). My own heart is sometimes full of antagonistic thoughts. My heart is sometimes restless with anxiety, distraction, racing thoughts, or frustration. It helps if I read a passage like the one above slowly. This quiets my soul. What God says is full of peace, grace, and goodness, and he puts my heart and mind at rest.

The main thing John wants me to experience freedom from in God's presence is self-condemnation. When I pay attention, I notice that my thoughts can be self-accusing. I find it easy to notice my inadequacies and shortcomings. I'm tempted to condemn myself. It doesn't help me much. Condemnation is different from conviction. Condemnation is a guilty dead end. True conviction leads me toward the path of holy change. Self-condemnation doesn't bear good fruit. Conviction is a gift from God to help me.

I find this prayer arising from within me: *Empower me by your life, Father, to walk as Jesus walked and to respond with obedience to what he says. When I fail to do so, give me an eye and ear for your mercy and grace. Keep me oriented toward you. Help me resist the voice of condemnation that would turn me away from you. There is life with you. There is only death in condemnation.*

. . . .

In what ways does your heart feel restless in God's presence? Rather than avoiding that restlessness, talk to God about it. Let God bring grace and peace to displace any accusing or condemning thoughts.

RELYING ON GOD'S LOVE

And so we know and rely on the love God has for us. (1 John 4:16)

IT'S GOOD TO KNOW that God loves us. It's even better to come to deeply rely on God's loving gaze toward us. But it's more than a facet of my statement of faith. It is a living reality I can lean into. I can settle into the affection of the Father for me. Divine love can be the place where my very body feels at home.

But at certain moments of my life I struggle to believe that God loves me. I imagine I've done something (or failed to do something) that has diminished God's care for me. Instead of letting God's love displace my anxiety and fear, I let fear displace my confidence in God's love.

I pray, *Father, may your Spirit enable me to be more deeply immersed in the height, the depth, the breadth, and the width of your love for me. Help me to know your love even if I can't fully comprehend it. Open my eyes to see your loving countenance. Open my ears to hear your words of affirmation.*

And when I stop to listen, I sense the Spirit saying, "My son, I enjoy you because I made you. You belong to me and I care for you. The Son has opened the way for us to enjoy unbroken friendship, so make yourself at home in my love today. Rest in my love and then share my love with others who will cross your path. That is how you can have confidence of my presence in you and my love for you."

. . . .

You likely know God loves you. Why not ask God to help you rely on his love for you a bit more?

LOVE DISPLACES FEAR

There is no fear in love. But perfect love drives out fear,
because fear has to do with punishment. The one who
fears is not made perfect in love. (1 John 4:18)

WHEN ONE OF OUR SONS was young, he struggled with nightmares and fear of the dark. He came into our bedroom nightly with fears of imagined monsters and scary dreams. I would explain there wasn't anyone in his room who could hurt him. I reminded him Mom and Dad were down the hall to keep him safe. Would it surprise you that my accurate comments were of little help?

One night our son came into our room crying again, and again my logical words did little good. I sensed the Spirit nudging me in a different direction, so I invited my son to crawl into my arms so I could embrace him. I then asked him to close his eyes and look for Jesus where the monsters were.

After a few moments of silence, my son said, "I see him." I asked what he was doing and my son said, "He's sitting on a throne."

"Is he saying anything?"

He answered, "He says I can come sit on his lap if I want to."

"Do you want to?"

My son mumbled, "Uh huh," and was asleep in minutes. That moment of prayer took a minute (far shorter than my helpful lectures).

A few nights later my son came to tell me he was afraid again. I asked him to look for Jesus. This time Jesus was walking on a crowded beach. I asked if Jesus was doing or saying anything.

My son said, "He's inviting me to join him."

Fear evaporated in the presence of the love of Christ.

. . . .

What are your fears these days? How might you look for Jesus present with you in those very fears?

GOD DOESN'T BURDEN US

*In fact, this is love for God: to keep his commands. And
his commands are not burdensome. (1 John 5:3)*

HUMBLY FOLLOWING GOD'S COUNSEL is the best evidence of my loving posture toward God. If I claim to know what God says but do not orient my life around that guidance, one would rightly assume I don't think God's counsel is as good as I claim. I love and treasure what God says, so I follow the goodness of that guidance as best I'm able.

God's commands are not a burdensome ordeal. They are training for a well-lived life. God's commands do not rob us of life. They lead us into a better life. It's tragic when we turn the commands of God into heavy "need-tos" and "have-tos" and "shoulds." If we got the chance to be coached by a mentor we admired, would we feel they were dumping obligations on us? Wouldn't we rather look forward to trying out their good advice because we believed in their message?

God's guidance is not burdensome for another reason. God does not tell us to do something and then leave us to figure out how to do it on our own. God's own Spirit is with us to continue guiding and empowering us in the good ways of God. We have an ever-present counselor and encourager.

. . . .

When have you felt tempted to view something God is telling you as too heavy or too hard? How might this apparently difficult saying be an invitation to more life than you currently enjoy? Talk with God about this.

NO HOME WITHOUT GOD

We know that God's children do not make a practice of sinning, for God's Son
holds them securely, and the evil one cannot touch them. (1 John 5:18 NLT)

JOHN WANTS US TO KNOW that anyone born of God doesn't make a practice of sinning. This has sometimes translated in my perfectionist mind into, "We know that anyone born of God never does anything wrong." But earlier John tells me if I claim to have no sin, I'm only fooling myself and refusing to accept the truth (1 John 1:8). He even says that if I claim I have not sinned, I am calling God a liar (1 John 1:10).

My scrupulous mind is left with a question. Understanding myself to be born of God, have I continued to sin? If the question means, "Have I done wrong or come up short since becoming a Christian in my teens?" the answer is "Yes, and often." But if the question is, "Has it been my purpose over the years of my adult life to manage my life without God?" the answer is, "No." I have come to my senses and longed to be free from wayward impulses that linger.

This is evidence of my birth into a new family. It has been my longing to be more at home in this heavenly family. I have sought to let myself be protected from every distorted desire that has not yet died. I have asked forgiveness many times for when I've fallen short. But I keep coming back. I have kept receiving mercy and grace in moments of need. Those bent on being at home without God don't do that sort of thing.

. . . .

How does this way of understanding "does not continue to sin" strike you?
Does it feel helpful? Does it feel hopeful? Talk with God about this.

AT HOME IN TRUTH AND LOVE

*Grace, mercy and peace from God the Father and from Jesus Christ,
the Father's Son, will be with us in truth and love. (2 John 3)*

THE APOSTLE JOHN HAS much to say about truth, but he is not talking about truth in the sense of historically rooted systematic theology, right beliefs about God, or anything of a merely cognitive, intellectual bent. He is talking about spiritual reality in Christ.

I love someone in the truth when my relationship with them more and more corresponds to the reality of God's kingdom in which grace, mercy, and peace are the reigning orientation. *That* is reality. Knowing the truth is not merely knowing about God. As James says, even demons know about God (James 2:19). Knowing the truth is having a heart, mind, soul, and body that are increasingly in harmony with kingdom reality.

Jesus, I'm grateful for the places of deeper spiritual reality into which your Spirit has enabled me to walk over my lifetime. Too often I have been satisfied with a vision of truth that is more "about" than "of" or "in." Now I see myself more truly, even in my shortcomings. I am learning to face my weaknesses like an adult rather than a scared child or insecure adolescent. I love how good this is. I want to walk in truth—in reality—today. Help me do just that, Jesus. Amen.

What kingdom reality has Jesus been trying to help you see lately? What is true in the presence of God that you'd like to grow more confident in? Talk with God about this.

TRUTH DEFINED BY LOVE

Many deceivers, who do not acknowledge Jesus Christ as
coming in the flesh, have gone out into the world. Any such
person is the deceiver and the antichrist. (2 John 7)

I REMEMBER HEARING a lot about the antichrist as a young believer. I came to faith in a church that majored on preaching about the end times and apocalyptic themes. It's taken a while, for example, for me to recover my love for the book of Revelation.

But hear what John says about the kind of person who is a deceiver and antichrist: it is the person who denies Christ came in the flesh. Perhaps more important, it is the person who does not walk in obedience to what Christ commands. The simplest definition of what it means to be "anti-Christ" is to be disobedient and unloving.

If we claim to be followers of Jesus, then the clearest evidence of that is living in the way of Jesus and seeking to follow Christ's example of obedience. Obedience is simply a way of staying put in the love of God—of receiving his love and showing his love to others. Love is the greatest command. Love is the surest sign we are living in Christ, wherever he has planted us.

The command of Jesus is that we walk in love, especially in relation to one another. It is in this light that I can recognize the nature of those deceivers who deny Christ's incarnation to be among us. They do not walk in love. They seek self-defined, self-serving outcomes.

We do not want to be like those who live counter to the purposes of Christ.

. . . .

How is Christ inviting you to join him in his intention to love the world today? How might you live in line with Christ's command to love? Think of a specific step you can take today.

WELCOMING GOD INTO OUR WEAKNESS

When I saw him, I fell at his feet as though dead. Then he placed his right hand on me and said: "Do not be afraid. I am the First and the Last. I am the Living One; I was dead, and now look, I am alive for ever and ever! And I hold the keys of death and Hades." (Revelation 1:17-18)

THE LAST OF JESUS' TWELVE DISCIPLES to die, the apostle John wrote that he had been exiled to the island of Patmos by Rome "because of the word of God and the testimony of Jesus" (Revelation 1:9). John had been preaching about the resurrected Jesus, so a fed-up Roman government sent him to Patmos where he would be preaching to no one.

While John was on Patmos, the resurrected Jesus appeared to him, and John "fell at his feet as though dead." I might have fallen over, too, had I seen this vision of the glorified Jesus who spoke to the terrified apostle: "Do not be afraid."

Jesus speaks similar words of courage, peace, and empowerment to help us in our life and our work. Even though it is work that I do imperfectly, it is work that Jesus has given me and is continually training me in.

I am keenly aware of my weaknesses and failures. I never want those to detract from the purposes of God in and through me. I invite you to join me in these intentions: I will focus on God's great faithfulness, on the power he offers me when he calls me to a task, and on listening for his guidance.

. . . .

List a personal weakness or two you tend to dwell on or a potential failure you fear. For each item, also record a line from Scripture you can focus on when that weakness or failure is at the forefront of your mind.

DOING FIRST THINGS AGAIN

*Yet I hold this against you: You have forsaken the love you
had at first. Consider how far you have fallen! Repent and
do the things you did at first. (Revelation 2:4-5)*

THERE IS A BATTLE within me in my contemplative journey with Jesus.
My experience of felt presence, clear guidance, and easy provision is not
always the same as the sweetness and warmth of my early days in Christ.
There come times when I feel the apparent absence of God more than God's
presence. There are moments when I wait for guidance or provision that
seems delayed.

With that in mind, I don't think Jesus is urging us to return to some idyllic
early season in our journey with him. As I write these words, Gem and I have
been married three and a half decades. The love we share today is different
from the honeymoon feelings of our early marriage. I think our love today
is far better, like a costly, well-aged vintage, than our early excitement and
easy romance.

Jesus' invitation here is to repentance, not necessarily early-stage romance.
God is inviting us to deepen our original commitment. In marriage language,
God is inviting us to say and do our "I do" again. The greatest graces of God
are not the most emotionally dramatic or intellectually stimulating. Rather,
great grace touches and transforms us at the deepest levels of our being.

In the process of helping me trust him more, God burns away attachment
to things rooted in human preferences. The contemplative life weans me from
being attached as an adult to something I needed only as a child. He seeks to
wean me from needing impressive insights and dramatic feelings to prove
God is present and loves me.

. . . .

**What would it look like for you to refresh your first devotion to Jesus?
How might you express this kind of loving communion?**

PART THREE

LIVING IN
UNHURRIED
COMMUNITY

HOPING AGAINST HOPE

Against all hope, Abraham in hope believed and so became
the father of many nations. (Romans 4:18)

ABRAHAM HAD BEEN GIVEN the promise of a son when he was in his seventies and Sarah was well past her childbearing years. God offered Abraham the hope of a child, but it was a thin hope from any human perspective.

There are times when I seem to see the unseen and believe with hope in what God has promised. The difference is one of focus—where am I setting my gaze? Am I more attentive to my seemingly hopeless circumstances or to the voice of the God of every hope? The latter is how I am learning to trust God and hope against hope.

Paul describes Abraham's trust in God as being "in hope." Hope is the soil in which faith grows, the atmosphere in which trust breathes, the refuge within which confidence grows. Abraham trusted God as he hoped in God and his faithfulness. His situation gave him little hope to trust God for the gift of a son.

Abraham had confidence in God when he gazed at God's promise and his capability to keep his promise. He didn't waver because he believed that God could accomplish what he promised, regardless of his circumstances.

Simply put, Abraham learned over the years and through his own faith failures that God was faithful. Even when the promise seemed to be a long-gone possibility, he honored the character of God (Romans 4:20). He grew to be fully persuaded that God, being who he is, was more than able to fulfill what he had promised (Romans 4:21).

. . . .

In what ways might you be hoping in outcomes from God more than hoping in God himself? Think and pray about that idea.

A DARKER SHADE OF GRACE

We boast in the hope of the glory of God.
Not only so, but we also glory in our sufferings,
because we know that suffering produces perseverance. (Romans 5:2-3)

IN THIS PASSAGE PAUL mentions two ways he's learned to live in joy, and both are rooted in hope. He speaks of having hope for our good end, and he finds hope along the present journey.

First, he speaks of the more obvious source of rejoicing, the hope of sharing in God's glory. What a remarkable hope that is! The very idea that we will come to share in God's magnificence and grandeur in an obvious and visible way overwhelms me.

But Paul also speaks of rejoicing in our sufferings. This source of joy is not so obvious. Paul's "not only so" acknowledges that this "glory in our sufferings" does not come as naturally. Connecting joy and hope with sufferings isn't easy. I'm more likely to say, "Get me out of here!" than "What a joy!" I'm still learning.

So Paul's words about rejoicing are two perspectives on the same reality. The joy we find in the hope of God's glory is an anticipated perspective. We rejoice in who we hope to become by the grace of God. The joy we can find in suffering is the recognition that testing in our journey produces in us that which we most deeply and truly desire. We rejoice in God's faithful shaping of our lives, even through painful means.

Suffering produces joy indirectly. I experience joy in my hardships and sufferings because I know, whether by unseen faith or by reflecting over my journey so far, that God is causing me to grow more rooted along the way.

. . . .

How have you experienced these two ways that Paul finds joy in his life?

SIN DOESN'T OVERWHELM GOD

But where sin increased,
grace increased all the more. (Romans 5:20)

NO MATTER HOW FAR we fall into failure and disobedience, coming into the presence of a holy God does not pollute him but cleanses us. A mountain of failure is dwarfed by God's measureless mercy. If I am tempted to make much of my sense of transgression, I can make more of God's grace.

One of the desert fathers said, "If a spark can set the sea on fire, that will be the day that your sins will pollute his purity." If I drop a match into the ocean, there will not be breaking news about a fiery cataclysm. The faint sound of the flame extinguished is easily drowned out by the roar of waves. When I bring my transgressions to the ocean of God's mercy, the same thing happens.

It doesn't take a lot of effort to fall into a pit. It takes even less effort to stay in it. What's inspiring is witnessing the one who finds courage to rise up—to repent. The enemy of our souls may laugh at our fall, but he'll be sorry when he sees us rise up stronger.

I am sometimes painfully aware of my line crossings. I try to fill my soul with stimulating experiences rather than good words from you. I let a season of plenty become more my focus than being rich toward you. I focus on the short-comings of others and react in condemnation. But these are like little matches I can drop into the ocean of your mercy and extinguish.

. . . .

What does confession look like in your life these days? How does it help to see God's mercy as greater than any wrong you've done?

RULES THAT DON'T WORK

But sin, seizing the opportunity afforded by the commandment, produced in me every kind of coveting. For apart from law, sin was dead. (Romans 7:8)

LAW HIGHLIGHTS SIN IN my life but doesn't cause it. A magnifying glass makes it easier to see something but does not create the something I see. Rules about what is good or not, excellent or ugly, simply highlight what may be wrong or even offensive. The impulse to do wrong is often provoked by the rules that prohibit that wrong. My lust, greed, or envy is not interested in those rules. In fact, those rules serve only to remind those misdirected desires what they think they want.

Paul is saying that sin is dead when the law is not in focus. If I live in relationship with God in the power and guidance of his Spirit, this puts my wrong impulses to death. When I turn the guidance of God into a system of rules to follow, I'm stirring up those impulses. My primary focus is not living under rules about the kingdom of God but under the reign of my loving King. Rules apart from life in God can become death-dealing. They are right in what they declare, but I can't keep them apart from the life of God in me.

Freedom and wholeness are not a personal construction project. I receive a life in the Spirit of holiness, one God is tending in me. Legalism empowers and gives center stage to sin all over again! Legalism looks for sins to overcome; grace-based living looks to Jesus, who has overcome sin.

. . . .

In what ways do you identify with Paul's idea that law orientation has a way of provoking what it prohibits? What would it look like to live in deeper communion with God's goodness?

PEACE OR CONFLICT WITH GOD?

*Those who live according to the flesh have their minds set on what
the flesh desires; but those who live in accordance with the Spirit
have their minds set on what the Spirit desires. (Romans 8:5)*

THIS CONFLICT BETWEEN FLESH and Spirit hits closer to home for me
the longer I live. I find myself on either side of this tension at different points
in my life, my week, my moments. I let my flesh steer my life when I wander
into places where my awareness of and allegiance to God's real presence,
abundant goodness, and faithfulness wane.

In such places I find myself driven by longings for pleasure, power, or
position. I begin to believe the peace I thirst for will come from something I
do not yet have. I imagine there is something else that will somehow fill the
vast space of my soul. That's the empty promise my flesh leads me to pursue.

At other times, I can and do set my mind on what the Spirit desires, which
is eternal, alive, and beautiful. This is a way of life and peace rather than a way
hostile to God and God's kingdom. The Spirit reminds me that only God can
satisfy my deep longings. When I remember God-with-us and who God is
with me, I find my mind and heart more alive and secure. I find myself at
home in the good, pleasing, and well-fitting purposes of God. Instead of
being resistant, I am receptive to eternal life.

When I allow my mind to be ruled by desires that distance me from God-
with-us, obviously I cannot submit to God. And I cannot satisfy apart-from-
God desires from a place of abiding in God—not shouldn't but can't.

- -

**In what ways have you found yourself resistant to the life God is inviting
you to? What would you like to say to God about such seasons?**

INVITING GOD'S GUIDANCE

The mind governed by the flesh is death, but the mind
governed by the Spirit is life and peace. (Romans 8:6)

I FEEL SAD FOR the ways I still allow my mind to be fixated on and steered by desires that are not rooted in the life of God. Pursuing pleasures, escaping from reality, or chasing recognition from others does not lead me to life but to death, not to peace with God but to conflict with him and his way. Why do I still allow myself to be driven by such empty thoughts?

Paul uses the word "govern" here to help me understand. When I allow my desires apart from God to direct and manage my life, I find life draining from me rather than constantly renewing me. When I allow my surface desires, which are twisted or hijacked by voices out there, to dominate my decisions, that turbulence distracts me from my truer desires in God.

I wonder what all this might sound like as a personal invitation from God.

"Alan, living according to the flesh means you've set your mind on desires apart from me. If you live in accordance with my Spirit, you set your mind on what I desire. You can discern what is ruling you by whether you find yourself experiencing life or death, peace or inner resistance. Let me rule your mind and so rule your life. You'll find you're able to live according to my guidance and in my way. And you'll find it to be a path of life."

. . . .

How would you like to invite God to give direction—to govern—places in your life that have been resistant to him? If God's voice were to come now, what might that invitation to trust and follow sound like?

ALIVE IN THE SPIRIT

You, however, are not in the realm of the flesh but are in the realm of the Spirit, if indeed the Spirit of God lives in you. And if anyone does not have the Spirit of Christ, they do not belong to Christ. (Romans 8:9)

WE DO NOT LIVE our lives—make ourselves at home—in the realm of the flesh but in the realm of the Spirit. If the Spirit of God lives in us (and the Spirit does), then our life is rooted in the life of God and is not separate from it. The Spirit who raised Jesus from the dead is alive in us. The Spirit will raise us where we have been lifeless.

When Paul says, "If indeed the Spirit of God lives in you," the word "if" could also be translated as "since." I've sought to live my life in Christ for more than forty years now. I have the Spirit of Christ and I am alive in Christ. This isn't a question but rather a statement of faith and trust. I am given life—a phrase Paul uses twice in these verses—by the Spirit of Christ who lives in me.

What a remarkable reality! The Spirit who raised Jesus Christ from the dead is *in* me, bringing life to me today. Now. Here. Actually. The very Spirit of Christ gives life to this mortal body of mine because of and by his presence within me.

. . . .

How alive do you feel these days? If you answered, "Very alive," take time to give thanks to the Spirit of Jesus who gives you life. If you answered, "Not very alive," how might you allow yourself to trust the real presence of the Spirit of Christ in you, bringing life to you? Take a few moments to talk with God about this.

A GOOD DEATH

And if the Spirit of him who raised Jesus from the dead is living in
you, he who raised Christ from the dead will also give life to your
mortal bodies because of his Spirit who lives in you. (Romans 8:11)

As I grow older, I feel the reality of my body's mortality in ways I didn't in decades past. Back then, mortality was about the last thing on my mind. Now I find myself reflecting on it. I am more aware now that this body will not live forever, even as I trust that I will live in God's kingdom forever.

But this mortal body that is dying is indwelt by the Spirit who raised Jesus from the dead. The death of my mortal body, while it is closer now than ever before, is not the biggest reality about me. For the Spirit of resurrection dwells in this body.

I'm not trying to be morbid. In fact, when I was on retreat at a nearby monastery, I remember hearing monks in their compline prayers closing out the day with the words, "May the Lord Almighty grant us a quiet night and a good death." When I first heard the monks pray these words, I found them a bit alarming and even distressing. Over time, I began to see them as words of grace and peace.

Today, God's Spirit lives in me. I can and will, by grace, remember this fact. *Spirit, enable me to know and rely on your life that is in me today, filling me to overflowing. May the work I do, the conversations I have, and whatever other tasks I engage in be touched by this reality.*

. . . .

Do you ever think about your eventual death? If you do, how does it make you feel? How might the presence of the Spirit of resurrection bless you in such seasons of thought and prayer?

TALKING BACK TO GOD

Who are you . . . to talk back to God? "Shall what is formed say to the
one who formed it, 'Why did you make me like this?'" Does not the
potter have the right to make out of the same lump of clay some pottery
for special purposes and some for common use? (Romans 9:20-21)

READ PAUL'S FIRST QUESTION again. Do you find it a bit jarring? I do.
We live in a day when the average person doesn't seem to hesitate to "talk back
to God." We have rights! We deserve freedom of speech, freedom to gather,
and freedom to talk back to God!

Paul's point, however, is that since God has made us, do we—that which
is made—have the right to talk back to the Maker? Paul says no. What if you
were a potter? Wouldn't you feel free to make special pottery and common
pottery as you saw fit? Can you imagine a common pot saying, "Hey, you
didn't make me special enough!" or a fine pot saying, "I would have preferred a simple existence of daily use by people. I don't like sitting on a shelf
being admired."

Note that Paul doesn't appear to be talking about the holy model of lament
we see in the Psalms but about a strident, self-willed contention. God welcomes our honest doubts and questions. Talking back to God is different. It's
when I call into question his good intention and his good work in and around
me. The reality of my own weaknesses and nearsightedness might enable me
to realize I just don't have as much perspective as God does.

Still, I'm tempted. I'm learning that no matter how I view my life or circumstances at present, I have a God who is fully loving and merciful, fully
mighty and sovereign, and still fully God.

. . . .

**What words describing God's nature are most helpful to you in places of
reaction that rise within? (Examples could include *loving, merciful,
gracious, mighty, sovereign,* and so on.)**

CHOSEN AND BELOVED

As [God] says in Hosea:
"I will call them 'my people' who are not my people;
and I will call her 'my loved one' who is not my loved one." (Romans 9:25)

GOD INCLUDES ME AMONG "his people" even though I was not born among his people. He calls me "beloved" even though I did not grow up knowing myself as one of his beloved. And he loved me in my childhood when I was still unaware of his presence with me. God chose me when I felt unchosen.

God wanted (and wants) me as one of his own. That is humbling and amazing to me. I have been adopted to be God's son. When I stop and think about this, I am awestruck and speechless.

But to be honest—and I'm guessing this won't surprise you—I don't always feel beloved by God. But feelings like these are usually rooted in an obsessive focus on my failings, which seem to say I'm not nearly as loveable as I wish. When I get to the point where I am no longer staring at myself but instead gazing at the blinding beauty, the sheer goodness, the deep love of God, then I am more able to feel and trust my belovedness. I long to know and trust this belovedness in the depths of my heart more and more. Perhaps this is your hunger and thirst as well.

. . . .

What, if anything, tempts you to feel less than beloved by God? How might you be focusing on these obstacles more than on the loving face of God shining on you?

CHOSEN BY GRACE

So too, at the present time there is a remnant chosen by
grace. And if by grace, then it cannot be based on works; if it
were, grace would no longer be grace. (Romans 11:5-6)

GOD SPEAKS OF MAKING choices based on grace. Grace is less often the basis of my own choices. I choose things that are impressive. I too often choose based on outward appearances. I'm drawn to what is eye-catching. And then I assume God makes choices for the same reasons I do. But God didn't choose me because of something exciting about me.

Whatever good there is in me is a gift of the same grace by which God has chosen me. And if the truth were fully known, there are plenty of reasons for God not to choose me if I'm comparing résumés. God chose me because God is generous.

God either chooses by assessing what we've done (or left undone), or God chooses based on generous grace. These are two very different reasons to make choices. If God is comparing our moral inventories, then grace isn't grace anymore. I'm not happy with the language of grace in the church as a theological category with little practical effect. Grace is not merely a critical salvation marker. It is a way to live and treat one another.

Paul speaks of grace that is no longer grace. It is a grace that has been emptied of gracious content. I would much rather live by grace that is more richly grace than ever before. I want to find myself at home in God's grace and then treat others with kindness, generosity, and holy acceptance. Let's aspire to live grace that really is grace.

. . . .

How might the reality of grace have grown thin for you? How might God wish to restore your sense of his generosity toward you and through you to others?

LIVING WORSHIP

Therefore, I urge you, brothers and sisters, in view of God's
mercy, to offer your bodies as a living sacrifice, holy and pleasing
to God—this is your true and proper worship. (Romans 12:1)

FIRST, IT IS UNFORTUNATE that the word "worship" has, for many, come to be limited to an experience we can have only in an auditorium with musical experts present. Worship is more than a shared musical experience.

Those who lead us in worship would do well to lead us in a way that cultivates a lifestyle of worship in our everyday lives. How good it is when those who lead the people of God in worship inspire them with a vision of God they can take with them and continue to respond to.

When we gather for worship, the most important thing happening is not just the amazing activity of a few trained and gifted leaders but the opportunity for us all to refresh our vision of God and respond to the goodness, beauty, and truth of this God we see more clearly. We learn to discern God's presence and see that presence more truly so we can respond with worship in all our moments.

Those who lead us in sung worship are a great gift to us. They do their work best when they point away from their giftedness to the Giver of every good gift. They serve us best when they focus their full attention on the God they are worshiping and resist the temptation to capture the admiration of God's people for themselves. They can refresh for us a vision of God's mercy and grace that inspires us once again to offer ourselves—body, soul, and spirit—in real and fitting praise.

. . . .

What has worship with music meant to you lately? What has worship without music looked like?

THE BEST FOUNDATION

*By the grace God has given me, I laid a foundation as a
wise builder, and someone else is building on it. But each
one should build with care. (1 Corinthians 3:10)*

HERE IS MY PRAYERFUL paraphrase of 1 Corinthians 3:10-15:

*By the grace you have given me, Father, I have ministered in the lives of
others—laying the foundation of Jesus Christ and building on that foundation.
Enable me to become more skilled to build in the same Spirit as you do. Thank
you for the honor of building in the lives of women and men over the years.*

*May you lead those who continue this building to use materials that last, like
gold, silver, and precious stones. May I continue to take care as to how I build
in my own life and in the lives of others. There is no better foundation on which
this life of faith can be built than Jesus Christ.*

*Jesus, you are my security, my stability, and the reference point of my life.
Everything I am and everything I do flows from you. I don't want to presume I
already know exactly what needs to be done. I always want to be learning from
you. Many popular ideas about what I should do are shaped more by the culture
than by the Spirit. Everything I do will face the test of eternity. Conventional
wisdom and its fruits aren't going to make the cut.*

*I long for what I am building to survive into eternity. I want to experience
the joy of seeing that you were at work through me in ways that endured. I
would be heartbroken if much of what my life has been about was temporary
and not eternal.*

. . . .

**What in this passage intersects with your experience these days? Talk with
God in the spirit of this passage.**

BEING A TEMPLE

Don't you know that you yourselves are God's temple and that
God's Spirit dwells in your midst? (1 Corinthians 3:16)

TODAY, I'LL CONTINUE TO personalize 1 Corinthians 3 as a prayer:

It's good for me to remember we are your temple and your Spirit lives in us—in each of us and in all of us. The church we're all building is a place of worship first and foremost. It is not a place of commerce or of busyness. It is a place to honor and acknowledge you as God alone. Anyone who seeks to destroy this temple made up of your people will have you to contend with. It's a place where you dwell and are honored. It is a sacred place.

I realize how easy it is to deceive myself. I can get caught up in popular standards and pursuits. But you don't treasure or affirm the same things my culture does. It is better for me to be considered a fool in this world if I am wise by kingdom standards. Conventional wisdom doesn't look so wise next to you. The big ideas of the know-it-alls won't mean much in the end. They'll have nothing to brag about.

Protect me from measuring myself against this important person or that important group. You are the one who measures me well, and I have a share in all that is Christ's. The most popular Christian leader, in the end, is simply my brother or sister. This doesn't demean them. It's a statement of our equal standing before you. There is one family of Christ, and we are finding ourselves at home together in God.

. . . .

Was there something in this prayer that caught your attention? How would you like to talk with God about that?

BREAKING BAD HABITS

No temptation has overtaken you except what is common to mankind. And God is faithful; he will not let you be tempted beyond what you can bear. (1 Corinthians 10:13)

REGINALD SOMERSET WARD in *A Guide for Spiritual Directors* writes:

> In the case of habitual sin the choice of the will is confronted not only by the temptation of self-love but also by the strong force of habit; and if the sin is to be conquered the first step must be to break the habit. It is found by experience that the only way to do this is to lay the whole stress of direction at first on the lengthening of the intervals between the occasions of the sin.

Ward offers simple counsel to overcome unhealthy habits. Bad habits may not be easy to break, but his advice is straightforward: Lengthen the space between offenses. This sounds like the helpful advice of recovery wisdom. Can you resist temptation today, in this moment? Of course. And when tomorrow becomes today and the next moment becomes the present, can you resist again? There will be grace for that moment when you get there.

This moment is where grace is. This moment is where goodness is. Now is when God is with us. We can practice the presence of God in the presence of temptation. Persistence in little, cumulative obediences makes a big difference. This is progress.

And we do not struggle alone. Again, this is recovery wisdom. There is a relationship of spiritual direction in which one says those little, moment-to-moment nos. We have companions on the way to wholeness.

. . . .

If you are facing a difficult temptation, with whom can you discuss your struggle? Who would listen and pray with you? Who would be willing to walk alongside you as you learn to replace bad habits with holy habits?

WORKING HARD OR WORKING HURRIED?

But by the grace of God I am what I am, and his grace to me was not without effect. No, I worked harder than all of them—yet not I, but the grace of God that was with me. (1 Corinthians 15:10)

PAUL SAYS HERE HE worked harder than any of the other apostles but his work was inspired and energized by the grace of God that was with him. This leads me to think about the difference between working hard (by God's grace) and working hurried (for other reasons).

"Working hard" sets holy priorities. Holy work can see that some work is of great value (caring for the good of another person). Other work is good but of little lasting value (like reaching the goal of inbox zero). "Working hurried" tends to see all work as equally urgent.

"Working hard" remembers that the good of all work is rooted in serving the good of other people. "Working hurried" tends to turn work inward and become self-serving. It tends to see work more as managing things than helping people.

"Working hard" maintains a sense of working *with* God. "Working hurried" tends to work *for* God with a sense of distance or a sense of trying to earn something.

"Working hard" maintains a holy perspective of grace empowerment. "Working hurried" tends to drive us into a tunnel vision orientation. We may see our work with blinders on, running from task to task to task.

"Working hard" is rooted in love. "Working hurried" is driven by lesser motives like selfish ambition or people pleasing.

What a gift to know that God is working in us to desire, intend, and have capacity for every good work he's prepared for us (Philippians 2:13).

. . . .

Is there one of these contrasts that feels like a divine invitation to allow grace to guide and empower your work these days?

HOW THE KINGDOM WORKS

So will it be with the resurrection of the dead. The body that is sown is perishable, it is raised imperishable. (1 Corinthians 15:42)

RESURRECTION IS CENTRAL TO our experience of God. It is a key cornerstone of our living faith and our growing trust. In my Anglican tradition, we remember together that "I believe in . . . the resurrection of the body and the life everlasting." The death of our bodies is not the end of our existence, regardless of what some people think. Our physical bodies will indeed die and be buried like a seed.

That perishable body is raised imperishable—a never-dying body at home in the kingdom of heaven. A decaying body is raised a glorious body. That weak body is raised in and with power. That natural body will grow like a seed into a spiritual body.

The first thing a seed does after it is planted is grow roots. Roots precede shoots. This is how our lives work as well. If we want our lives to be fruitful and productive, death will precede life—resurrection life. Life begins with roots—invisible life, foundational life, the beginnings of sustainable life.

While I like this as a theory, I never seem to like when some part of me, or some dream or plan or vision, must die. I assume this is the end of it. But that is not how God's kingdom works. The death of anything is the first step in a different kind of life—an eternal kind of life. This requires patience and humility.

. . . .

In what ways have you experienced something that felt more like death than life in your journey? Have you begun to see anything that looks like resurrection from that place of death? This might be a good conversation to have with God.

DEATH DOESN'T WIN

The sting of death is sin, and the power of sin is the law. But thanks be to God! He gives us the victory through our Lord Jesus Christ. (1 Corinthians 15:56-57)

IF DEATH WERE A BEE, its sting would be sin. If the law were part of a human body, it would be the muscular system. What does this mean?

Let's think about the idea of sin as separation or disconnection, like a branch detached from a vine. When a loved one dies, our separation from them stings. For those of us who hope in eternal life through Christ, death stings less, but it still stings.

As a system of restrictions or imperatives, the law is what gives power to the separation of sin. Up against any unbending law, I realize my weakness and frailty. I see how imperfectly I abide in the one who gives life.

Thankfully, the truth about sin as sting and law as power gets reversed in 1 Corinthians 15:57 with the simple conjunction *but*. Those things are true about death and sin, *but* that is not the end of the story. Our risen Lord Jesus Christ has triumphed over these dynamics of sin, death, and law and has graciously given us the gift of life. Life is an engine that overcomes death's sting of sin and sin's power in the law.

I am offered the comfort and freedom of the life of God in the risen Christ. I am free from the sting of separation from God. I am free from the ways in which law empowers sin. I am free to live in relationship with God rather than trying to perform for God.

. . . .

How might the life and grace of Jesus meet you in places that sting and bring you freedom and comfort there?

WORKING IN GOD'S PRESENCE

Always give yourselves fully to the work of the Lord, because you know
that your labor in the Lord is not in vain. (1 Corinthians 15:58)

I FACE MANY SITUATIONS that make me feel shaky, but Paul encourages me to stand firm and unmoved. I have a secure place to stand in God. The kingdom of God is a place of stability and confidence for my soul. When feelings of anxiety, fear, self-doubt, or insecurity arise within me, they are not evidence that I'm no longer secure. I'm always safe in the presence of God.

I imagine Paul speaking personally to me: "Alan, keep giving yourself fully to the work the Lord has given you. Be confident that doing this work will not be empty effort." This brings focus to my work. I can learn to discern where my work is rooted in my own ideas and perspectives and where I'm learning to work *with* Jesus. I pray, *Grant me wisdom amid all the opportunities that arise each day. Help me see where you are working, what you are doing, so I might join you there.*

Because whatever work I do in communion with God will be fruitful in the end, I can confidently and freely give myself to such work. The "work of the Lord" is available to me here and now. God wants to work in and through me in the context of my present job and current relationships. May God's Spirit open our eyes to what he wants to do in and through us exactly where we find ourselves today.

. . . .

Think about the work that lies ahead of you in the next twenty-four hours. How might you envision those meetings, appointments, projects, or tasks as places for you to work *with* God?

CONTEMPLATION TRANSFORMS

And we all, who with unveiled faces contemplate the Lord's glory, are
being transformed into his image with ever-increasing glory, which
comes from the Lord, who is the Spirit. (2 Corinthians 3:18)

PAUL INVITES US INTO glorious transformation through the contemplation of God's glorious countenance. Contemplation is far from impractical or unproductive. People who have lived profoundly fruitful lives did so in the fertile soil of contemplation. The produce of frantic busyness doesn't have staying power.

The integration of contemplation and service is fruitful in both directions. Service keeps contemplation engaged with reality. Contemplation keeps service from becoming self-promotion. I've witnessed many find fresh vision and energy for their God-given work through contemplative communion with God. Service is not a replacement for but the truest outward expression of contemplation.

When our living encounter with God in contemplation grows thin, we tend to lose touch with reality and find ourselves less fruitful. Knowing truth is more than a cognitive process. Our eyes are opened to truth in the light of God's presence. We *receive* truth. We don't *achieve* truth. Truth is living and personal. Jesus is truth. We want to define truth in our human theological and doctrinal categories. But at their best these must be rooted in real communion with the one who is Truth.

We know we are in communion with this God who is Truth when our lives bear the fruit of his Spirit. Contemplating a God who is humble and gentle of heart will smooth our proud, harsh edges. Gazing on a God of mercy and grace will soften our judgmental tendencies. Contemplation transforms us, not only for our own good but for the good of our neighbors.

. . . .

Take a moment in stillness and silence to let yourself be in God's presence.
How do you feel? What might God's invitation to you in this moment be?

NEVER LOSE HEART

*Therefore, since through God's mercy we have this
ministry, we do not lose heart. (2 Corinthians 4:1)*

PAUL HAS LEARNED NOT to lose heart because the work he is doing was always a gift of mercy. Paul didn't establish a qualifying résumé and then get hired to work for the kingdom. Paul was invited in grace to join Christ in his work. When I lose heart in my own share of God's work, it's usually a sign I've forgotten I didn't choose this work, but God chose me.

When I lose heart in my service of God's purposes, I have forgotten that I serve at the pleasure of another. My place of ministry has always been something God has guided. God chose me, and God wasn't wrong about that. God decided to work in and through me for the good of my neighbor and world.

When I lose heart as I age and my physical capacities change, I make the mistake of thinking my physical energies are the most important thing about me. I am alive because God is with me. Paul acknowledges that "though outwardly we are wasting away, yet inwardly we are being renewed day by day" (2 Corinthians 4:16). As my energies diminish over time, who I am within is being renewed daily.

When I find myself losing heart because of suffering I face—whether sharp, crisis pain or long-term, perseverance-testing pain—I may have forgotten that Christ understands such pain even more than I do. He empathizes with all that tempts me to grow weary and lose heart.

- -

How have you recently been tempted to lose heart? How does it help to remember that God has chosen you and is determined to help you be as fruitful as you can be?

DAILY RENEWAL

Though outwardly we are wasting away, yet inwardly we
are being renewed day by day. (2 Corinthians 4:16)

"WASTING AWAY" FEELS LIKE a dramatic phrase to describe aging. For each of us, though, this is an outward reality. In my sixties, I'm noticing different capacities than in my twenties and thirties. I have to think about doing things I did easily without thought before. I experience aches and pains as I age that are new and surprising.

The more important part of Paul's counsel today is the wonderful news that we are being renewed on the inside day by day. I don't think Paul is talking about how our bodies renew themselves by creating new cells. Instead he is saying that the life of our soul is refreshed daily. In some ways I feel I'm growing younger inside even as I grow older outside.

That inward renewal isn't always obvious, but sometimes I feel it easier to be childlike now in ways I was too proud to be in young adulthood. The life of God is always seeking to fill me and flow from me to others. And the life of God is always young. As G. K. Chesterton suggests in *Orthodoxy,* "It may be that God has the eternal appetite of infancy; for we have sinned and grown old, and our Father is younger than we."

Renewal looks like peace arising more readily than anxiety used to do. Renewal looks like a simple interest in the concerns of others when I used to be so focused on what mattered to me. God wishes to renew us in the very life of the kingdom day by day.

. . . .

In what way are you hungry to be refreshed or renewed in your life? Offer this hunger to God in prayer.

THE NEW HAS COME

If anyone is in Christ, he is a new creation. The old has passed
away; behold, the new has come. (2 Corinthians 5:17 ESV)

JESUS WAS—AND IS—THE SON OF GOD and therefore truly worthy of
worship, but the Jews treated him just like any other young man who had
been raised among them. Some of them thought they knew Jesus because
they had watched him grow up. They hadn't seen anything divine about Jesus
during those years.

Similarly, I'm guessing that many people who knew me when I was
growing up wouldn't expect me to be who I am today. They might be surprised that the quiet, shy kid they knew then is now a preacher, teacher, and
author. They might also be surprised about my commitment to follow Jesus
and introduce him to those who don't yet know him.

I am not defined by the experiences I had growing up, nor am I defined by
anyone who sees me only in human terms. I am someone who is alive forever
because I have been—and continue to be—nourished in soul by Jesus. His
very life is feeding me so I might grow strong for the good and glory of his
kingdom. This is my reality.

If you are "in Christ," this is your reality too. Whatever your past, whatever
your growing-up years were like, you are a new creation.

What are some signs in your life of being a new creation in Christ today?
How might that surprise those who knew you earlier?

A BIAS AGAINST JUDGMENT

For our sake he made him to be sin who knew no sin, so that in him we might become the righteousness of God. (2 Corinthians 5:21 NRSV)

GOD MADE CHRIST TO BE SIN. Christ, the one who was never guilty of any sin, was made to *be* sin. He identified himself with the sin that separated us from God so that we might become identified with God's righteousness. This is more than transactional language. This is identity language.

Far from coming to judge the world, Jesus came to identify with the core problem of the world and resolve it. To the Pharisees, who had a habit of judging others, Jesus says, "You judge by human standards; I judge no one" (John 8:15 NRSV).

Like the Pharisees, we often judge things by our own standards. I might expect Jesus to begin by saying how he judges differently, but Jesus prefers not to judge. But if the judgment of Jesus must come, it is true because it comes from perfect wisdom. God does not turn to judgment as a first response. His first response is loving care. If he judges, it is an expression of that care in the face of everything that dirties or distorts what he created good.

In your life, when you encounter Jesus and become aware of your own shortcomings, how do you imagine his posture toward you? Is he disappointed or compassionate? Does he cross his arms in displeasure or extend his arms in care? He comes not to accuse but to heal, restore, forgive. What good news!

As you become aware of your own disobediences, ask Jesus to reveal himself to you as one who identifies with your sins rather than one who stands apart to accuse. What does this do to your perspective? Your emotions?

HOLY WEAKNESS

But he said to me, "My grace is sufficient for you, for my power is made perfect in weakness." Therefore I will boast all the more gladly about my weaknesses, so that Christ's power may rest on me. (2 Corinthians 12:9)

WHEN I AM TEMPTED to despair because of what feels like weakness growing in me rather than strength, I can find hope. The more I recognize my need, the more I can lean on the abundant grace of God in my life. I can't be strengthened by grace for which I feel little need. So the feeling of my weakness might just be a gift to be received rather than a curse to be rejected.

God's letting me feel the depth of my real weakness is soul training. It establishes and deepens my awareness of the breadth of my need for the strengthening presence of his divine generosity. Discovering the depth of my need feels humiliating, but it is mostly just humbling. It's only my pride that is humiliated.

Weakness may make us feel miserable, but it is not a sign of worthlessness. Rather, it is an opportunity. Instead of revolting against misery or seeking to numb, avoid, or escape it, I can acknowledge it in the presence of grace that meets me right in the middle of it. Perhaps in this way I can even boast in weakness like Paul does. I don't love feeling weak, but I love living and working in the power of God's grace.

My goal is not to solve my every weakness and always feel strong. God invites me to bring my weakness into the presence of his great grace. This becomes a point of fruitful communion with God.

. . . .

What is your usual response when you feel weak? What would it look like to meet God in that place of weakness and receive his empowering presence?

ABUNDANT GRACE

That is why, for Christ's sake, I delight in weaknesses,
in insults, in hardships, in persecutions, in difficulties.
For when I am weak, then I am strong. (2 Corinthians 12:10)

HOW DOES GOD GROW my receptivity and openness to grace? What does God uncover and cultivate in me that enables this process? I'm often tempted to think favor lies in the direction of my strengths. I imagine that God is at his best when I'm at mine. But Paul seems to have learned a different secret. He's learned that generous grace is made complete in us where we are weak.

We want to always feel strong, but I've found that my feelings of strength are often rooted more in my abilities, capacities, expertise, even self-confidence. Grace produces God-rooted, God-focused strength.

I find myself expecting to see God in my big, strong, invulnerable independence. I've sometimes looked for God in my places of success and satisfaction, of good performances and personal power. But I've rarely found God there. These places are too often areas of self-focus, self-reliance, and self-satisfaction.

I've experienced God's generous and empowering presence far more often in felt weakness. I've felt vulnerable and found myself crying out for encouragement or protection. I've felt small and in need of divine companionship. I've felt confused and in need of a wonderful counselor. I've felt dependent and realized I could depend on an ever-present, good God with me. A focus on successes and power hasn't been a grace place in my life. God's generosity blossoms in the soil of my weaknesses. It grows quite well there and bears rich fruit that lasts.

. . . .

When you come to God, do you find yourself bringing your accomplishments and successes or your places of need and weakness? What might praying in this spirit look like today?

SUSPICIOUS OF GRACE

This matter arose because some false believers had infiltrated our ranks to spy on the freedom we have in Christ Jesus and to make us slaves. (Galatians 2:4)

PAUL HERE IS TALKING about a conversation with church leaders in Jerusalem about the gospel he is proclaiming. Some "false believers" are suspicious of just how free Paul's message seems. He is not focusing on their treasured Jewish traditions. This bothers many Jews who have come to follow Jesus and still hold to those traditions.

Paul's message of grace sounds dangerous to their ears. They want him to rein that message in with traditions and practices that are important to them. But Paul refuses to make Jews out of the Gentiles who embrace his message. He is trying to help them become followers of the way of Christ. He is unwilling to negotiate this message of God's gift of life in Christ, a gift to be embraced, enjoyed, and shared with others.

There are those who see such a message of grace as suspicious. They have a whole set of treasured traditions that feel threatened by a message of God's grace being given to anyone who wants it. They feel a message of grace will only lead to moral and doctrinal laxity and sloppiness.

One sign we are living in the grace of God may be that someone is scandalized by the freedom grace produces in us. We don't seem to be as worried about things that worry them. We don't seem faithful to certain moral distinctives by which they measure themselves and others. But good living is rooted in divine grace and freedom, not in temporary human standards.

What does it look like for you to grow in grace and freedom? When have you felt stuck in human religious observances that did not lead to joyful living?

GOD AT WORK IN ME

For God, who was at work in Peter as an apostle to the circumcised,
was also at work in me as an apostle to the Gentiles. (Galatians 2:8)

JUST AS GOD WAS AT WORK in Peter and Paul in their ministries, so God is at work in us. What a humbling and encouraging thought. Paul had learned to cooperate with the work of God in and through him as he spoke to non-Jews about the good news of Jesus. Jesus is inviting us to grow in a collaborative friendship with him. We can learn to cooperate with God's work in our unique expression of service right where he has planted us.

This is good to remember. This is a good way to shape our prayers. *Father, you are working in me. You are working through me to bless others. Keep me awake to this reality throughout this day. Show me how to cooperate with what you are initiating. Enable me to work with you and not in tension with you.*

Later, Paul says James, Peter, and John recognized the grace God had given to him. I wonder if some of us struggle to recognize grace in others because we haven't recognized it in our own experience. I've come to recognize God's grace when something good happens in or through me that surprises me at least a bit.

What a gift to acknowledge the grace of God at work in each other. How powerful to tell someone else how you see God's generosity, goodness, and humble power at work in and through them.

. . . .

Where have you noticed God's generous presence at work in you or through you lately? How would you like to offer thanks and offer yourself to cooperate with God's empowering presence more fully? How would you like to ask for God's help in this?

FALLING FROM GRACE?

You who are trying to be justified by the law have been alienated
from Christ; you have fallen away from grace. (Galatians 5:4)

"TRYING TO BE JUSTIFIED" sounds like a contradiction to me. Maybe that's because I'm thinking of Paul's message of justification by grace while he is talking here about an attempt to be justified by doing perfectly everything God says. Being right with God is not a thing we can *try* to do. When I am trying to be justified, I am placing myself under law and, therefore, under bondage. Justification that is a strained, sweaty effort isn't what it thinks it is. It's self-enslavement to the law. To use another of Paul's words, trying to be justified is really alienation from the Justifier!

So if I want to be right with God, I have two choices. I can try to be justified by law (which doesn't work, according to Paul), or I can be justified as a gift of Christ's grace. The first option has the net outcome of alienating me from Christ and distancing me from the privileged place of grace altogether. The second option positions me as a recipient of continuous divine generosity. I can choose between trying and receiving.

When you think about your own relationship to God, do you have a sense that God has done what must be done to address the reasons you feel distant from him? Or are you, even in subtle ways, trying to make up for something by your own design? It's good to listen to Paul and remember which of these approaches will work for us.

. . . .

Are you trying to earn God's smile, or are you learning that God's smile is a gift of his own giving? How might you grow in your confidence in such a generous posture?

GRACE SAVES ME

For it is by grace you have been saved, through faith—and this is not from yourselves, it is the gift of God. (Ephesians 2:8)

HERE'S A PRAYER INSPIRED by Ephesians 2:4-9:

Father, there was a time when I was dead in my disobedience and ignorance. The ways of the world around me were all I knew. I was moved by my impulses in every direction but toward true life in you. I thought life was about satisfying whatever whim arose within me. I embraced that which grieves you and harms me. Nothing in that way of living recommended me to your kingdom. I was hopeless and helpless!

That's why it's remarkable that you acted out of your own rich mercy and great love to make me alive out of the empty life I was living. You raised me from my unknowing failures and willful rebellions. You rescued me from the deathlike existence I was powerless to change. Such grace! Instead of allowing me to continue seeking life where there was only death, you raised me up to a place with Christ in your heavenly presence. You invited me to be with you in eternal life now. You welcomed me into the majesty and grandeur of your great and generous grace.

Don't ever let me forget that it was you, in your great grace, who rescued me from this path of death. Remind me of your simple invitation to reach out my little-faith hand to your mighty, rescuing hand. Entering this life wasn't about my abilities, my achievements, or my résumé. These were nothing but a liability to me. Keeping teaching me how to grow in your grace.

· ·

What line in this prayerful response to Scripture is most helpful to you? How would you like to make it your own in prayer right now?

CAPTURED BY CHRIST

I, Paul, the prisoner of Christ Jesus
for the sake of you Gentiles. (Ephesians 3:1)

PAUL WRITES HIS LETTER to the Ephesians as an actual prisoner. But rather than seeing himself as a man stuck in a Roman jail, he thinks of himself as a prisoner of Christ. He's been captured by Christ Jesus. And he understands this imprisonment to be on behalf of his Gentile fellow believers.

I've never found myself in prison for the sake of Christ or for any other reason. Paul has, and more than once. But I've sometimes found myself feeling struck, even trapped in painful or unjust circumstances along the way.

For example, I felt like a prisoner of the Northridge earthquake of 1994 when Gem and I lost the only house we'd ever owned. I felt stuck in the financial realities of that painful experience.

I often felt trapped during the isolating season of Covid-19 quarantine. There were things I'd done often that I could no longer do. I felt like a prisoner in my own home. The limitations we took upon ourselves for the greater good didn't always feel good for me.

It helps me to think of all of this while considering Paul's perspective as a prisoner of Christ. He's locked up in a Roman prison, but rather than feeling stuck, he is at home there.

When I find myself in hard places, it helps me to think, as Paul does, that one, I am there with Christ, and two, I am there for the sake of others. I can find myself at home in Christ when I am in difficult situations.

. . . .

Where have you felt trapped like a prisoner, needing to find yourself at home in Christ?

A STEWARD OF GRACE

Surely you have heard about the administration of God's grace that was given to me for you. (Ephesians 3:2)

HAVING BEEN CAPTURED BY CHRIST, Paul reminds us that he has been given "the administration of God's grace." This is the language of stewardship. Paul is entrusted with the message of God's generosity in Christ, and he enjoys and shares it with fellow Christ-followers everywhere.

In the church, we tend to use the word "stewardship" in relation to finances. We rightly say we have been entrusted with financial resources not just for our own use but to be generous with and to help others. Paul understands that the wealth he's been entrusted with as steward consists of "the boundless riches of Christ" (Ephesians 3:8).

One of my mentors liked to define grace as God's empowering presence. God's way is to treat us with generosity. God doesn't give because we deserve or have earned it. God is simply gracious in himself.

And grace does not just make up for our shortfalls. Grace fuels kingdom living. The reality of God's grace tells us we are never alone in our journey. The generous presence of God is present like the air in our lungs or the blood coursing through our bodies. God's grace is the kind and good way in which God is always present with us, making us truly alive.

God is present to us in mercy and grace. God has a bias for that kind of generosity and kindness. Ours is a God of amazing grace.

. . . .

What of God's grace has he entrusted to you for your enjoyment and to share with others?

A SERVANT OF GOOD NEWS

I became a servant of this gospel by the gift of God's grace given me through the working of his power. (Ephesians 3:7)

PAUL PROCLAIMED THE MYSTERY of Christ. He extended God's invitation to everyone so they might become partakers of the promise in Christ through the gospel. Paul says God has given him grace to proclaim this gracious message of the boundless riches of Christ. Paul wants everyone to know that, in Christ, they might discover bold and confident access to God. What a gospel! What good news!

We have good news to share with the world. During what have felt like "bad news" seasons of my life, I've often sensed an invitation to find myself at home in God's good news. I want my life to be more and more gospeled. I long for my way of living to reflect and commend the good news I proclaim.

I tend to be a cup-half-empty sort of person. I can become engrossed in bad news that crosses my path or catches my ear. I can ruminate and get caught up in how *bad* the bad news is. When I do this, my mood sinks and my energy wanes. My hopefulness for the future grows thin. I am easily discouraged or troubled.

But even in my natural tendency to gaze at the dark side of things, I can learn to rehearse the reality of good news in Christ. It's not wishful thinking. God's good news is greater than the bad news that surrounds us. And we live in a world desperate for good news.

. . . .

In what ways has life felt like bad news for you lately? What would it look like to remember and rehearse Christ's good news amid the bad news around you?

LEAST OF THE SAINTS

Although I am less than the least of all the Lord's people,
this grace was given me: to preach to the Gentiles
the boundless riches of Christ. (Ephesians 3:8)

PAUL'S SELF-DESCRIPTION MAY SOUND self-deprecating, even self-condemning. But I think these humble words highlight just how much grace Paul recognizes he needs.

When I was a young Christian decades ago, I had a fuzzy idea that as I grew in faith, I would need less and less grace than I did in the beginning. I imagined that my growth might make me one of the *greatest* of all saints. It's arrogant, I know. I'm embarrassed to admit it.

But having entered my sixties this year, I haven't found that to be the trajectory of my life. I identify more and more with Paul's description of himself here. I think calling himself "the very least of all the saints" (ESV) is a way of saying the opposite of my immature vision of what it would look like to grow in Christ over a lifetime.

I need the empowering, forgiving presence of God more today than I ever have. I am coming to recognize that I need the help of God's grace in every situation, task, interaction, moment, and day.

Jesus wants to touch each of our lives in those areas where feel disabled. We need courage in the face of what frightens us. We need peace in the presence of what worries us. We need strength where we feel weak. We need the grace of God in more ways than we even now know.

Someone who is the very least of all the saints just might become great in the kingdom of God's grace.

How have you recently felt weak or "least," as Paul does here? In what way might this be an area where Christ wants to show you grace?

QUIET VIRTUES

Be completely humble and gentle; be patient, bearing with
one another in love. Make every effort to keep the unity of the
Spirit through the bond of peace. (Ephesians 4:2-3)

WHO WE UNDERSTAND OURSELVES to be will transform how we respond to those around us. God has chosen us because he wants to live in communion with us. God has made us holy—special—because this is what God wants. And, perhaps best of all, God dearly loves us.

When we are more at home in these realities, we find humility, gentleness, patience, and forbearance—what Francis de Sales calls the "little virtues"—aren't nearly as hard as they might be in a self-improvement project. But these are not popular virtues. They rarely grace the headlines of our newsfeed. We live in a time when these virtues seem more like liabilities than assets.

Yet Jesus describes himself as humble and gentle in heart (Matthew 11:29). It's not hard to find examples of each of these virtues in Jesus' treatment of others. So why are they so hard to find among God's people nowadays?

Defensiveness seems more common than compassion. Cruelty is more prevalent than kindness. Pride outshouts humility. Harshness outglares gentleness. Short tempers run right past patience. Think of our freeways. Think of our public conversations. Think of social media.

What would it look like to clothe ourselves with the virtues Jesus made famous? How might we live as a kind of antidote to the public poison prevalent today? How might our power, rather than a force by which we *over-power* others, be a gracious influence that grows out of our union with a gentle, humble Savior?

. . . .

Which of the virtues listed by Paul do you find it hardest to see in God?
How might this be an invitation to rethink your present vision of God?

GIVEN TO SERVE

Christ himself gave the apostles, the prophets, the evangelists,
the pastors and teachers, to equip his people for works of service,
so that the body of Christ may be built up. (Ephesians 4:11-12)

GOD GIVES SERVANT LEADERS to the church and gifts them in that service. Their primary focus here is to "equip his people for works of service" that build up the body of Christ. Sometimes we have focused more on preparing works of service for God's people to do. The difference is critical. God's focus is on developing people more than on getting jobs done.

Servant leaders are to focus on cultivating the grace gifts God has given each of his people. Every individual is to be equipped to extend grace to others in a unique, God-given way. As Paul said earlier, each of us is "God's handiwork, created in Christ Jesus to do good works, which God prepared in advance for us to do" (Ephesians 2:10).

God is the one who is at work renewing us and giving us opportunities to bless others. God is overseeing this project. The arrangement is not that we think of good things to do and then ask God's blessing on our plans. Instead we learn to discern the good things God has in mind and has prepared for us to enjoy and share with others.

The church—the people of God—need to experience God-given gifts of grace and walk in the personally prepared works of ministry and service that he prepared for each of us in advance. What a change in morale and motivation it is to develop people's God-given giftedness and calling and to cooperate with God's preordained ministry for them.

· ·

How has God used you to bless others in the past? How might he want to help you cooperate even more with the ways he has gifted you?

HAVING OTHERS IN OUR HEARTS

*It is right for me to feel this way about all of you, since I have you in
my heart and, whether I am in chains or defending and confirming the
gospel, all of you share in God's grace with me. (Philippians 1:7)*

WHEN I'M NOT TAKING time to pray for the people God has placed in my life, I find that my prayerlessness affects my interactions with them and my thoughts about them. To be specific, I notice my empty heart: I don't find much holy concern for their souls or interest in their spiritual growth. I don't even feel much joyful attraction to them or real desire to spend time with them.

But when I am praying often and well for other people, I experience something like what Paul speaks about in today's verse. I experience Jesus' life and love flowing through me. I find myself very much concerned about their souls and spiritual growth, and I want to spend more time with them—for their good rather than my own.

Investing time in praying for the people in my life increases my kingdom energy and awareness when I'm with them. I find myself wanting to bless, help, and encourage them and to invite them more deeply into God's kingdom purposes.

Try an experiment: Choose someone in your life—in your workplace or at church, in your neighborhood or even your family—whom you find hard to love right now. Then pray for this person regularly for two weeks. At the end of two weeks, watch for how your heart has changed because of your praying.

. . . .

Do you know of anyone who has prayed often for you? If possible, thank that person and offer some specific evidence of the positive impact their prayers have had on your life.

THE FRUIT OF UNION

Therefore if you have any encouragement from being united with Christ, if any comfort from his love, if any common sharing in the Spirit, if any tenderness and compassion . . . (Philippians 2:1)

WHEN PAUL SAYS "IF" here, he's not talking about something unlikely or uncertain. It's one of those "ifs" that actually mean "since." He's confident his readers will know intuitively what he's talking about in these four ways of describing Christian community.

It's a great gift to experience union with Christ in community with others. Christ is nearer to me than my own breath. Sharing Christ in common draws us closer to one another more than any mutual interest. I have been made one with Christ in his unity with the Father and the Spirit.

What a comfort the love of Christ for me has been over the years. When I've been anxious, the love of Christ has quieted my soul. When I've been fearful, his love has displaced that fear. When I've been sad, his love has lifted my spirits. I find such comfort in the certainty and faithfulness of the love of Christ.

What a grace to experience the Spirit of God I share with others in Christ. It still surprises me when I meet a fellow Christ-follower and find a simple closeness that feels as warm as friendships I've enjoyed for years. There is a true fellowship that is rooted in our shared belonging to Christ.

I'm grateful that Christ's posture toward me is tender and compassionate in the harsh and coldhearted world in which I live. Christ's is a kingdom rich in gentle, kind, gracious love. The more confident I am in these four kingdom realities, the more at home I feel.

Which of these four phrases either rings true for you or touches a place of longing in your heart? Talk with God about this.

RELATING LIKE CHRIST

In your relationships with one another, have the same
mindset as Christ Jesus. (Philippians 2:5)

THIS IS THE FIRST line of a hymn that speaks about the humbling, then exalting, of Christ. It is given as an example of the mindset that should mark our relationships with one another. This is especially fitting since Paul is talking to a church that is having a lot of disagreements as people fight for their own perspective rather than the good of others.

For our sake, Jesus didn't demand his rights as God but instead made himself nothing by becoming a servant. He took on and identified with our weak human bodies and was willing to experience a brutal death in that body. Jesus went to the greatest possible lengths to serve our good. Paul is urging us to be willing to lay down our selfish expectations and ambitions to actively seek the good of others.

When things are challenging, I can become self-serving. I suppose this isn't unique to me. Jesus has been a gracious servant to me, but I have not always done well stepping outside my preferences for others.

I work within a nonprofit called Unhurried Living. We provide many good things at no cost to those who benefit from them. But I must admit my hidden hope that it will all lead to great visibility. My tendency to seek benefit for myself runs deep. Perhaps yours does too.

May Jesus keep fresh before our eyes his way of serving us so we can sink into that same spirit as we learn to serve one another.

. . . .

How have you experienced Jesus serving you recently? How might that focus and empower you to seek the good of others who cross your path?

HOPE ROOTED IN GOD

I hope in the Lord Jesus to send Timothy to you soon, that I also may be cheered when I receive news about you. . . . And I am confident in the Lord that I myself will come soon. (Philippians 2:19, 24)

PAUL IS SPEAKING TO his friends in Philippi about his intentions and plans. Twice he mentions these hopes as being "in the Lord Jesus." First, he says he hopes in the Lord Jesus to send Timothy to visit them soon. And then he speaks of being confident in the Lord that he himself will visit in person.

Paul could certainly have said this more simply. Couldn't he have just told them, "I'm sending Timothy soon, and I expect to visit shortly as well"? Aren't we tempted to hear the other language as mere religious talk?

But Paul isn't speaking empty words. Paul is expressing something dynamic and substantial about his life and his plans. He conveys his intentions and expectations, but he does so with abundant hope that Jesus will make those intentions fruitful. He has plans like the rest of us, but he has learned to walk closely with Jesus. As a result, he has a strong sense of collaborative intention borne out of constant communion with the Lord.

Chuck Miller, a friend and mentor of mine, used to say we should plan well but hold our plans loosely. Planning is good, but we do not know the future. Jesus does. He may wish to guide our steps differently than we had planned. And so we make our plans in the Lord and we carry them out in communion with the Lord.

. . . .

How can you follow Paul's example and see your plans as a place of communion with Jesus? How can you view the implementing (or changing) of those plans as subject to the guidance of Jesus?

LOVE COMES FIRST

But I think it is necessary to send back to you Epaphroditus, my brother, co-worker and fellow soldier, who is also your messenger, whom you sent to take care of my needs. (Philippians 2:25)

A MENTOR OF MINE loved to talk about the way Paul describes his friend Epaphroditus. There is a sequence implied in the three words he uses: brother, coworker, fellow soldier. The language of relationship precedes language of work or battle. Paul and Epaphroditus are brothers first, and as brothers, they enjoy working and fighting good battles together.

I have gotten these out of order in my life and work. I've behaved as though the work comes first and relationship comes second. I have sometimes had high "program capacity" but low "people capacity." But the kingdom is rooted in relationships. The great commandment is about love. God wants to cultivate in us a love for one another that is central. Our shared work and battle are fruit of loving relationships.

When we live in loving relationship with God and one another, our work looks like love in action. When we focus first on the work we're doing, we begin to see signs of impatience, unkindness, and competitiveness that do not look like the way of God.

When we find ourselves working at our jobs, or perhaps in works of service related to our churches, are we focused first on the tasks, or do we give good time to cultivating our relationship first as brothers and sisters? Do we start with love, or do we start with getting something done? Praying well together before we do our work together can make a big difference. Here we acknowledge we are working in and with God. What could be more fruitful?

. . . .

How have you been tempted to put tasks and projects ahead of God's priority of living in loving relationship with one another?

A SOUL HAPPY IN GOD

Rejoice in the Lord always. I will say it again: Rejoice! (Philippians 4:4)

PAUL URGES US TO find happiness for our souls in God. We might believe happiness can't be commanded. But Paul shares a word of good counsel from experience. Before we do anything to serve God or seek to honor God, God invites us to experience his presence.

I tend to be a bit of a pessimist (and my wife says I have a gift for understatement). It helps me to begin a day by rehearsing the joyful goodness of God rather than ruminating on what bothers, burdens, or overwhelms me. Remembering who God is and that God is with me here and now nourishes my soul, brightens my perspective, and energizes me for my collaborative opportunities with God for the day.

Sometimes my prayers and my journal entries feel like spinning around my own emotions, intentions, thoughts, and evaluations. I mean to bring them before God, but I too easily stare at my troubles rather than gazing toward God.

There is a way of reading the Scriptures, for example, that focuses on what I'm doing well or what I'm doing poorly. But I can also read the Scriptures as a way of hearing the voice of God speaking words full of grace and truth to me. I can read them as a way of seeking the countenance of God shining in love toward me.

I look to God as the joyful presence that surrounds and indwells me. In this way I can find joy, live joy, and express joy in God today.

Can you imagine God smiling at you in this moment? Can you envision God truly happy to be with you now? Ask the Spirit to help you.

DISCERNING THOUGHTS

Finally, brothers and sisters, whatever is true, whatever is noble, whatever is right, whatever is pure, whatever is lovely, whatever is admirable—if anything is excellent or praiseworthy—think about such things. (Philippians 4:8)

I HAVE FREEDOM TO think about my thoughts. That's important. If I assume my every thought is me, the whole me, and nothing but me, I might allow tempting thoughts to draw me to something that seems irresistible. But if I acknowledge that some thoughts arise from my true self, some are echoes of something old and dying, and some are whispers from my soul's enemy, then I can discern my thoughts and decide how to respond.

We can attend to what is true and turn from what is false. We can aspire to what is noble and turn away from the dishonorable. We can embrace what is just and reject what is unjust. We can focus on the simplicity of purity and leave the messy mix of motives at the perimeter. We can let ourselves be inspired by what is lovely and admirable and see what is truly unlovely or unworthy.

What I think about God, myself, others, and the world is perhaps the most important reality about me. How I think will shape and move how I speak and live. This is not just a personal morality exercise but a way of remaining on God's transforming path and learning to set my thoughts on that which is good, beautiful, and true.

. . . .

In what ways have your thoughts been good, beautiful, and true? In what ways have not been? How would you like to offer God your attention now, allowing the Spirit to guide you into truth?

THE FAMILY OF GOD

Paul, an apostle of Christ Jesus by the will of God, and Timothy our brother,
To God's holy people in Colossae, the faithful brothers and sisters in Christ:
Grace and peace to you from God our Father. (Colossians 1:1-2)

PAUL SEES HIMSELF IN the role of apostle because this is what God wished. It was God's will that Paul work for the kingdom in this capacity. Paul announced the good news of this kingdom over most of the Roman Empire in his lifetime.

I am in my own roles and relationships by the will of God. He chose me to be his son and a little brother to Jesus. He chose Gem and me to be partners in life, marriage, and ministry. He chose me to pastor, first in local churches and now in a more itinerant fashion. He chose me to write.

The evidence of grace in these places encourages me that these things have been his wish. This is how he has wanted to bless the world through me. And it is far more about him than me.

Paul is not a lone ranger in this work. Timothy "our brother" is with him. There is much goodness in those two little words. Paul sees this younger man, Timothy, not as a subordinate but a brother. Despite the clear authority difference between them, Paul sees him as a member of his family and says so.

Timothy is brother also to these friends in Colossae. We are brothers and sisters to one another. This is the nature of authority in the kingdom of God. We are not rulers and servants to one another. We have one King, we are all his beloved sons and daughters, and this makes us brothers and sisters.

· ·

In what ways has your church experience felt like "brothers and sisters"? Have you had experiences that felt more like "ruler and ruled"? How were these different?

ALWAYS GRATEFUL

We always thank God, the Father of our Lord Jesus
Christ, when we pray for you. (Colossians 1:3)

"WE ALWAYS THANK GOD." This perpetual gratitude is a beautiful sign of the kingdom richly present to Paul. Growing gratitude in my own life renews my awareness of God with me. Gratitude doesn't cause the kingdom to be present but is a sign of my awareness that God's kingdom is here.

What is Paul's vision of God? "The Father of our Lord Jesus Christ." As for Jesus, God is "Abba" for Paul. God is the one Jesus came to make known to us. God is not just the Almighty and transcendent God of Israel but a Father in heaven who is closer to us than we are even to ourselves.

Paul prayed for others in a spirit of gratitude. He didn't pray tentatively or with uncertainty. He knew he was speaking to a God of generous grace. He had reason to trust that God would do more than he could think to ask or imagine for the good of those for whom he interceded. I find that I voice many of my requests for others these days as a kind of anticipatory gratitude rather than a doubtful hope.

As we cultivate a life of prayer day by day, whether a prayer of quiet presence or of grateful intercession, may it be inspired and energized by the Spirit. May God grant us a prayerful, grateful heart in this day. May we be enabled to cooperate with God in prayer in ways we haven't yet learned so far. May this inspire great gratitude in our hearts and minds.

. . . .

In what ways have you experienced gratitude when praying for others? How might you welcome it when you pray?

FRIENDS AND FELLOW SERVANTS

You learned the gospel from Epaphras, our dear fellow servant,
who is a faithful minister of Christ on our behalf, and who
also told us of your love in the Spirit. (Colossians 1:7-8)

EPAPHRAS WAS THE ONE who brought the good news of the gospel to
the Colossian community. Once again Paul uses intimate terms to describe
someone with whom he is working to proclaim this good news. Epaphras is
a dear fellow servant in the eyes at least of Paul and Timothy. There is love
and togetherness among them. The love of the Spirit should mark the work
we do as servants of the kingdom.

Epaphras is also a faithful minister of Christ on behalf of Paul and Timothy
there in Colossae. He represents them and Christ. He is faithful to the nature
of the message and to its proclamation. He is a minister in that he has been
entrusted with this good news and is giving it out in Colossae. And even
before he is a minister to the Colossians, he is a minister of Christ. His focus
is more on speaking on behalf of Christ than it is speaking to this church.

Epaphras was the one who told Paul and Timothy about the great love
among the brothers and sisters in Colossae. It was love birthed by the Spirit
of God. Love in the Spirit is a way of saying their lives were so full of God's
presence that God's measureless love filled them to overflowing. This is
always the primary evidence of the presence of God at work in a community. We are confident in the love of God for us so that we love one
another profoundly.

. . . .

Who in your life has shared good news about Jesus with you? Why don't
you find a way to express your gratitude to them for this gift?

THE GIFT OF PRAYING FOR OTHERS

*For this reason, since the day we heard about you, we have
not stopped praying for you. (Colossians 1:9)*

A SPIRITUAL PRACTICE THAT has meant much to me over the years is praying and personalizing Scripture. Sometimes I take a passage and imagine it being spoken directly to me, using my name. Sometimes I let a passage serve as a guide for how I pray for others. Here I imagine being Paul praying for my friends like he prays for the church in Colossae in Colossians 1:3-8.

Thank you, Father, for the privilege to pray for my brothers and sisters in faith. What a gift my family in Christ has been for me. I love being a witness to their faith in you and their love for one another. May you continue to deepen our faith and love as we live together in the sure hope we will one day fully realize in your presence.

I learned of this great news thanks to those who were witnesses of it to me so many years ago. It's amazing that this good news has reached through the centuries and around the globe to find me. It's impacting the entire world—bearing good fruit and constantly growing, just like it has done over my adult life.

What a gift that the reality of your grace has been growing me ever since I heard the good message from friends who shared with me. I learned how to love from your Spirit at work in and through people like them.

. . . .

Was there a line in this prayer paraphrase that seemed especially timely for you or someone you care about? Why not take a moment to return to that line and pray it for yourself or for another?

RECONCILED TO GOD

Once you were alienated from God and were enemies in your minds because of your evil behavior. But now he has reconciled you by Christ's physical body through death to present you holy in his sight. (Colossians 1:21-22)

THERE WAS A TIME when my thoughts and way of life were utterly contrary to the heart and mind of God. My thoughts were opposed to the truth of God's kingdom. That wasn't necessarily what I was trying for, but it was my effective reality.

What a gift it is that God renews my mind over time. I understand reality better than I did back then. My mind has been reconciled to God by Christ's body being put to death in a shameful, painful way. He took death and destroyed it. That which made me an enemy of God in my mind was made impotent by Christ in his body.

Christ reconciles me to God. I am in rather than out of God. I am with rather than against God. This is not my virtue but Christ's effective work on a cross. The cross is not magic. It is the place where Christ did what no one could have imagined possible—defeat death for us.

This is what I am invited to trust and entrust myself to. Believing this has changed me in every way. Belief here is more vision than mere profession. It is a way of seeing differently than I did before. This good news is hopeful and trustworthy.

Lord, have mercy and show me how to engage in my part in this kingdom work. Free me from the provincial versions of the gospel that deaden instead of enliven, that are sadly impotent instead of divinely powerful. May I proclaim the good news that reconciles people to you.

. . . .

In what way have you experienced reconciliation with God through Christ? Reflect on your journey through the lens of reconciliation.

A MYSTERY REVEALED

To them God has chosen to make known among the Gentiles the glorious riches
of this mystery, which is Christ in you, the hope of glory. (Colossians 1:27)

IN THIS PASSAGE, PAUL speaks of a mystery hidden for ages and generations (Colossians 1:26) but now made known to God's people. What exactly is this mystery? What was hidden from God's people for centuries before the coming of Christ? The mystery, as Paul describes it to these fellow followers of the risen Christ, is "Christ in you, the hope of glory."

"You" here is a singular verb. This is not just general and communal. It is personal. It is true of every follower of the way of Jesus, and it is true for each one of us. It is both personal and mysterious. Christ is in me. Not just in us, though that is true, but in *me*. By the power of God's Spirit, Christ has come to be at home in my life. This is a gloriously rich reality. There is a holy Christian mystery rooted in this reality.

Paul says the message of "Christ in you" is the message he and his colleagues proclaim (Colossians 1:28). The gospel is not just a set of ideas. The gospel we proclaim is a person. There is an element of mystery about this even though it has been revealed. The good news is news about Jesus Christ. The good life is a life lived in communion with God in Christ. It is good news that God has wanted to make known to us. God does not wish to withhold anything good from those who long for him.

· ·

In what ways have you experienced the reality of Christ in you in your everyday life? How would you like to remember this mystery more often? Ask for the Spirit's help in this.

LIFE HIDDEN IN GOD

Set your minds on things above, not on earthly things. For you died,
and your life is now hidden with Christ in God. (Colossians 3:2-3)

PAUL INVITES US TO carry with us a "things above" perspective rather than living in the tunnel vision of that which surrounds and sometimes overwhelms us. *My life is now hidden with Christ in God.* Each of those phrases speaks to me.

My life. The whole of who I am—my identity, activity, relationships, and vocation. Paul is speaking about who I really am—my being.

Is now. My life in this very moment. God does not want me to linger in the past with regrets or try to time-travel to the future in anxiety. My life is here and now.

Hidden. The deepest reality of my life is not obvious or what others see when they look at us. We are not our accomplishments, possessions, or reputation. Our true life is hidden.

With Christ. My life—my true and hidden life—is hidden with Christ. My most real life is found in relationship with Christ. My life is in communion. I am a branch alive in my union with Christ the true vine. Christ is the hidden reality of my real life.

In God. The setting of my life is not mostly the house where I live, the city in which I make my home, the workplace where I spend hours each week. My life is in God. I am most at home in God. This is my place. This is my real life.

My life is truly hidden in Christ with God. How good to have this vision refreshed for me.

. . . .

When you hear the words "real life," what comes to mind? How does this compare with Paul's vision of our lives hidden in Christ with God?

BECOMING SPIRITUAL ADULTS

You have taken off your old self with its practices and have
put on the new self, which is being renewed in knowledge
in the image of its Creator. (Colossians 3:9-10)

I'VE SOMETIMES IMAGINED THAT my old self—the one that needs to be put off—is a child or adolescent and that the new self is a mature adult. Below, I've paraphrased Colossians 3:1-11 with this perspective in mind.

Since I am a mature man who has been raised with Christ, I must set my heart on higher things. This is where Jesus Christ is. It's a place of favor at God's right hand. I can learn to set my mind on higher things instead of base things.

That childish way of life is past—as good as dead. It no longer exists. My real life—my mature adult life—is hidden with Christ in God. And since Christ really is my life, then I will be where he is—now and in future glory.

So it makes sense to put to death whatever has its roots in that juvenile way of life: misuse of sex, every desire that leads away from God, and idolatrous greed. This is the stuff that provokes God's anger.

I used to live this way when I didn't know any better, but now I must get rid of everything that grows out of anger, evil intent, or hurtful words. Lies are never helpful, since they come from that old way, which I've taken off, and are completely out of place with the new self, which is always being made new in contemplating and knowing my Creator.

In this new life, all merely human distinctions are meaningless—Gentile or Jew, circumcised or uncircumcised, barbarian, terrorist, slave, or free. Christ is everything and is in everything.

. . . .

Was there a line that seemed to especially hit home? Why?

CLOTHED IN COMPASSION

Therefore, as God's chosen people, holy and dearly loved, clothe yourselves with compassion, kindness, humility, gentleness and patience. (Colossians 3:12)

I WAS IN SANTA BARBARA once, preparing to speak for a chapel service at Westmont College. Gem and I were sitting down to breakfast at a spot our hotel recommended. We saw many customers who we could tell were wealthy by the way they were dressed. It made me think of the old saying, "Clothes make the man."

When we saw well-dressed men and women walking into breakfast, we made certain assumptions about their status and finances. Appearances make a significant impression on us.

But the young man who was serving as host that day showed us to our table with a bright smile and an easy greeting. We saw him give others the same treatment. He was dressed in his host uniform, but I found myself far more impressed by him than I was by the wealthy customers he seated. It made me think maybe we'd be better to say, "Countenance makes the man."

Nice, expensive clothes create an appearance but do not actually communicate anything about a person. There are well-dressed awful people in this world. On the other hand, this young man, dressed in his simple uniform, was communicating something beautiful with his welcoming smile, inviting words, and joyful demeanor. Countenance communicates more reality than clothes do.

I've seen well-dressed people whose faces are angry, anxious, or distracted. Their countenance speaks louder than their clothes do. God doesn't assess us by our outward appearance. We've heard that before. But we would do well to learn to look deeper than first impressions.

. . . .

What might it look like today to clothe yourself not only with attractive clothing but with qualities Paul recommends: compassion, kindness, humility, gentleness, and patience?

MAKE THE MOST OF YOUR MOMENTS

Be wise in the way you act toward outsiders; make the
most of every opportunity. (Colossians 4:5)

I HAVE SOMETIMES SEEN "make the most of every opportunity" through the lens of the Protestant work ethic and a modern productivity mindset. Paul did not speak from these frameworks.

In his far more generous vision, opportunities are God-given moments. They are encounters inviting us to unhurried presence, especially with those who haven't yet embraced the good news we proclaim about Jesus. Our time is a gift given us rather than a possession to hoard. We have all the time we need for every good opportunity God brings our way.

Often someone will say to me, "I know you're *very* busy, and I don't want to bother you, but . . . " When I was sitting over coffee with a young leader recently, our coffee was moving past ninety minutes toward two hours, and he began to apologize about keeping me so long. While I often have more requests for my time than in the past, I still like to be generous with my time.

I have plenty of time to be in conversation with people. This doesn't mean I never decline invitations or say, "I need to go now," but it does mean I've learned more often to be present where I am rather than nonpresent through soul hurry or anxiety.

I'm learning to be where I am. That may not sound like master's level coursework, but it has taken quite a while to learn and live into. In this way, I'm learning to make the most of every opportunity God brings my way.

. . . .

How do you hear Paul's invitation to "make the most of every opportunity"? How might you hear the grace and peace underneath these words?

SEASONED WITH SALT

*Let your conversation be always full of grace, seasoned with salt, so
that you may know how to answer everyone. (Colossians 4:6)*

I'M DRAWN TO THESE phrases: "full of grace, seasoned with salt." Paul has
just talked about the good news Christ has given him to proclaim. He longs
for a wide-open door to share this good news. He wants to be able to proclaim
the message clearly. He urges his friends in Colossae to be wise when it comes
to how they act and speak with those who don't see themselves being in the
faith (Colossians 4:3-5).

Paul has a simple guide to offer: let your conversation be full of grace and
seasoned with salt (which I read as a way to talk about truth). When we are
talking with those who are uncertain how they feel or what they think about
this good news we proclaim, we cannot be gracious enough. Paul wants his
friends to be overflowing with grace.

But he urges them to season their conversations with salt. There is a way
of speaking the "whole truth" that is like pouring a whole saltshaker of salt
onto a plate of food. Not very appetizing! Unfortunately, there are some who
think Paul got it backward. They pour on the salt and are sparing with grace.
Is it any surprise that not too many of these outsiders are drawn to take another taste of what's being offered?

Words that are full of grace will lead with love. They are humble and gentle
words. They are patient and kind words. They are words from a humble
knower rather than a proud know-it-all.

．．．．．．．．．．．．．．．．．．．．．．．．．．．．．．．．．．

**When you next share the good news of God's kingdom to another, what
might it look like for your words to be full of grace and seasoned with salt?**

THE SHAPE OF OUR PRAYING

Rejoice always, pray without ceasing, in everything give thanks; for this is the will of God for you in Christ Jesus. (1 Thessalonians 5:16-18 NASB)

WHAT GIVES SHAPE TO our praying life? What will it look like to grow in our conversational relationship with God for our own sake and for the sake of others?

What do we pray about? What problems feel unresolvable? We can share our honest feelings and pour out our heart to God because God cares about what touches our lives. We can welcome God's grace to be present as we navigate the challenges that lie ahead. We are not alone in them.

What are our plans for this day? We can talk with God about each task, appointment, or responsibility. We can ask that God grant us energy, creativity, or guidance as we need it. We can ask that God grow our capacity to collaborate with what he is doing. We can pray that we'll learn to join God in his work.

Who do we expect to be with today? We can remember them in God's presence. We can ask that God would provide us an opportunity to express tangible kindness to them. We can envision ways in which the Spirit of God might fill us and flow to these brothers, sisters, or friends.

What excites or pleases us in our lives at this moment? Let's offer a word of thanks. *What frustrates or grieves us right now?* Let's remember that we are in the presence of a God of comfort. In these ways we can learn to pray more and more as the Scriptures encourage us to do.

· ·

What are some of the "everythings" that will fill this day that you can remember in God's presence now? Why not take a few moments to enjoy doing just that?

PRAYER AND DESIRES

We constantly pray for you, that our God may make you worthy of his calling, and that by his power he may bring to fruition your every desire for goodness and your every deed prompted by faith. (2 Thessalonians 1:11)

PAUL CONSTANTLY ASKS GOD to realize the Thessalonians' every desire for goodness. He wants everything they do, prompted by their trusting friendship with God through Christ, to be brought to a good outcome. Where does this desire for goodness come from? Elsewhere, Paul says it is God working in us to want, intend, and do what is good (Philippians 2:13).

God's Spirit inspires us, if we'll welcome his work, to desire that which is truly good. God's Spirit empowers us to do that which is truly good. And Paul joins the Thessalonians in this work by his prayers. I imagine Paul seeing himself as collaborating with what the Spirit is doing in and through his brothers and sisters. Paul asks God to enable them to do every good, God-inspired thing the Spirit has put on their hearts and do them fruitfully.

It's too easy to see the bad intentions of others and rehearse our frustration, irritation, even disgust toward them. This is the opposite of Paul's prayer. He sees the good God's Spirit has been working into his friends, and he rehearses this good through his prayers. Paul seems to want to add his spiritual help to the initiative and engagement of God's Spirit in their lives. What a remarkable example for us to follow.

Be attentive for evidence of God's Spirit working within others to move them toward what is good and loving. Ask God to enable good intentions to bear fruit. And then watch for signs that your prayers are helping. What a fruitful opportunity!

. . . .

Why not simply do what Paul does in his prayer here? Pray the good intentions you see in others would bear lasting fruit.

OVERCOMING RESISTANCE

*And as for you, brothers and sisters, never tire of
doing what is good. (2 Thessalonians 3:13)*

I LOVE LEARNING. WHEN I engage my work from a learning posture, I'm energized and alive. When I imagine that I'm "cranking out" rather than receiving my work, I find this draining and discouraging. In *What Does Your Soul Love?* I talked about how resistance is like a wall that looks like unbreakable brick but is just tissue paper painted to look like brick. It looks impenetrable until I lean on it. But if I don't test it, it still blocks my way.

What dynamics in my life tempt me to grow weary in doing the good God has given me to do? Often it's feelings of fear, anxiety, insecurity, and self-doubt. They feel substantial, formidable, even insurmountable. But when I lean into my resistance, I realize those feelings aren't giving good counsel about freedom in God's kingdom.

One way of working fruitfully in something God has entrusted is the work of writing. When I lean into my writing as a learner seeking to share, I find myself coming alive. If I let anxiety, self-doubt, or insecurity have their way, I avoid starting the work. Instead, I fritter away my moments with okay activities that aren't my best work—answering emails or responding to social media, for example.

God has entrusted each of us with good work that will help many others if we stay with it. His Spirit will guide us, inspire us, and energize us. But sometimes we must press through that tissue paper brick wall to make our way forward.

. . . .

What "brick walls" have blocked your way lately? What would it look like to lean on them and discover they aren't as formidable as you thought?

COMING FOR THE BROKEN

Here is a trustworthy saying that deserves full acceptance: Christ Jesus came into the world to save sinners—of whom I am the worst. (1 Timothy 1:15)

IT'S ALWAYS GOOD WHEN someone tells us the truth. Here Paul shares something he has tested and that we can trust: Christ Jesus came into the world to save sinners. He didn't come to affirm the (self-)righteous. He didn't come to applaud the good guys. He didn't come to hand out prizes to the most upright. He came because we were broken, wounded, and alone. We were sinners. We needed a Healer and a Savior.

With Paul, I sense my need growing the further I go in my journey with Jesus. Paul considers himself the neediest of all. My awareness of my need for mercy and grace expands as I awaken to the depths of brokenness within me.

And, with Paul, I feel a sense of being the worst of sinners the longer I travel this journey. I am aware of how many ways I fall short, wander off, and even choose the wrong. Jesus shows mercy to the worst of sinners because that dark backdrop serves to highlight just how immense is his mercy and grace. He wants everyone to know that his mercy and grace are available to them no matter what reasons they have for feeling unworthy.

Earlier Paul says that even though he was once a blasphemer, persecutor, and violent man, he was shown mercy because he acted in ignorance and unbelief (1 Timothy 1:13). Jesus gives us grace in our great need, and he entrusts that message of grace that we might share it.

. . . .

In what ways has your awareness of need for God's mercy and grace grown over time? How might a growing need for grace be good news for you?

PEACE AND PRAYER

I urge, then, first of all, that petitions, prayers, intercession and thanksgiving
be made for all people—for kings and all those in authority, that we may live
peaceful and quiet lives in all godliness and holiness. (1 Timothy 2:1-2)

PAUL URGES TIMOTHY TO make it a priority to pray. All kinds of prayers need to be offered for all kinds of people. Paul wants Timothy to know prayer is a strategic priority for spiritual leaders. And prayer is more than merely saying words. Prayer is aligning ourselves with the heart and mind of God. Prayer seeks to discern what God is saying and doing so we might speak and act in union with God.

Prayer helps us remember the kingdom of Jesus is the foundational reality on which are built all political, organizational, relational, and personal realities. We're tempted to label our building as "reality" and to imagine that prayer is the unreal, detached-from-reality dynamic. The opposite is true. Prayer attunes us to the Real that supports and surrounds us.

One fruit of praying for everyone is that the quiet and peace of God's presence just might infuse our world. We pray for those with earthly power so they might use that power to help people and honor God. Such godliness is a fruit of prayerful friendship with God. We don't seek godliness. We seek God by cultivating a life of prayerful communion with God. Godliness is then a subsequent fruit.

Through prayer God transforms us. Our vision is cleared and focused on heavenly reality. This is what happens when we always live to be in communion (and communication) with God. This is what it looks like to offer all kinds of prayers for all people all the time.

· ·

What does prayer look like in your life? What next step might God be inviting you into as you learn to listen to, respond to, and work with God?

ALL CREATION IS GOOD

*For everything God created is good, and nothing is to be rejected
if it is received with thanksgiving, because it is consecrated
by the word of God and prayer. (1 Timothy 4:4-5)*

THESE LINES FROM PAUL'S first letter to Timothy come as Paul says a few things about false teachers inspired by false spirits. Creation is good, but good things can be distorted, twisted, and misused. Creation is misused when we exploit it according to our self-centered whims rather than with gratitude for God's good intentions.

A life that is faithful to the goodness of what God has made deals with a good and beautiful kingdom. It deals in knowledge of the truth that resonates with life. Everything made by God is good. Creation reflects the goodness of its Creator. Such goodness blesses us and others when we welcome it gratefully.

We acknowledge a goodness we did not make ourselves, and we thank God for it. We experience that goodness because God calls it good, and we enter it in union and communion with God. It's a union Jesus prays for and the Spirit works toward.

God invites us to live and then proclaim goodness. God doesn't invite us to speak eloquent words empty of goodness. We aren't to use words to idealize our circumstances. We express trustworthy truths. Wisdom is the fruit of lived truth.

God invites us today to be diligent and persevere in the good things that fill our lives today. There is good work to engage. There are good conversations to be had. May the Spirit of God stir us, awaken us, and open our eyes to the goodness that fills the day ahead.

. . . .

Reflect on your last twenty-four hours. What are a few good things God has opened your eyes to for which you'd like to say thank you?

KNOWN AS GOD'S FRIEND

But you, man of God, flee from all this, and pursue righteousness, godliness, faith, love, endurance and gentleness. (1 Timothy 6:11)

PAUL CALLS TIMOTHY a man of God. This is how Paul sees him. He sees him as God's friend. I wonder if we see ourselves that way. I wonder if we are learning what it looks like to live that way. I've aspired to be God's friend. In this passage of Paul's letter to Timothy, he's warned against living to get rich. It is tempting to believe the gospel of the culture that says we are what we have.

But what does it look like to be truly rich? Paul offers six words that describe kingdom wealth. They aren't what you'd hear on a financial news channel. They are marks of what makes us wealthy in God.

God's friend is growing in righteousness. She seeks to be aligned with God's purposes, work, and way. God's friend is growing in godliness. In friendship with God, her life comes to take on the aroma of God's presence. God's friend is growing in faith. She models growing confidence in who God is and in faithfulness to that trust.

God's friend is known for a life of love. She is confident in the love of God and is learning to love God back and love others. God's friend doesn't give up but learns endurance to stay on a good path with a heart full of hope. Finally, God's friend is gentle because God in Christ is humble and gentle in heart. Let's pursue this friendship with the one who has come toward us first in friendship.

. . . .

Which of those six marks of friendship with God feel like a divine invitation to you? What do you wish to say to God about this?

GOD-GIVEN LIFE

In the sight of God, who gives life to everything, and of Christ Jesus, who while testifying before Pontius Pilate made the good confession, I charge you. (1 Timothy 6:13)

GOD GIVES LIFE TO EVERYTHING. Trees, plants, birds, and every other living thing I see out my back window are all divinely alive. Every living thing draws its life from the living God. Life is the breath of God. Just as surely as the air that inflates and exits my lungs keeps my body alive, so the breath of God's Spirit keeps everything alive—keeps my soul alive. Paul said to his audience in Athens, "In him we live and move and have our being" (Acts 17:28). In God we have our very existence.

We live in a culture that offers a different message. It says we'll only really be alive if we seek certain experiences or associate with certain people or purchase certain products. It insists our life is elsewhere. When the world warns us we're not as alive as we could be, it can sound convincing. But our life is not in some other time or place or situation. Wherever we go, there is air to breathe. Wherever we go, there is the living presence of God-with-us.

Excitement will come and go, but joy can arise from within us, where Christ has been making himself at home in every moment. In friendship with God through Christ, we are being renewed and revitalized day by day. Life is being renewed in us. What a beautiful, generous, reliable reality this is.

· ·

How might the presence of the living God with you become the focus of everything you hunger and thirst for? How would you like to bring those desires into conversation with the living God?

LEARNING WITHOUT KNOWING

. . . always learning but never able to come to a
knowledge of the truth. (2 Timothy 3:7)

PAUL HERE TALKS ABOUT those who love their own desires and impulses more than they love the God who made them. He describes them as lovers of pleasure rather than of God (2 Timothy 3:4). I wish none of this were ever true of me, but that wouldn't be honest. There are times when I'm more interested in what I think I want than I am in knowing what God made me for.

In this I'm drawn to Paul's description of someone continually learning but somehow failing to enter experiential knowledge. We can become well-informed about various theological theories, biblical ideas, and doctrinal frameworks and somehow miss loving communion with the real God. I have sometimes felt self-satisfied with knowing about God without slowing down to cultivate communion with God. Sometimes stopping at "knowing about" feels less risky.

I'm sometimes tempted to read yet another book of spirituality without giving deeper attention to my own spiritual formation. It's as though I'm a collector of cookbooks who doesn't cook any of the recipes. I can talk with great intelligence and detail about the wonderful recipes they contain, but I cannot say how they taste. It's as though I'm a collector of maps but never travel anywhere.

There is knowing about and there is knowing in relationship. There is the knowledge that stocks my cognitive storage shelves and the knowledge that is the fruit of a loving encounter with God in Christ. I long to grow in learning that bears the fruit of growing in loving knowledge.

. . . .

In what ways do you recognize the temptation to learn about God in a way that doesn't bear the fruit of loving knowledge of God?

START WITH REST

Let us, therefore, make every effort to enter that rest. (Hebrews 4:11)

ENTERING GOD'S REST REQUIRES effort. It's more effortless to jump into tasks than to begin in God's rest. Restlessness is often easier than rest. But I've learned I do better work from a restful soul than I do from a restless one.

The gift of God's rest isn't something I collapse into at the end of a day but the place my soul begins to live in and continues to work from. I don't seek rest after what I accomplish in any given day. I work from settled rest in each moment of the day. Rest is a way of talking about our graced relationship with God that can guide and energize everything we do.

In practical terms, my first moment of each day isn't a moment of work but rest. I used to have my smartphone as my alarm, but this meant that I would take a "quick peek" at email before even getting out of bed. Inevitably I'd see something needing my attention and my mind would begin working on it.

Now I have a simple digital clock on my nightstand for those days when I need an alarm, and my smartphone charges downstairs in our library. I will not pick up that phone until later in the morning after I've enjoyed some moments in Scripture, quiet reflection, prayerful conversation with God, and a bit of writing from my soul. I remember rest, then I engage my work. This is always a more productive, creative, and energizing way than jumping straight into my work in the first moment of a new day.

. . . .

What's one way you could begin your day with rest rather than work?

THE LIVING WORD

For the word of God is alive and active. Sharper than any double-edged sword, it penetrates even to dividing soul and spirit, joints and marrow; it judges the thoughts and attitudes of the heart. (Hebrews 4:12)

WHAT MAKES THE WORD of God "alive and active," as the writer of Hebrews puts it? The biblical metaphor that comes to mind is "living water." Living water is water that is moving like a living thing. It is running water like a stream or river as compared to pond water that can stagnate because it doesn't move.

What God says is living and active. God's words haven't sat like pondwater, but the Jewish leaders of Jesus' day didn't always experience the Scriptures as living. They had a more stagnant approach. Jesus had a living relationship with the living God. The Pharisees were diligent in their searching of Scripture, but they didn't find what God was offering to them.

If they had been open to what the Scriptures said, they would have recognized Jesus as the living Word being spoken by the Father among them. There is a way of studying the Bible that stops at the Bible. The Bible is not a destination. It is a door or a window into the living presence of God. Life has an unpredictable element to it. Always. This makes many uncomfortable. It should.

If we think we can control God in the way we understand the Scriptures, we have a real problem. Jesus is the Word, and the Pharisees would have none of that. The Pharisees thought life was found in the written Scriptures. Jesus said life was found in him and that the Scriptures pointed to him.

. . . .

In what ways have the Scriptures felt more stagnant to you than alive? How might Jesus, the living Word, enable you to experience just how "alive and active" the Scripture can be?

EMPTY OUTLINES

The law is only a shadow of the good things that are coming—not the realities themselves. (Hebrews 10:1)

THE JEWISH LAW HAD people offering the same sacrifices for their sins year after year. Those offerings didn't make people whole because they were only a shadow of the future reality to which they pointed. Those continual sacrifices had the opposite effect. Instead of removing sins they reminded the people of their sins.

I've never been tempted to offer an animal in sacrifice for my offenses, but there are other sacrifices I've tried offering to make up for something I did and wish I hadn't.

"I resolve, here and now, to never do or say something like that again."

"I'll carry shame for a while to pay for my failure."

"I'll give up television for a week."

Paul once pointed out that sacrificial resolutions like, "Don't handle! Don't taste! Don't touch!" look wise with their self-imposed requirements, glaring humility, and implicit harshness, but they prove utterly powerless to change people (Colossians 2:21-23). Sometimes I foolishly offer up my self-esteem as a sacrifice, choosing to wallow in shame in hopes this will make me feel free of sin. Maybe I sacrifice my peace as payment and live in anxiety, or sacrifice my joy and live in depression.

When I make personal sacrifices in response to my shortcomings or offenses, I'm still focused on me. Hebrews counsels us to find holiness in the sacrifice of the body of Jesus Christ once for all (Hebrews 10:10). I can either remember Jesus or keep remembering some wrong I've done.

. . . .

When you become aware of shortcomings or offenses in your life, what sacrifices are you tempted to offer? Has that helped or not? How might the sacrificial love of Jesus be enough for you here?

A GREAT CLOUD OF WITNESSES

*Since we are surrounded by so great a cloud of witnesses, let us also
lay aside every weight and the sin that clings so closely, and let us
run with perseverance the race that is set before us, looking to Jesus
the pioneer and perfecter of our faith. (Hebrews 12:1-2 NRSV)*

WHAT DO YOU PICTURE when you read that you, as a follower of Jesus,
are "surrounded by so great a cloud of witnesses"? I picture something greater
than a stadium filled with a hundred thousand fans cheering for their home
team. Imagine a thousand such stadiums, and that cloud of witnesses is still
far smaller than the one described in Hebrews.

We can be glad to be surrounded by this cloud. All the faithful who have
gone before us testify of the blessings of living life with and for Jesus. If they
could, they would probably tell us how much they wish they'd set aside every
burden and distracting shortcoming sooner.

May we learn from these godly people and "look to Jesus" with a laser-
focused single-mindedness. Jesus, our Good Shepherd, invites us to know the
joy that satisfies, the joy that can help us endure whatever suffering may come.
Paul compared us to the elite athlete who looks past the pain of training to
the goal of peak performance and its prize (see 1 Corinthians 9:24-27).

We will know the pain of training in Christlikeness but remember that we
are not running for a temporary reward or fleeting praise. Ours is an eternal
reward of abiding in the very presence of God's loving favor. Jesus will coach
us in this race as much as we'll let him. As we run this race, he is right
alongside us.

. . . .

**Name some forerunners of the faith who are especially encouraging to
you. Consider the saints you know or have known in person, the saints
from church history through the years, and the saints in the Scriptures.**

DAY 352

GENEROUS WISDOM

*If any of you lacks wisdom, you should ask God, who gives generously
to all without finding fault, and it will be given to you. (James 1:5)*

I CAN'T THINK OF a single area of my life that I've got completely figured
out. I'm still learning how to love my wife, Gem, after being married nearly
our whole adult lives. I'm still learning how to love my three sons well. I'm
still learning how to cooperate with God in the work of ministry entrusted
to me. I need a lot of wisdom and I need it constantly.

What good news it is that wisdom is something God wishes to give and
give generously. God wants to help me live well. God is wonderful in coun-
seling me in the best way forward in each area of my life. Wisdom is a gift
God keeps giving.

*I sense your invitation to ask for the wisdom I need today, Father. You
remind me that you are generous with your guidance. So I'm asking again. I'm
glad you don't lose patience with how unwise I sometimes am. You don't meet
my request for wisdom with faultfinding. You'll never say to me, "Why can't you
figure this one out yourself? Didn't we already talk about this?" I have been
guilty of faultfinding with others and even with myself, but this is not your way.
You have a bias for mercy and grace.*

*You invite me to ask with confidence and not double-mindedness (James 1:6-7).
You invite me to singleness in my intention to be guided by your wisdom. I'm
not asking to collect insights. I'm asking for help in living well in your presence.
And this is something you love.*

. . . .

**In what way do you feel in need of God's counsel today? Why not simply
ask for God's gift of wisdom now?**

TESTING OR BEING TESTED

Come close to God, and God will come close to you. (James 4:8 NLT)

IT ALWAYS HELPS ME to remember that prayer is a relationship I'm cultivating more than a discipline I'm practicing. Sometimes, to help myself enter into this reality, I imagine myself having a conversation with Jesus. Below is a prayerful conversation I've had about realizing I've been testing God rather than following God.

Jesus, I realize I'm still like the Pharisees, guilty of testing you rather than drawing close to you.

"I understand why you keep your distance, and those reasons aren't rooted in truth. You are afraid of a distorted image of me that you haven't yet let go of. You are anxious that I will somehow fail to provide what you need. You could be free of fear and worry if you would trust me."

I hear your invitation to trust you. I know you call yourself my Good Shepherd, and I want to trust you. I want to believe that I am not alone, that you will never abandon me, and that yours is a kingdom of abundance. Open my eyes to see. Open my ears to listen. Open my heart to trust. I am willing to follow you—and follow you closely.

"I'm happy you're choosing to follow me. Be ready. Be attentive. Trust me. You have my help."

When you think about prayer today, imagine Jesus welcoming you into his presence. Envision his great interest, deep concern, and availability to encourage you and guide you in your life and work today.

. . . .

What untruths—regarding your sense of worth, your picture of God, your willingness to trust, even your emotions toward God—keep you standing at a distance from Jesus rather than entering into conversation with him?

GENUINE SURRENDER

Humble yourselves before the Lord, and he will lift you up. (James 4:10)

HUMILITY DOESN'T SOUND VERY inviting to the average ear. But humility is simply living in the light of reality. It is a simple surrender to how things actually are. It isn't devaluing self. It is ceasing to be obsessed with ourselves.

Humility therefore invites us to surrender. That's another word most of us don't like much. Sometimes the surrender I've offered has looked more like empty resignation than loving offering. Jesus longs to draw out of me a hearty surrender to himself.

Sometimes my surrender looks like spiritual narcissism, when I want to be seen as heroically humble by those around me. What an embarrassing admission!

Humility doesn't need a spotlight. It just needs to be grounded, quietly and perhaps even invisibly, in divine reality. Humility responds to the might and majesty of God. It is focused more on who God is than who I am.

Humility is something we choose. It is offered in trust. Humility is an expression of freedom. It can't be forced but is rather invited. It is an act of offering my God-given authority for God's use.

I cannot fully comprehend the nature of humbly offering myself to God. In a sense, surrender is a matter of faith, not of sight. I may see the outlines of my surrender, or may know one side of my surrender, but I cannot fully know and define my surrender to God.

. . . .

How do you respond to words like *humility* or *surrender*? If resistance rises, why not talk with the God of grace about this?

PRAYER: PEOPLE-FOCUSED OR THING-FOCUSED?

Pray for each other. . . . The prayer of a righteous person is powerful and effective. (James 5:16)

WHAT SHOULD WE PRAY about? Who should we pray for?

To answer those questions, we need to discern what we genuinely care about. We can ask ourselves who we want to be more caring toward. We can pray from a place of genuine care for an event, concern, or person. Our list can be focused on people in our life: family, neighbors, coworkers, and so on. When we choose this perspective—when we consider prayer an opportunity to give attention to what and who matter to us—we may desire to pray more.

When my prayers are mostly about things coming up in my calendar or on my to-do list, I often end up feeling like I'm praying about selfish concerns. I want this appointment to be successful and well-received; I want people to like what I planned; I want the outcome of my current task to reflect well on me. That's not bad as far as it goes, but it doesn't go far enough.

How much better when our prayers come to reflect the servant heart of our Shepherd for the good of those we serve. And a good place to start is to pray for people before we pray for things. We can let something of the care and concern of God for another arise within us in the form of our prayers.

. . . .

Do you struggle to keep your prayers focused on the people affected by your plans and your work? If so, why do you think this is?

COMMON PRAYER

Elijah was a human being, even as we are.
He prayed earnestly that it would not rain, and it did not rain
on the land for three and a half years. (James 5:17)

I'M TEMPTED TO DISAGREE with James on this one. Elijah seems super-human to me when I read his story. I imagine him in a completely different class of human from me. But maybe James is right.

James wants us to believe that what happened in through Elijah's prayer was not because he was different from us but because God acted in response. He asked in earnest that rain would cease, and it did. He then prayed that it would return, and it did.

Praying earnestly doesn't seem to be about speaking lots of passionate words. In the famous story about Elijah and the prophets of Baal, they shout louder and louder, hour after hour, from morning until evening, eventually cutting themselves to prove they mean what they say. Such prayers may look impressive, but they aren't rooted in confidence. They are an expression of insecurity or uncertainty.

Earnest prayer in the spirit of Elijah is about simplicity and profound attentiveness to God. In contrast to the daylong prayers of the Baal prophets, Elijah's prayer acknowledges who God is, affirms Elijah's service and obedience to God, and asks God simply to act so God's people awaken and turn their hearts to him.

Earnestness rooted in wishful thinking will not accomplish much. If we align ourselves with the heart of God, we may discern ways to join with the mighty and even surprising work of God through our prayers. Perhaps we'd find ourselves cooperating with God's intention to move even mountains.

. . . .

Do you see Elijah as a normal human or as superhuman? How might you offer yourself to God's service and seek to align your prayers with his heart and mind today?

ANSWERING SELF-DOUBT

Humble yourselves, therefore, under God's mighty hand,
that he may lift you up in due time. Cast all your anxiety
on him because he cares for you. (1 Peter 5:6-7)

IT'S IMPORTANT TO SPEAK the truth to ourselves about our identity rather than letting self-doubts and insecurities win. Often a voice whispers in the back of my mind, "Insecurity and self-doubt are a form of humility, and you're *supposed* to be humble." We are invited to holy humility, but we aren't invited to anxious insecurity.

This thought about insecurity and self-doubt is a distortion. Insecurity and self-doubt are both varieties of pride, not humility. Rather than puffing up or promoting selfish agendas, self-doubt clings to a low vision. Just about every self-hyphenated quality—self-promotion or self-denigration—is pride because of its focus on "self."

The reality is that I am secure in the presence of God. Insecurity is a perspective detached from reality. Insecurity doesn't serve God's purposes or please God's heart. My security in him honors him. This is a major piece of rethinking I continue to do. It helps no one to make a virtue of insecurity, just as it helps no one to make a virtue of anxiety or fear.

And what fruit does insecurity or self-doubt bear? Mostly, it prevents me from bearing the good fruit of holy confidence. Because insecurity dims my awareness of God with me, it does not bear the fruit of abiding communion.

In the end, God invites me to humble myself by focusing my attention on him and not on myself. I don't congratulate myself or depreciate myself. I focus my attention on God with me and learn to bear the fruit of that graced friendship.

. . . .

What has been your journey with self-doubt or insecurity? How might you pivot your gaze to the gracious, affirming presence of God with you in this moment?

GRACE AND PEACE: THE ABUNDANT BASICS

May grace and peace be yours in abundance in the knowledge
of God and of Jesus our Lord. (2 Peter 1:2 NRSV)

MANY NEW TESTAMENT LETTERS begin with a prayer that "grace and peace" will be with the recipients. I like that this good, basic reality is the starting point. After all, we very much need God's grace manifested in his generous and empowering presence. We also need the deep well-being and wholeness God's peace brings to us.

The apostle Peter wanted his readers then and now to experience both abundant grace and abundant peace, and he realized that grace and peace are rooted in our personal experiential knowledge of God and our Lord Jesus. This abundance is not just for our own benefit but also for the sake of others, as implied in Peter's words below:

> You must make every effort to support your faith with goodness, and goodness with knowledge, and knowledge with self-control, and self-control with endurance, and endurance with godliness, and godliness with mutual affection, and mutual affection with love. (2 Peter 1:5-7 NRSV)

How good it is—for us and for those around us—when we become people characterized by faith in God, goodness, self-control, affection, and love.

. . . .

What would you say if someone asked you to explain what grace is— specifically God's grace? Spend some time finding a way to talk about grace that feels natural and that people new to the concept would understand.

EVERYTHING WE NEED

His divine power has given us everything needed for life
and godliness, through the knowledge of him who called us
by his own glory and goodness. (2 Peter 1:3 NRSV)

I LOVE THE RHYTHM between "has given us everything needed" here in 2 Peter 1:3 and "you must make every effort to support your faith" that comes in 2 Peter 1:5.

This passage contains such a wonderful promise! God's people are abundantly supplied to be able to work hard for God's glory with confidence and effectiveness. The confidence and effectiveness come because we know that our efforts are fully supported by all the resources we need for the tasks of life and for godliness.

In other words, I do not need to wait for resources to do the work God has given me to do. Our never-changing God has given his people who went before us everything they needed for life and godliness, and he won't stop doing so for you or me. God promises his resources, but they may not fall from the heavens effortlessly like manna. We may be required to do some patient farming before we are able to draw on those abundant resources.

We can count on God to enable us to work persistently and wait patiently for that farming to bear fruit. Then we can be good stewards of the good harvest that comes.

. . . .

When has God surprised you with unexpectedly abundant provision, either in the work you were doing for him or in your pursuit of godliness? Comment on that experience or another that you have witnessed.

EXPERIENCING GOD

*Thus he has given us, through these things, his precious and
very great promises, so that through them you may escape from
the corruption that is in the world because of lust, and may become
participants of the divine nature. (2 Peter 1:4 NRSV)*

PETER REMINDS US THAT it is through our encounter with God's own glory and goodness ("these things") that he has given us priceless and powerful promises. God has made a great commitment to us that we might enjoy deep and transforming communion with him in Christ.

The Christian life is not mainly believing things about God but entering into life-transforming relationship with God. This is how we break free of all the ways the world around us might seek to misdirect us to that which isn't life. Not only do we have what we need now—in this moment—to live richly and deeply in God, but we are promised all that we need to continue living this sort of life.

Lust is shorthand for all the ways our human desires become detached from God or redirected away from God. We were made to want, but our wants are fulfilled in the Person who created us.

It's as though God is saying, "I promise you that I will be with you as you journey through this world that is so often alienated from me. My Spirit will help you live in interactive friendship with me along the way. This will change you. Your life will grow richer in divine qualities like love, joy, and peace. Grow in freedom from that which would degrade your life. Enter more deeply instead into my very life." Let's enter more deeply into the lasting life into which God is already inviting us.

· ·

What has participating in the life of God looked like for you recently? How might you ask God's faithful help in growing even deeper in this communion?

THE LORD IS NOT SLOW

With the Lord a day is like a thousand years, and a thousand years are like a day. The Lord is not slow in keeping his promise, as some understand slowness. Instead he is patient with you. (2 Peter 3:8-9)

"THE LORD IS NOT SLOW." This is an intriguing statement in the context of unhurried living. God is not guilty of an unholy, unloving slowness. The Lord is not slow as it relates to faithfulness. What may seem slow to us is God's patience. His patience may look slow, but it is slow with a purpose.

A thousand years is like a day, and day is like a thousand years with God. The year 1020, when the church was only decades away from the Great Schism between East and West, is like yesterday to God. This is the direction in which I usually understand these words about God and time.

But a day is also like a thousand years. With God, a single day is so full of life that it could take us a thousand years to unpack it. A single day is dense with meaning in God. There is more kingdom life available to us in one day than we can imagine.

God isn't lackadaisical about his promises. We often assume that the delays we perceive are always bad news. But here Peter says the delay of God is about opportunity. What we see as uncaring lateness is loving patience. God is always working to help us turn more fully toward him, to be more deeply rooted in him, to find our life in him. And these things take more time than we realize.

. . . .

Can you envision a way in which an apparent delay might actually be an expression of God's patient love for you and faithfulness to you? Talk with God about this.

DEEPENING GRACE

But grow in the grace and knowledge of our Lord and Savior Jesus Christ. To him be glory both now and forever! Amen. (2 Peter 3:18)

GOD OFTEN SEEMS TO give great measures of easily perceived grace to those in early stages of their faith or new places in their growth. I remember being a new believer who often experienced remarkable answers to my prayers. I felt God's presence in every spiritual practice I engaged. I couldn't understand why those who had been Christians longer than me didn't have the same joy, energy, exuberance, or faith as me. It was, at least in part, because I was riding the wave of beginner's grace.

It is as though such obvious grace helps to initiate or establish us. God often rewards the efforts of those just beginning their spiritual journey with remarkable generosity. But these easily felt graces aren't meant to last forever. God wants us to learn how to live well in challenging circumstances as well as we do in greatly facilitated ones. Maturity can live well on less easily felt grace. Such grace can establish holy patterns, habits, and rhythms in our lives that don't require extraordinary grace.

God may remove the comfort we once relied on or the grace we felt to refine our trust. It's one thing to believe in God when your every prayer is answered quickly. It is another thing to trust God in his apparent absence. Dryness may replace constant refreshment. Darkness may replace the ready glow of divine blessing. It is too easy to cling to the gifts of God rather than clinging to God alone.

· ·

When in your journey have you easily felt God's generous presence? When have you experienced a withdrawal of this felt grace? How might God be just as present to you in both?

THE WEDDING HAS COME

[The Lamb's] bride has made herself ready.
Fine linen, bright and clean,
was given her to wear. (Revelation 19:7-8)

WHAT DOES A BRIDE do to get ready for her wedding? She may spend a great amount of time choosing just the right dress. She may give careful attention to the details of the wedding ceremony and reception. She might take extra time to look and feel as beautiful on the outside as God has made her on the inside.

We, the church, are preparing ourselves for a wedding as well. A wedding is one of the ways our heavenly reunion with Jesus, face-to-face, is described. The fine linen that we will wear is not a garment we've saved for and purchased ourselves. Like the bride in this passage, fine linen is given as a gift.

This fine linen is the righteous acts of the saints. John tells me that the work of preparing myself and beautifying myself for the marriage feast of the Lamb involves receiving the fine linen of the righteous life I'm learning to live in communion with a good God. Such righteousness is not rooted in my own initiatives and strategies. It is inspired by love.

Our being made righteous over time is as much a gift as our being declared righteous is. Justification and sanctification are both pure gifts to be embraced, treasured, and lived. God our Father is footing the bill for this wedding. We are being invited to stand in the beauty that God has made possible for us.

. . . .

How are you hungry for the gift of God's "fine linen, bright and clean," to be given you? Where in your life do you long to find more harmony with the heart and mind of God? Why not talk with God about this?

ACKNOWLEDGMENTS

NONE OF MY BOOKS have been the fruit of my efforts alone. There are many who have contributed to who I am becoming and, therefore, to what I write. I'm grateful for countless mentors and friends who have counseled me, encouraged me, supported me, and prayed for me along the way. Since mentioning all your names would take pages, know that I remember you often in my prayers with gratitude.

I continue to be grateful for the team at InterVarsity Press. They published many of the books that, decades ago, shaped my young faith. I am honored to be part of their author community. I especially appreciate the help of Cindy Bunch and Rachel Hastings as my editors, and Lori Neff for her guidance and help in getting my books out there into the wide world. Thank you for inviting me to write this book.

Gem and I are grateful for the gift of our Unhurried Living team, board, donors, and other partners. Thank you for all the ways you have walked alongside us over these last six years. It has been perhaps the most life-giving season of our journey so far.

I am grateful for the partnership that Gem and I have enjoyed as husband and wife over the last thirty-seven years, and the growing partnership in ministry over those years. Gem, I can't number the times when I was ready to give up on a project like this one when you spoke words of affirmation and encouragement that got me rolling again. As I sang to you when I proposed marriage so many years ago, "These two hearts never apart."

And, finally, to my unhurried Savior, I give thanks for the gift of my life. I'm grateful for the joy, peace, and hope of your presence. Thank you for the help of your Spirit in this work of writing. Apart from you, this book would not be possible. May you find pleasure and honor in my little efforts.

ALSO AVAILABLE FROM ALAN AND GEM FADLING

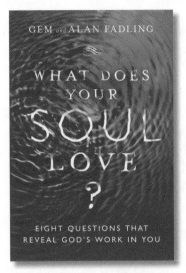

What Does Your Soul Love?
978-0-8308-4659-7

Hold That Thought
978-0-8308-3169-2

unhurriedliving

Many leaders feel hurried, and hurry is costing them more than they realize. Unhurried Living, founded by Alan and Gem Fadling, provides coaching, resources, and training to help people learn to lead from fullness rather than leading on empty.

Busy is a matter of calendar. Hurry is a matter of soul.

Built on more than twenty-five years of experience at the intersection of spiritual formation and leadership development, Unhurried Living seeks to inspire Christian leaders around the world to rest deeper so they can live fuller and lead better.

Spiritual leadership is the influence that grows in the life of a leader being transformed by the power of God's Spirit. Spiritual leadership is learning to robustly practice spiritual disciplines that deepen the roots of leaders in the love of God.

Effective spiritual leaders learn to experience the depths of God's love so they know how to lead others into those same depths. Such leadership bears the fruit of transformed lives and expanded kingdom influence.

We seek to respond to questions many are asking:

Rest deeper: Why do I so often feel more drained than energized? Can I find space for my soul to breathe?

Live fuller: I have tried to fill my life with achievements, possessions, and popularity, and I feel emptier than ever. Where can I find fullness that lasts?

Lead better: How can I step off the treadmill of mere busyness and make real, meaningful progress in my life and work?

Rediscover the genius of Jesus' unhurried way of life and leadership.

Come visit us at unhurriedliving.com to discover free resources to help you

Rest Deeper. Live Fuller. Lead Better.

Web: unhurriedliving.com
Facebook: facebook.com/unhurriedliving
Instagram: UnhurriedLiving
Email: info@unhurriedliving.com

BECOMING OUR TRUE SELVES

The nautilus is one of the sea's oldest creatures. Beginning with a tight center, its remarkable growth pattern can be seen in the ever-enlarging chambers that spiral outward. The nautilus in the IVP Formatio logo symbolizes deep inward work of spiritual formation that begins rooted in our souls and then opens to the world as we experience spiritual transformation. The shell takes on a stunning pearlized appearance as it ages and forms in much the same way as the souls of those who devote themselves to spiritual practice. Formatio books draw on the ancient wisdom of the saints and the early church as well as the rich resources of Scripture, applying tradition to the needs of contemporary life and practice.

Within each of us is a longing to be in God's presence. Formatio books call us into our deepest desires and help us to become our true selves in the light of God's grace.

VISIT

ivpress.com/formatio

*to see all of the books in the
line and to sign up for the
IVP Formatio newsletter.*